The universal Baroque

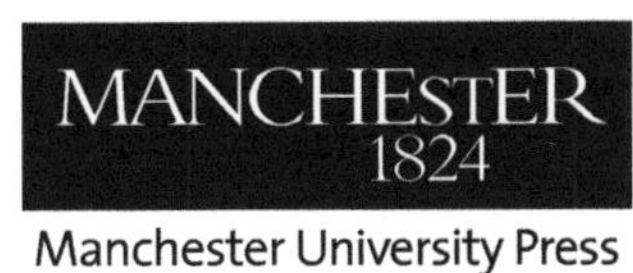

Manchester University Press

TO

Femmes fortes who would have adorned any baroque academy:

Jill Bepler, Patricia Brückmann, Jennifer Carter, Anne Dillon,
Patricia Hanley, Alison Saunders, Alison Shell, Jane Stevenson,
Robin Smith, Anne Sweeney, Laura Tosi, Jelena Todorović

The universal Baroque

PETER DAVIDSON

Manchester University Press

Published by Manchester University Press
Altrincham Street, Manchester, M1 7JA
www.manchesteruniversitypress.co.uk

British Library Cataloguing-in-Publication Data
A catalogue record for this book is available from the British Library
Library of Congress Cataloging-in-Publication Data applied for

ISBN 978 0 7190 7572 8 hardback

ISBN 978 1 5261 2693 1 paperback

First published in hardback 2007

First published in paperback 2018

Typeset 10.5/13pt ITC New Baskerville by
Graphicraft Limited, Hong Kong
Printed by Lightning Source

Barrocos fuimos siempre y barrocos tenemos que seguir siendo, por una razón muy sencilla: que para definir, pintar, determinar un mundo nuevo, árboles desconocidos, vegetaciones increíbles, ríos inmensos, siempre se es barroco.

Interview reported in Carlos Rincón, 'La poética de lo real-maravilloso americano', in *Recopilación de textos sobre Alejo Carpentier* (Havana: Casa de las Américas, La Habana, 1977), p. 176.

Pero, quién no advierte, en coyunturas análogas, que qualquier país, al expender en la lajanía su proprio espíritu, reciebe a su vez el contragolpe de la expansión y que siempre, en cierta manera, el colonizador es colonizado, el influencador influenciado, el vencedor vencido? Alejandro sojuzgó al Oriente, adentóse en el: del Oriente, empero, volvió . . . llevando en la frente la tiara de los Emperadores asiáticos.

Eugenio D'Ors, *Lo Barocco* (Madrid: Tecnos/Alianza, 2002), p. 130.

The Paraguayan art historian Josefina Plá asks: 'was the Indian's manifest inability to reproduce the model in its plastic, canonical and rhythmic entirety the logical result of the form of his artistic apprenticeship . . . or does it reflect, on a deeper level, the fight between the rhythms imposed by the imported culture, on the one hand, and the indigenous artisan's formal will on the other?' Such questions again force us to go beyond concepts such as 'folk' or 'primitive' art and examine how these works might represent a distinctive dialect of the common Late Renaissance and Baroque language that is equally indigenous and part of that global phenomenon.

Gauvin Alexander Bailey, *Art on the Jesuit Missions in Asia and Latin America, 1542–1773* (Toronto: University of Toronto Press, 1999), p. 165.

Contents

List of illustrations

Plates

Figures

Acknowledgements

The first idea for this book arose, appositely, on the staircase of the Jesuit Archives in the Borgo Santo Spirito in Rome. Gauvin Alexander Bailey, now of Boston College, was telling me about the research which later found written form in his *Art on the Jesuit Missions,* and asked me casually if I knew the name of the wife of Don Martín de Loyola, the nephew of St Ignatius, the founder of the Society of Jesus. I was astonished to be told that she was 'the niece of Tupac Amaru'. In the course of the long, ambulatory Roman conversations which followed, the essentials of this book emerged as I began to see the degree to which Gauvin's highly nuanced reassessment of the art of Ibero-America in the time of the Viceroys offered a series of insights equally applicable to the arts of early-modern Scotland and Ireland. His formulation about the art of the Guarani people, which is quoted as an epigraph to this book, has been essential to the whole process.

It has only been possible to make these connections in the light of years of conversation with my wife Jane Stevenson, whose own extraordinarily broad interests include international Latin of the seventeenth century and, in addition, the high cultures of first-millennium Scotland and Ireland. It is impossible to quantify what she has contributed to this book. Earlier work of my own which found published form as the Clarendon edition of Sir Richard Fanshawe raised the question of what had to be done to the English language to accommodate the baroque poetic of Góngora, and also, of necessity, noted that Fanshawe had been sent as an envoy from Charles I to the Confederate Irish. When I first worked on that material, I was ignorant of what now seem to me to be its most vital and interesting aspects. My sense of dissatisfaction which started then with the attempt (as bizarre and self-defeating as any restricted writing of the *grand siècle*) to study early modern English literature in isolation from continental culture and international Latin is what has brought this study into being.

This has been followed up in many travels and researches in continental libraries, chiefly the Biblioteca Apostolica Vaticana, but also the Roman archive of the Society of Jesus (ARSI) and the libraries and archives of the exiled English and Scottish colleges of Rome, Valladolid and Salamanca, as well as in the 'returned' Jesuit college at Stonyhurst in Lancashire and the 'returned' monastery of Downside in Somerset. My debt to the librarians, curators and abbots and rectors of these institutions is profound, especially to Dom Aidan Bellenger, Abbot of Downside; Fr T.M. McCoog SJ, archivist of the English province of the Society of Jesus; Mrs Janet Graffius at Stonyhurst; Mgr Denis Carlin, former Rector of the Royal Scots College in Salamanca; Mgr Nicholas Hudson, Rector of the Venerable English College in Rome; Sr Mary Joseph, also at the Venerabile; and Dr Javier Burrieza Sánchez at the College of St Alban in Valladolid.

The Most Rev. Mario Conti, Archbishop of Glasgow, has done an enormous amount to foster the study of that alternative history of Scotland which took place at Rome, Valladolid and Regensburg. I am more than grateful to him for personal encouragement, for introductions and for much kindness.

In many of these travels, I have been aware that I am lagging in the footsteps of Dr Alison Shell, whose monograph *Catholicism, Controversy and the English Literary Imagination* (1999) brought the culture and literature of the exiles into the mainstream debate on the histories of the arts. Much of this book has been developed in conversation with her and she has, *nota bene*, contributed most of the 'Theses on the Baroque' in the introduction.

But as the central point of this book is the internationalism and the supraconfessionalism of the Baroque, the time spent at the University of Leiden in the Netherlands was equally essential. Dr Robin Smith welcomed me there with memorable kindness and first took me to see the great garden of Het Loo. My dear friend Prof. Adriaan van der Weel led me into the world of the Dutch Baroque, culminating in our collaborative translation of Constantijn Huygens. And, although I barely realised it at the time, Prof. Alastair Hamilton was leading me to consider the far frontiers of the baroque world, particularly in the Middle East.

Also of the first importance for the apprehension of the Protestant Baroque is the Herzog August Bibliothek at Wolfenbüttel, and the unrivalled hospitality of Dr Jill Bepler. A wonderful conversation there with Prof. Dietrich Briesemeister made me feel considerably less alone in the pursuit of these ideas, especially with respect to the Latinity of the Americas.

Prof. Alison Saunders and Prof. Michael Bath have both continued my education in emblemata, begun under the kindly tutelage of Prof. Bart Westerweel at Leiden. Prof. Saunders, with exemplary patience and kindness, unravelled for me the matter of Montaigne and the 'baroque' syllogism. Prof. Allan MacInnes has taught me more about the history of Scotland than I can readily acknowledge and has convinced me of the vitality and importance of the alternative cultural tradition embodied in the Jacobite diaspora. The Hispanists of the University of Nottingham, especially Dr Jean Andrews and Dr Alex Coroleu, have held a pioneering series of events concerning the frontiers of the baroque world which it has been my privilege to attend, including a performance of the opera of *San Francisco Xavier* in the original Chiquitana language, a most moving occasion to which the epilogue to this study tries to pay due tribute.

The exceptional generosity of Prof. Bernardo Illari of Texas is most gratefully acknowledged: at a time when the Jesuit operas were known in Europe only by the specialist recordings of the *K617 Chemins du Baroque* in Lorraine, he sent me the score of his edition of *San Ignacio* and his own original study of the text. I have benefited also from the unstinting kindness of another great expert on Jesuit music, Prof. T. Frank Kennedy SJ. Much of the work on this book was indirectly made possible by the remarkable conference on *The Jesuits: Cultures, Sciences and the Arts* at Boston College in the summer of 2003. I am profoundly grateful also to the co-organisers of that event, Prof. John W. O'Malley SJ, Prof. Steven Harris and, once more, Gauvin Alexander Bailey.

Simon Rees and Yoko Kawaguchi in Cardiff have very kindly found for me texts of Welsh music of the eighteenth century and advised on Welsh parallels to the hybrid cultural phenomena of the other Celtic countries, while Andrew Losowsky in Madrid and *ma belle cousine* Paula in Andalucia have done much to sustain the Spanish parts of this project. Research in Dublin was greatly cheered by the hospitality and advice of Aoife Goodman. It is a very specific (and curious) exercise of the historical imagination to dead-reckon one's way across Ireland with the old *Shell Guide*, trying to conjecture which Church of Ireland parish one might happen to be in at any given time. Fr Fergus O'Donoghue SJ kindly arranged my access to the Jesuit library in Dublin and to his own invaluable work on the Irish Jesuits of the seventeenth century. Jill and Stephen Wolfe and Dr Juan Christian Pellicer have been more than generous in finding and sending material from Norway. Laura Tosi and Renato Campaci have been superb hosts in Venice and the Veneto, and took me to see the stupendous baroque garden of Valsanzibio. Dr Gabriele Cingolani of the University of Macerata arranged a private visit to the gardens, grottoes and automata of the Villa Buonaccorsi, an extraordinarily privileged access to one of the most extraordinary baroque places in Europe. Dr Jelena Todorović of the University of the Arts in Belgrade has, with extraordinary patience and kindness, guided me into the territories of Orthodox Baroque. Her generosity in obtaining texts, illustrations and translations is worthy of particular thanks. Dr Andrew Biswell and Nicholas Graham have held forts, rescued computers and remained memorably steady under fire.

Dr Arnold Hunt of the British Library performed a prodigy of lateral thinking to second-guess an auctioneer's catalogue description (so bizarre as to constitute in itself an epilogue to the history of the Protestant Ascendancy in Ireland), and to find for me the crucial manuscript witness to the culture of Confederate Ireland. This is very far from being Dr Hunt's only contribution to this book. At the Beinecke Library, Dr Robert Babcock and Anne Marie Menta both did everything possible to expedite my access to that manuscript.

Dr Louise Bourdua has very kindly lent me materials on the arts of *la Nouvelle France*, while Pat Hanley in Toronto has done much to assist my access to early Canadian music. Jamie Reid Baxter offered much encouragement and advice on Alejo Carpentier. My heartfelt thanks also to the curators of Rare Books and Museum Collections at the University of Aberdeen, Dr Iain Beavan and Neil Curtis, both of whom have been exceptionally kind.

Prof. Stephen Orgel is the kindest of friends, whose own *Illusion of Power* offers an ideal of the short book, and his conversation over the last decade has been as vital as his writings. Dr Anne Dillon has helped on the history of recusancy out of her vast knowledge, and supported the project in every way, as has Prof. Patricia Brückmann, the book's first reader, than whom no better reader could be imagined. I have been grateful also to Anne Sweeney for her own excellent monograph on St Robert Southwell and for our harmonious collaboration on our edition of his collected poems. My publisher, Matthew Frost at MUP, embraced this awkward proposition with enthusiasm, admirable tolerance, *mysterious calm.*

I end, inevitably, with my indebtedness to the only ancient university of the British Isles to have a recusant Catholic burial ground on its campus. It is also, in a sense, the only ancient university of the British Isles to have a tradition sufficiently dissident from the metropolitan consensus to provoke in itself the kinds of reflections which this book embodies. The crown spire (although I would have sacrificed even that had James Byres been allowed, in the 1770s, to rebuild the whole college in the style of the Collegio Romano, as was the baroque proposal of a moment) presides over the ideal ambiance in which to develop an account, such as this, of alternatives and exceptions. I cannot begin to express my thanks to the Principal of the University, C. Duncan Rice, Vice-Principal Chris Gane and Prof. Robert Frost, not only for giving me time in which to think and write but also for placing in my hands (literally) the keys of the *wunderkammer.* The least I can do to repay them all is to claim the inheritance (if not the laurels) of the Aberdeen doctors of the seventeenth century. So stand by, *lector benevole,* for the deployment of a good quantity of miscellaneous erudition in the defence of an unpopular cause.

Introduction

Considering the word 'Baroque'

This book is a set of variations on a word, a series of divisions on a ground: *Baroque.* It is not an attempt to use the word exclusively as a term of period definition or a stylistic descriptor, but to use it to set free a whole sequence of thoughts about how arts, ideas and energies circulated in the early modern world. While concurring with the great Spanish critic Eugenio D'Ors that one possible use of the term *Baroque* is to describe a kind of art, not a period of art, and, therefore, that one can perceive a poet such as the late-antique Claudian as high-baroque,[1] I would argue that there is a further, potentially even more liberating, usage. That is to use *Baroque* to identify the wholeness of the arts of early modern Europe, the whole cultural system prevailing in those parts of the world in dialogue, whether willingly or unwillingly, with early modern Europe, and those geographically distant parts of the world which were at least corresponding (in the sense of the far-flung 'corresponding' members of an *accademia*) with Europe, however much on their own terms and in their own idioms. So *Baroque* is poten-tially also a word to describe a system of international discourses, a 'way of proceeding', a symbolic language, an agreed set of conventions over-riding all the allegiances of religious confession or nationality which have come to seem, since the turn of the nineteenth century, unavoid-able descriptors of all cultural endeavour.

It is potentially useful to resist using *Baroque* only as a term for a period, or as a term defining, or denigrating, a single style.[2] Much of the argu-ment of this book will be that to see Baroque in its real historical context is to see an intricate complex of interconnected 'Baroques'. Perhaps the chief point which it seeks to advance is that Baroque is *not* confined to one geographical area or religious confession: most of all, it resists the idea that Baroque is the style of the Catholic south of Europe, and of the New World territories and protectorates of the Catholic south. For Baroque to function, as it did, as an international system of communication in all the arts, it was essential that it should be supra-confessional and genuinely international. That means the inclusion of as much of the Orthodox east as wished to engage in a dialogue with western Europe, as well as of the Protestant north.

The ways in which Baroque is supra-national account for many of the problems attending the use of the term. All critical traditions born of the nation state, of focus on the study of national schools of art and architecture or on vernacular literatures, especially if those literatures are studied in cultural isolation, are structurally and inevitably hostile to notions of baroque universalism. This phenomenon is as visible in the Orthodox countries of central Europe as it is in the Protestant countries of northern Europe and their former colonies. Since the early nineteenth century, so much energy has been invested in the creation of histories of independently indigenous cultural traditions for each nation (national traditions which are often religious traditions as well) that the notion of participation in an international movement, style or mode is resisted, sometimes violently, sometimes, in retrospect, even comically.[3]

To make the term *Baroque* work hardest to unlock the early modern arts, it is most useful to see it as a term which identifies a flexible and permeable *system*, which comprehends all the major and minor arts of that epoch, rather than as a marker for a limited temporal period or a single style. Much energy has been invested in definitions of *Baroque*, particularly in writing about the visual arts. The discussion of what to call the art which developed after the Italian art of the Renaissance has been long and sometimes acrimonious. 'Mannerism' and 'Maniera', both of which are anachronistic uses of a word which sixteenth-century writers on art simply used to mean 'style' in a more general sense, have been advanced as descriptors somehow distinct from *Baroque*. The influence of the Counter-Reformation on European art has variously been applauded or deplored with attendant, but not consequent, uncertainty as to where the border between 'Mannerism' and 'Baroque' might lie.[4]

It would be more useful still, and equally liberating, to postulate that the manifestation of *Baroque* as the world-wide system of the late sixteenth to the eighteenth centuries was the most concentrated manifestation of an artistic mode (or artistic phenomenon) which has – to a greater or lesser degree – manifested itself at different epochs and in widely scattered places.

In seeking to use the term *Baroque* as a radically useful shorthand for the whole cultural system which operated in different degrees within the arts world-wide from the mid-sixteenth century to the later eighteenth century, and intermittently thereafter, often in unexpected places, there is an element of difficulty with the history of the word itself, which is predictably ambiguous.

The oldest use of the term would seem to be a part of a logician's mnemonic, an invented name for a particular sort of syllogism, a variant on: if all As are Bs, and C is an A, therefore C is a B. The 'baroque' syllogism runs: if all As are Bs, but some Cs are not Bs, therefore some Cs are not As. As a logical structure, the baroque syllogism leaves a considerable amount of play to the far-fetched or intricately paradoxical. It also leaves considerable scope for both mischievous and poetic use of the structure to prove that things are true which are only true within the restricted terms of that particular syllogistic argument. This is the use of *Baroque* with which Montaigne was familiar. He used the term to denigrate mere manipulations of logic which usurp the august name of philosophy:

> La plus expresse marque de la sagesse, c'est un ejouïssance constante; son estat est comme des choses au dessus de la Lune: toujours serein. C'est 'Barocco' et 'Baralipton' qui renderent leurs supposts ainsi crotez et enfumés, ce n'est pas elle; ils ne la conoissent que par ouïr dire.[5]

> The most evident token and apparent sign of true wisdom is a constant and unconstrained rejoycing, whose estate is like to all things above the Moone, that is ever cleare, alwaies bright. It is Baroco and Baralipton, that makes their followers prove so base and idle, and not Philosophie: they know her not but by heare-say.[6]

So here 'Barocco' is a perverse piece of cleverness, a logical proof which is not quite a proof. One might add irreverently that there is, however, a kind of poetic truth at work here. The energy of much baroque art, especially baroque poetry, comes from saying that some thing is, in a restricted sense, another thing altogether.

To a considerable extent this is the sense of *Baroque* expressed by the quotations given in the *Oxford English Dictionary* from 1765 onwards. There is also a repeated assertion that *Baroque* begins as a jeweller's term for an irregularly shaped pearl, a usage which remains current. In the run of examples in the *Dictionary*, there is a barrage of negativity for a century: 'whimsical, grotesque, odd'; 'baroque or absurd'; 'the degenerated Renaissance known as Baroque'. It is not until the 1920s, and

Bannister Fletcher's *History of Architecture*, that the term is used as any sort of neutral descriptor. It is not until 1953, in the work of Sir John Summerson, that the idea of 'English Baroque' (up to that point, quite clearly considered an oxymoron), is applied to architecture – tellingly, in opposition to the Palladianism sponsored by Lord Burlington. The last quotation, interestingly enough, is from T.S. Eliot's *On Poetry and Poets* (1957), attributing the eighteenth-century unpopularity of Milton's *Lycidas* to its 'baroque' combination of classical and Christian imagery.

The shift towards allowing *Baroque* to be a term more calmly describing a period and a style most probably comes in the work of the German critic Heinrich Wölfflin. His *Renaissance und Barock* (Munich, 1888), although it quotes many bitterly negative assessments of the arts, and particularly the architecture, of seventeenth-century Italy, is certainly very early in suggesting that *Baroque* might be applied to the description of music and to literature as well as to the visual arts.

One of the most original contributions to the debate, and one which is of great importance to the arguments of this work, is Mario Praz's pioneering study of the degree to which the literature of seventeenth-century England, Latin as well as English, might be thought of as part of a continuum embracing the writing, Latin and vernacular, of contemporary continental Europe. In 1925, Praz (1896–1982) published *Secentismo e Marinismo in Inghilterra* (*Baroque and the Style of Marino in England*) at Florence. Two wide-ranging and erudite essays on Donne and Crashaw relate their works to those of their contemporaries Europe-wide. Praz makes the quiet, wholly historically informed, assumption that Latin is an essential medium for any educated early modern reader, or almost any early modern poet. He assumes the internationality of the baroque mode and mounts an informed challenge, albeit one that he later withdrew to some extent in his 1958 English-language study of England and Italy, *The Flaming Heart,* to the whole notion of considering early modern British culture in isolation.

As we will see in the chapter on British Baroque (pp. 25–93), the resistance to this internationalist position (even before Praz published it in full) has been consistent, varying in quality from T.S. Eliot's awareness of, but distance from, this material in his careful writing on early modern English literature, to the hysterical, and, retrospectively, hilarious, insularity of Sir Herbert Grierson (1866–1960).

Praz's fellow Italian Benedetto Croce (1866–1952) took a consistently negative view of the baroque arts, although he eventually allowed (reluctantly) that the term was established as a descriptor of period and that even those manifestations of the cultural life of early modern Italy to which he was personally attracted had to be subsumed under the heading of Baroque. The title of his *Storia di l'età barocca in Italia* (1st ed., 1929) accepts as much, although Croce remains personally deeply suspicious of baroque as a mode:

> quella perversione artistica, dominato dal bisogno dello stupore.

> [this perversion of the arts, dominated by the need to astonish.]

> Per tale sua natura, non solo esso (diversamente da altre forme di brutto, che tavolta scuotono, eccitano e turbano) riesce, in ultimo, freddo, nonostante la sua agitazione e il suo calore superficiale, e lascia in senso di vuoto, nonostante la follia delle immagini e delle combinazioni di immagini che mette in opera.[7]

> [By this its nature, not only to be (in contrast to other forms of ugliness which variously stir, excite or trouble) in result, in the end, cold, despite its agitation and its superficial warmth, and it leaves a feeling of emptiness, in spite of the plethora of images and the combinations of images with which it works.]

Ultimately Croce sees the Baroque as a confessional style, the cultural manifestation of the Counter-Reformation, which, almost unconsciously, he stigmatises as an enemy of the modern nation state:

> Peggiore aspetto prendeva la Controriforma, coi suoi gesuiti, la sua inquisizione e i suoi roghi, con l'oppressione della parola e del pensiero, con rinvigorimento del Papato, antico ostaculo all'unione dell'Italia.[8]

> [The Counter-Reformation gives it a worse appearance, with its Jesuits, its Inquisition and its stakes, with the oppression of speech and thought, with the revival of the Papacy, that ancient obstacle to the unification of Italy.]

Thus we have the lucid statement of one of the problems which this work must consider: the retrospective values and assumptions of the post-nineteenth-century nation state intrinsically at best suspicious of baroque internationalism, especially if that internationalism is identified, wholly wrongly, with revived Catholicism.

The Spanish critic Eugenio d'Ors gave the whole phenomenon of Baroque a considered, virtuosic and remarkable treatment in his short treatise, *Lo barocco*, first published in full in the French translation of Agathe Rouart-Valéry, *Du baroque* (Paris, 1935). D'Ors offers the liberating idea that Baroque can be seen above all as a *category*, a mode of feeling and expression which recurs throughout human history, alternating with the rigours and (usually fallacious) simplicities of Classicism.

> Et Rome, principe de l'unité, et Babel, symbole éternel de la dispersion. Et le Classicisime, langage de l'unité, langage de l'éternelle Rome idéale. Et le Baroquisme, esprit et style de la dispersion.[9]

> [Both Rome, principle of unity, and Babel, eternal symbol of diaspora. Both Classicism, language of unity, language of the eternal and ideal Rome. And Baroque, style and spirit of diaspora . . .]

D'Ors sees Baroque as a 'constant', a term for a recurrent phenomenon which embraces, for him, a variety of emotive and expressive artistic expressions, including the works of Rousseau, *Robinson Crusoe* and *Paul et Virginie,* which would be more readily categorised as romantic today. But the quotation above goes to the heart of his perceptions: Baroque is the style of the fallen world which we actually inhabit, of reality, of 'things exactly as they are'.[10] It is Classicism, with its idealism, its imposition upon the citizen of the rules of the ideal state, the ancient Rome of the imagination in all its imaginary order, which is delusive and at an oblique angle to reality.

D'Ors also emphasises that, while the most lasting and visible manifestation of the constant which he identifies as 'Baroque' occurred in the course of the late sixteenth to eighteenth centuries, Baroque is a recurrent phenomenon, returning and recurring throughout history: 'Le Baroque est une constante historique qui se retrouve à les époques aussi réciproquement éloignées que l'Alexandrisme de la Contre-Réforme'.[11] (The Baroque is a historical constant which is found in eras as far from each other as [late-antique] Alexandria and the Counter-Reformation).

D'Ors also sees the plurality of the Baroque, in his distinction between '. . . une "langue" centrale et unifiée de la spontanéité périphérique des "dialectes" ', that is, between the cenralised and standardised 'language' of Classicism and the peripheral spontaneity of the multifarious 'dialects' of Baroque. He also applies this essential perception to the worldwide devolution of the Baroque and the capacity which the Baroque has to generate local manifestations blending the vernacular and the international.

> Tout pays qui, en de semblables conjonctures, étend au loin son propre esprit, reçoit lui-même le contrecoup de cette expansion et que, toujours, le colonisateur est en quelque sorte colonisé, le vainceur vaincu?

Alexandre tient l'Orient sous son joug; il y pénètre: et voici qu'il revient empereur et le front coiffé de la tiare des empereurs asiatiques.[12]

[But, who does not see, in similar conjunctions, that all nations which expend their own spirit in distant places, themselves receive in their turn the counterblow which always attends such expansion – the coloniser colonised, the conqueror conquered. Alexander the Great subdued the Orient; he penetrated it: mark how he returned an emperor, bearing on his forehead the tiara of the emperors of Asia.]

This book seeks to explore and expand the use of the term *Baroque.* Therefore, to a considerable extent, it accepts D'Ors as a guide to Baroque as a phenomenon reaching its height of expression in the seventeenth and early eighteenth centuries, but with a cyclic life in different ages. However, the focus of this present book is on the Baroque of the seventeenth and eighteenth centuries: the point when the system was working most internationally and at its fullest power.

Robert Harbison's recent *Reflections on Baroque* is an architecturally focused series of essays, written without reference to any of the twentieth-century critics cited above. It is therefore a curious production, eager to see particular manifestations of baroque architecture, especially Borromini, as forerunners of the freedoms of the twentieth century, but remarkably insular and traditionalist in its general approach:

> The baroque can be viewed as an episode in the history of art, or of religion, or of absolutist politics or of consciousness more generally . . . In religion it is tied to Counter-Reformation reassertions of Catholic orthodoxy against Protestant incursions . . . Northern Protestant variants are more problematic – debates still continue over whether there is an English Baroque at all . . .[13]

The great value of the book is the way in which, focusing mostly on architecture, it indicates that versions of Baroque are part of the visual histories of Russia and Turkey,[14] even if they are categorised with 'Neo and pseudo baroque', that is, with a dubious classis of baroque revivals stretching to the present. The approach to the Baroque of Ibero-America is indicated by the opening sentence on what he calls 'Colonial Baroque': 'In the eighteenth century European Baroque enjoyed a surprising afterlife or apotheosis outside Europe'[15]. And he goes on to define what can only be called honest confusion as to the status of the arts of Ibero-America:

> So if we had hoped to find here a Baroque interpreted by or filtered through a lively native culture, we are doomed to at least partial disappointment . . . of course there is disagreement about the nature and the

extent of Mexican baroque's independence of Spanish models . . .
Perhaps it is often some variant of Mexican patriotism (and for this one
needn't be Mexican) which tempts one to deny this. One wants to insist
on the Mexicanness of Mexican baroque *even before one has begun to think
about it.*[16]

If the built arts and the visual arts are considered in isolation from the
writings of early modern Mexicans, *indio, criollo* and *mestizo* alike, this
is not as naive a position as it might appear. For all that Harbison tries
to bring music and poetry into his discussion, what *Reflections on
Baroque* really demonstrates is the immense difficulty of considering the
phenomenon of Baroque from within early twenty-first-century discip-
linary boundaries, and the great obstacles, most of them conceptual,
which the established body of Anglophone critical terminology places
in the way of such a discussion.

By contrast, Giovanni Careri's *Baroques* is a cosmopolitan and magnificently inclusive work. The plural of the title is in itself is both
significant and consoling. Its scope is illustrated by its opening words:

> From Rome to Würzburg, Andalusia to Latin America, and Portugal to
> Brazil, baroque art was the first artistic expression to go global . . .
> baroque art was long considered decadent in comparison to renaissance
> expressions, but today we know that it is the ultimate manifestation of a
> civilisation that explosively expanded the boundaries of reality. In that
> sense, the culture of the baroque age is the source of our own, and the
> better we know it, the better we will be able to understand our own time.[17]

Careri uses the term *Baroque* in much the same way as I am trying to
use it: an explosion of possibilities ensues in his inclusive book. While
I can never hope to match the sheer scope of his discussion of the visual
arts, I hope that this book can offer itself as a pendant to Careri in
that it tries to consider some of the phenomena which he identifies as
applied also to literature, music and eloquence. He is incisive about
the processes at work in the Iberian Americas, and how helpless the
European critic's terminology can seem when trying to discuss them:

> In the hands of the artists of the Americas, the Baroque became mestizo,
> open to myriad cultural admixtures. It became a site where images are
> both stratified and joined, at the level of both form and content, in such
> a way that in the end a third term appears, neither European nor indige-
> nous, and outside the categories of either.[18]

One important question of emphasis and method remains: a word
of context is needed for the Society of Jesus, in the early modern world
and in this book. We have already seen Croce assuming axiomatically

that no good and no good art can come out of any institution involved with the Jesuits. Inevitably, this book has to deal with the phenomenon of 'Jesuit baroque', as D'Ors categorised it, not without humour: *barrochus tridentinus sive jesuiticus*. As the argument of the book develops, it will become clear that the enemy of the Baroque as I define it is the nation state. The Jesuits, enemies of the nation state themselves, were among the chief proponents of the baroque arts. They were therefore inevitably considered with aesthetic suspicion from the nineteenth century onwards, just as they had been considered with political suspicion before the suppression of 1773.

International Protestantism is a phenomenon to an extent overshadowed and obscured by the activities and priorities of the Enlightenment, but Enlightenment was very clear that Catholic internationalism was its principal enemy. And within the Catholic church, the most consciously international, supra-national and internationalist movement was the Society of Jesus, the intellectual powerhouse of the Counter-Reformation.

The Jesuits functioned to a considerable degree independently of local bishops and national churches, and even published their supra-nationalism in a tree-diagram of worldwide command and connection, the *Horoscopium catolicum Societatis Jesu*. Axiomatically the Jesuits are therefore the bogey of the Enlightenment, with its romantic nationalism and primitivist reappropriation of the pure lines and simplicities of antiquity. If the Baroque is the style of the Jesuits, it is axiomatically to be condemned.

'Jesuit style' was blamed for making extravagant appeals to the senses as a vehicle for control and domination. Wanton luxury, illusionism, vulgarity and a specifically Italianate or Roman style were key features of this pejorative concept – as late as 1921, Werner Weisbach was still directly linking the spirit of the Baroque with Ignatius of Loyola.[19] The English critic and political activist Anthony Blunt similarly argued that Jesuit art was low-brow and anti-humanist.

> This worldly, emotional, anti-intellectual kind of religion produced its equivalent in the arts. In the seventeenth century, the whole Baroque movement must be closely associated with the Jesuits, but even before that time there was a branch of Mannerist painting in which many of the same qualities could be found.[20]

This is a particularly fascinating English use of the term *Mannerist*, as though the mere association was dragging even degenerating renaissance art headlong towards the full degradation of Jesuit Baroque.

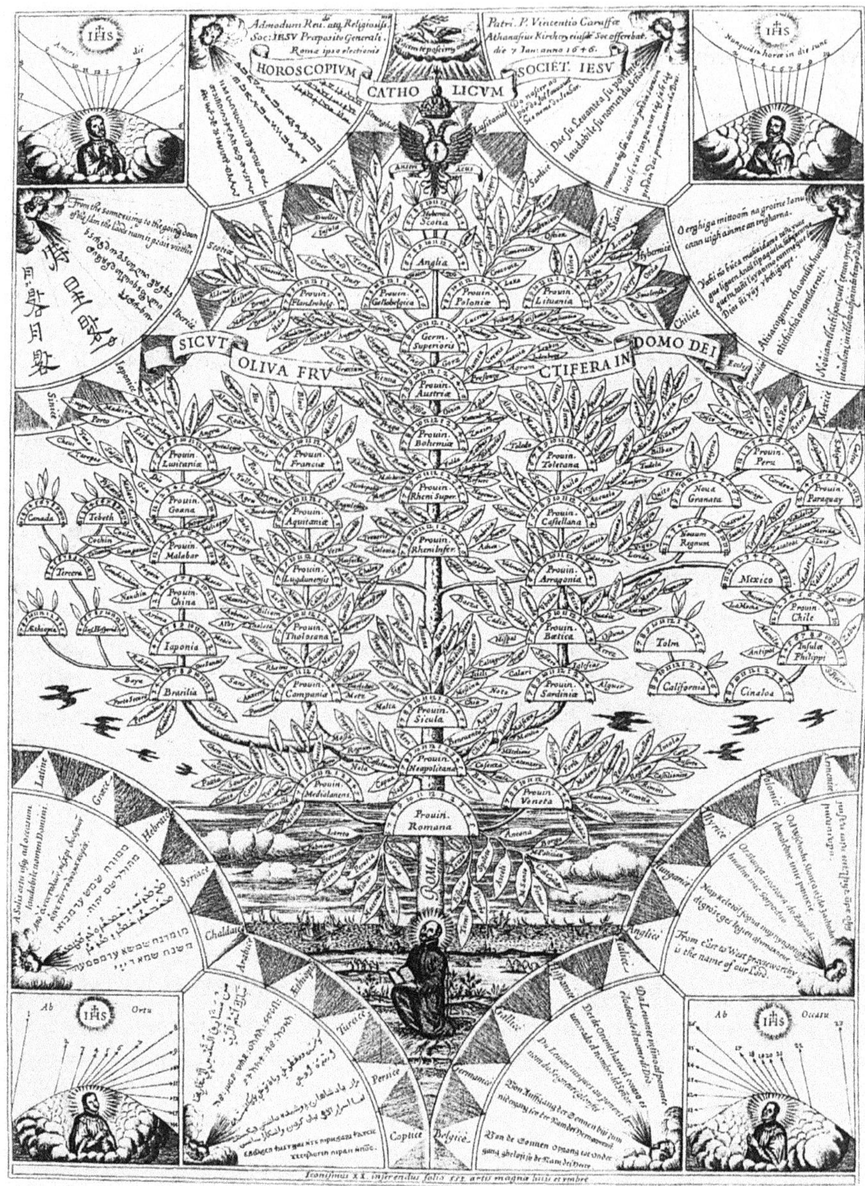

1 A map of the worldwide system of Jesuit communications: *Horoscopium catolicum Societatis Jesu,* engraved illustration from Athanasius Kircher, *Ars magnis lucis et umbrae* (Rome, 1646), p. 553.

Despite this sustained history of critical hostility to the Jesuit arts, they will play a central and quietly heroic part in this book, precisely because of the very internationalism which elicited such hostility; and also because the Jesuits' practice, their 'way of proceeding' in the mission field, was to learn languages wherever possible, to establish equivalences, and to work within the cultures with which they were in contact; because their educational commitments worldwide made them peerless disseminators of symbolic and figurative languages; because they kept records of their disseminations; but above all, because the final focus of this book is on what we might call the margins and fringes of the Baroque. On those frontiers, the Jesuits were active and at their most brilliant as agents of the hybridisation of cultures, producers of the new.

Hostile critics of the Baroque reiterate their suspicion of striving after effect, but can we then stretch this definition further and say, in a more positive sense, that there are *ambitions* common to all the works of art, whether visual verbal or musical, in any medium, which can usefully be described as 'Baroque'. Effect plays a part, because the baroque artwork strives towards magnificence, *la meraviglia*, competence, curiosity, a sense that medium or detail is very much less important than impression. The end justifies the means so axiomatically that it can be taken for granted. In the achievement of the stupendous, categories are bound to become fluid, things are (literally and in the arts of illusion) inevitably going to flow into each other, so that with magnificence and decorum comes an element of the deliberately astonishing, a pleasure in the astonishing, something that might elicit the English words 'flouting' and 'flaunting'.

This is something perceptible in certain lights – for example, the golden lights from concealed windows of tinted glass which bathe certain silver statues, certain flying stuccoes, certain revolving altarpieces in the sunlight of the otherworld – as *queer*. The pleasure of the cabinet of curiosities is also a pleasure in queerness, in juxtaposition, in an investigation of the surreal poetry of an expanding perception of the world, in the continuous arrangement of discontinuous objects as though they were connected.

We must face squarely the problem of trying to use the term *Baroque* to free and open up discussion of the arts of early modern Britain and Ireland: British cultural history has gone to Alexandrian lengths to invent terminology to avoid it. Some of this terminology in its own way almost attains the status of a xenophobic poetry, such as 'artisan Mannerist',[21] and the catastrophic 'metaphysical'. This unease with terminology has crucially obscured the degree to which the arts of the British Isles were themselves full participators in the baroque worlds of learning and delight.

Definitions of Baroque

I should like now to continue this re-examination by listing some of the features which identify a work of art as 'baroque'. One of the first and most crucial features it will exhibit is a grounding in reference to *antiquities* – the plural is as deliberate as the plural in Giovannio Careri's title. The baroque world, reflective as it was of the Latin past of Europe, and dependent as it was on Latin as a central means of international communication, also invoked, where relevant, the ancient history of the Far East, of the Germanic and Celtic past of Europe, of Southern America and of Egypt as well as that of the Mediterranean. Above all, baroque evocations of Egyptian antiquity (hieroglyphics, obelisks, myths of origin) keep the gates of the past open, suggesting that there is yet another civilisation and its writings which we have not yet explored. This baroque fascination with Egypt stems from the direct statements of Herodotus and Plato that Egyptian culture was older than that of the Greeks, more mysterious and more sacred, a perception which militated against perceiving the Periclean Athens as straightforwardly 'the cradle of civilisation'. In a sense, baroque evocations of ancient Egypt serve to keep the mysterious plurality of antiquity in mind, so that there is a place for the antiquities of the Americas and the East when they are brought into the baroque view of the world.

Another marker is that work is identifiable as a set of variations on established themes. The Baroque is a permeable system, a set of infinitely flexible stock responses in literature, visual art and music, which make all arts potentially variations on a sequence of known, tested grounds. Personifications and mythologies, types and figures, strategies of rhetoric and imagery, are ever at the baroque artist's disposal, offering a ground-bass over which astonishment can be improvised. A cultural system so much in love with the remote and exotic that it draws strangeness unto itself, it is eager to explore and coexist with extremes, at the same time as it is a daily, serviceable set of conventions for discussing and celebrating quotidian experience. Among the many features which distinguish baroque from classical art is the capacity to work in more than one artistic tradition at the same time – Baroque inevitably embraces hybridity.

Baroque is a cultural system which is supra-national, supra-confessional. Indeed, one of the functions, or characteristics, of baroque art, deriving from its deployment of a common verbal and visual language, is that it was the system through which enemies could communicate with each other at moments of truce (this is seen most effectively in masque and festival texts). It is not a system spreading out from European capitals in washes of dilution and enfeeblement. Each centre of cultural production worldwide produces its own Baroque.

I should now like to continue this re-examination of the concept of baroque art by setting forth some theses to try to begin a definition of Baroque for our times. As a framework for the detailed discussion in the chapters which follow, I now put forward twelve theses, or propositions, or ideas,[22] with some commentaries.

1 Baroque art is never at a loss: it has evolved a way of dealing with reality
It is the art of the Enlightenment (the art which displaced and vilified the Baroque) which is escapist and unreal, with its fogs of morning and evening and its dubious sentimentalities over landscapes and children. It is the art of the Enlightenment which looks for escapes in drugs and trance states, opium or hysterics or delicious fear at the edge of a precipice. These are very different states from the ecstasies of the Baroque.

What the baroque arts deal with is 'things exactly as they are'. The baroque system can find an artistic response for any occasion. A baroque artist (in any medium) can and should be able to produce something apposite for any occasion. It need not be original, but it must be accomplished. This is the aspect of the Baroque which (along with its capacity to elicit embarrassment) has caused most trouble to subsequent criticism, for the simple reason that subsequent criticism has been trained to look for individualism as a criterion of achievement.

2 The Baroque has no metropolis
In this it is utterly unlike the art of the Renaissance as imagined by Northern Europe, with its 'cradles' in Florence, Rome, Urbino and Ferrara. It is also the case that both America and Europe have chosen to see twentieth-century art as very much a matter of cultural capital cities. For all that it is the style which served the *ancien régime* and the era of absolutism in religion (reformed as well as Counter-Reformation), Baroque is not intrinsically authoritarian: rather Baroque is a manner susceptible of almost infinite local adaptation and naturalisation. *It is permeable*. The Baroque of Cuzco is not a primitive imitation of the

Baroque of Madrid, it is a localisation of a universal manner. The most exciting works of baroque art are often bilingual in the international and local artistic idioms. The crucial works of baroque art speak in both idioms at the same time, creating thereby a third, new, language.

One important aspect of this is the ability of the Baroque world-wide to reinvent the discourse of the festival: the state entry, the annual celebration. The 1670 festival for the canonisation of the first saint of the Americas, St Rose of Lima, was achieved American Baroque, not Spanish Baroque diluted. There were great stands ornamented with the blue and white oriental porcelain brought from the East by the 'Manila galleon';[23] a pattern-poem was displayed in praise of the rose blooming as 'queen of flowers nourished by the dews of heaven . . . resplendent in both worlds . . . enduring coral of mortifications . . . symbol of silence of death to the world . . . incomparable felicity of the rose now growing in the gardens of paradise'.[24]

The baroque world has the capacity to invent festivals where the degree of localisation is yet greater, as in this arch of triumph from the Guarani mission towns in the jungles of Paraguay:

> Woven from tree branches into the form of a tripartite Roman triumphal arch, the central arch was draped all over with dried and fresh fish, dried and fresh wild game, live pullets in cages, hens tied by the neck, ostrich eggs . . . colourful birds which are in the greatest abundance in the region, and foxes and dogs . . . The arches, columns and plinths are adorned, they have hung from them tigers, serpents and the greatest variety of wild skins, which are stuffed to regain their former appearance so they look alive. Interspersed between these are bags stuffed full of food . . . clothing, bows, arrows and quivers . . .[25]

Or this extraordinary blending of European local traditions with the observances of Catholicism in Eugenio d'Ors's account of a living altar for the feast of St Peter:

> Extrémité du baroque à Valence, extrémité encore dans ce petit village de pêcheurs, à la côte catalane, ou naguère on garnissait, pour la fête de S. Pierre, l'autel churrigueresque, – aux grasses spires, aux colunnes entortillées, aux ors si éclatants sur le mur blanchi à la chaux – avec une guirlande de langoustes vivantes, dont la carapace obèse se crispait de temps en temps, au milieu du remuement des pattes, antennes et pédoncules. A la lueur des cierges, cette agitation tressait une sarabande opulente de formes et des reflets. Il y avait encore des oillets rouges à la senteur poivrée. De fauves odeurs fermentaient dans un mélange de marée, d'encens et de cire. Et la mort s'insérait dans la liturgie des offices. Cela pouvait tenir lieu de musique, n'est-ce pas?[26]

[The most extreme Baroque is at Valencia, and also in this little fishing village on the Catalan coast, where formerly the Churrigueresque altar was decorated for the feast of St Peter – the altar with its rich spirals, its salomonic columns, their gilding dazzling against the whitewashed wall – with a garland of live lobsters whose rounded shells contracted from time to time, amongst the stirring of claws, legs and feelers. In the light of the candles, this this movement wove into an opulent sarabande of shapes and reflections. There were also red carnations with a peppery scent. The savage smells fermented in a mixture of fish, wax and incense. And death took its place in the observances of the liturgy. This could serve for music, could it not?]

3 Those who find the Baroque embarrassing are testifying to its success
This is the more so, the more that they are discountenanced by its blithe indifference to degree, material or genre. Baroque still embarrasses people by refusing to ignore the senses or the physical world. Embarrassment is perhaps the one response left that hasn't been postmodernised out of existence; and the quintessential baroque saint, St Ignatius, tells us to pray with the senses.[27]

More generally, embarrassment attends things made of the 'wrong' material: the marble curtains and carpets of the Venetian Jesuits; the stucco and metal clouds of Weltenburg Abbey on the Danube: the stucco curtain (one of the greatest curtains in all European art) in the Abbey

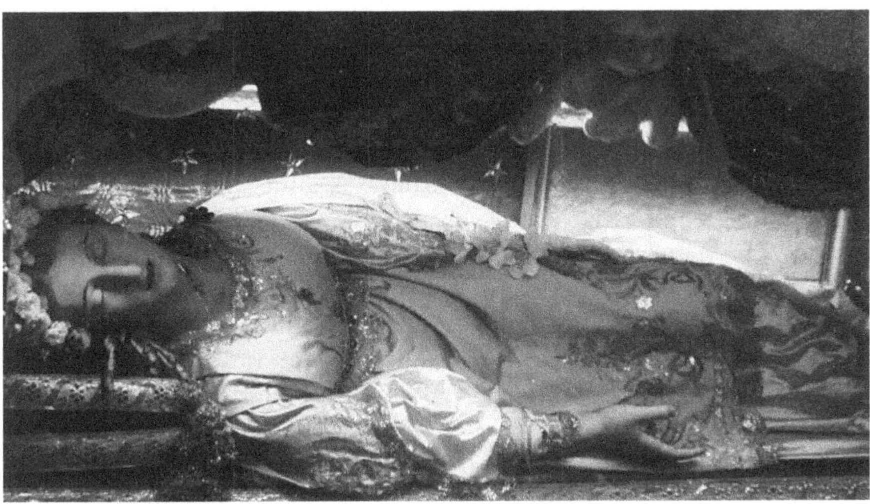

2 Sacred waxwork: seventeenth-century clothing of a catacomb martyr's skeleton in wax and silk. Santa Maria della Vittoria, Rome.

Church at Rohr. Or the real silks and brocades of the clothes of Hispanic dressed and draped religious statues.

Extremes of wrong material coincide with extremes of conventional embarrassment in the wax-clad skeletons under the altars of Roman churches in their costumes of silk and sequins. In their beauty and strangeness, their garments cross the line into theatrical costume of the day. Embarrassment and repulsion stem from the fact that these exquisite waxworks are built up on an armature of real body parts, and that their clothes are opera clothes. But the beauty of the objects themselves is obstinate.

This is even more apparent in the ossuary at Kutna-Hora, Sedlec, in the Czech Republic, created in 1718 by Johann-Blasius Santini-Aichel (1677–1723),[28] with its arrangements of human remains in chaste and elegant friezes, urns and fictive architecture. The gadrooning round the base of the urn is achieved by ball-joints alternating with pelvic bones. This ossuary is the sacred expression of the secular grotto enthusiasm which led the elite of half of Europe to press shells and glittering minerals into the plaster of their pleasure-houses and artificial caverns, to make themselves glimmering, subterranean spaces in which to meditate upon virtue, retirement and transience. The difficulty is retrospective and to a considerable degree anachronistic.

But the works which we read as decadent ossuaries, exhibitions of preserved corpses are, in the language of their time, *edifying*. The armoured or spangled skeletons of Roman and Bavarian churches read anachronistically as a decadent clash of materials (the dead body clothed with what should clothe the living body at its most alive, its most heroic or most beautiful), but actually all these works are 'about' the dignity of holy death and are offered as a consolation.

The other embarrassment of Baroque is affect: the affront of what is seen as 'Catholic kitsch', the religious emotion which comes forward to meet the spectator, already formed. Where is the affront – is it really that things are being made easy for the poor, the tired and those who have no education? That they are, in the noblest sense, vulgar? That is the mode in which oratorio started in Rome, however much it may have ended up as the Lenten diversion of the elite at Covent Garden. This accessibility, this free and copious offering of images, is half of what is read as 'wrong' with Crashaw. The problem of many Anglophone critics with Crashaw is the product, in fact, of social embarrassment: Crashaw is offering spirituality to the common people. Accessible, broken down into bite-sized units, open to all.

The effects of baroque works of art can be confrontational or affirmative, depending rather on the positioning of the spectator, but although ultimately consoling, it is often their immediate function to provoke that perfectly reasonable baroque emotion, *disquietude.*

4 The Baroque is pragmatic

Therefore, the Baroque is aware of the fact that no one is freed from minor day-to-day moral decisions, and that it makes sense to systematise. Hence the systematisations of spirituality of St Ignatius and the systematisation of emotions offered by Crashaw, by Bernini, by all the sculptors and architects who offer movement and emotion to the spectator rather than the static icon.

Also, the pragmatism of the Baroque can be seen in the willingness to systematise oratory, occasion and the literature of ceremony: originality is not the question, the questions are more complex ones of decorum and the encodement of political or social assurances.

5 The Baroque has reached the last possible point in eclecticism

In baroque art, notions of the exotic have become meaningless, which is consistent, nevertheless, with shying away from homogeneity. For the first time, by the late sixteenth century, a cultural system had evolved which could be enacted (and was) by any race, in any dress, in any context. There are constants, such as *magnificence* and *compunction,* but these are capable of infinite translations. A feather cloak is, in its own context, as magnificent as a cope of Genoese cut velvet.

The Baroque (as a political descriptor) has gaps and porosity, it is permeable because it is an accommodating set of systems capable of infinitely varied local application. Enlightenment, constitutional and constitutionalist, has *fewer gaps.* Baroque cannot ever be intrinsically racist: its systems of signs are happily too flexible, and far too accommodating. Enlightenment sentimentality about the virtuous inhabitants of Otahiti, on the other hand, is fatally the child of the perception that the peoples of the 'new worlds' are childlike.

6 Since asymmetry and imperfection are one meaning of 'Baroque', it may be held to valorise the grotesque

This is where its ingenuity is most compassionate. Baroque religious art so often depicts the moment of crisis, ecstasy, passion (in every sense) that Baroque habituates the spectator to depiction even of the conventionally comely body in states of extremity, whether of gesture or situation. Caricature heads of extremes of emotion are one way to the truth.[29] The Spanish statues of the tortured dead body of Christ, the Holy Week mysteries which are paraded still through the streets with drums and torches, have names which are themselves calmly contrastive mottoes for *imprese*. 'The Serene Lord of Light', 'The Christ of Humility and Patience'.

7 Baroque was always post-Reformation

This is one aspect of the way in which the baroque mode inhabits 'things exactly as they are': it can come to terms with the *datum* of irreconcilable views – as Classicists, followers of the Enlightenment and many revolutionary Protestants never can, because of their conviction that they are right and that, outside their just republic, the world is wrong and mired and despicable in its wrongness. Hence, commendation and eloquence are of the utmost importance to the argumentative arts of the Baroque: 'there will always be heretics, but this is what *we* think'.

The shrine of St Ignatius in the church of the Gesú has on one side of the lapis-lazuli sarcophagus, Europe falling into schism and error, with a ferocious cupidon attempting to tear the Reformation out of the marble book of history. But on the other side are African kings and Asian savants embracing the light which, refracting in gold, streams from the windows at the east end of the church.

8 That being so, Baroque believes that emblematics – taken in its widest sense – is the most honest and acceptable form of imaginative endeavour

The question is not whether moral messages derivable from the natural world are divinely installed or not – rather, once they've been read as such, what follows? Much of the text which follows will be devoted to attempting to understand the emblematising genius of the baroque epochs, the complex, developed and essential capacity to read things, plants, gardens, buildings, gestures, utterances, arches, stars and events, as well as to interpret retrospectively the literatures and images of all the plural antiquities.

9 The Baroque is not ignorant, and it is unshockable

It is simultaneously sophisticated and optimistic. It evolved (or it comes, or it returns) at moments when contemporary culture has been saturated with imaginative depictions of evil. It doesn't take its fathers' descriptions of evil on trust: it condemns evil, but it is only frightened by the poverty of what evil elicits imaginatively. Virtue is copious. The Baroque is copious in the commendation of virtue.

10 *Hence, it coincides with decadence although it is not necessarily decadent of itself*

It believes that temptation is played out. It's explicitly anti-Romantic, hence its Miltonic proof-text is not *Paradise Lost* but *Paradise Regained*.

Versions of European baroque architecture recur in successive eras as architectures of splendour. Baroque has been used, in revival, as the decor of decadence but is not of necessity decadent in itself, indeed it is too multifarious and energetic to be decadent.

Thus there has arisen a tendency, particularly in northern Europe, to read magnificence and astonishment as intrinsically rather than coincidentally decadent. Baroque itself has remarkably little nostalgia and remarkably little regret, although the Baroque is fearless in the exploration of melancholia, recognising (as Classicism in all its idealistic forms has never really done) that melancholia is an inextricable part of human experience: Pope and Swift were often melancholy, but they were never serious. Melancholia is a very different thing from decadence.

With colleagues at the Herzog August Bibliothek at Wolfenbüttel, we convened a conference on 'Triumphs of the Defeated' in 2005 to study the public lives and ceremonial of groups of people in baroque Europe and America who had, by any normal standard, lost their particular battles and ended in exile or captivity. We had reckoned to some degree without the baroque capacity never to be at a loss, so what we actually ended up with was a colloquium on the arts of those who thought they *should* have won (indeed, morally *had* won) and refused, ceremonially, emblematically or culturally, to accept defeat. Baroque as consolation.

*

Those few baroque works which appear genuinely decadent are exceptions. What they appear to have in common is a playing (luxuriously, frivolously, masochistically) with the notion of destruction divorced from any mitigating philosophical element of edification or transformation. Thus the '*parco degli mostri*' at Bomarzo in Lazio with its hell grotto, its falling tower, its snarling metamorphic creatures cut out of the living rock, is genuinely childish and nasty and appears to have been intended to be so from the start. The inscriptions about *meraviglie* at the entrance seem disingenuous. This is a discourse designed to make sense on a large scale deliberately reduced to nonsense: the garden guest (an important subdivision of baroque reader) is being bombarded with contemptuous nonsense. This argument could extend to seeing the later, content-free Whig landscapes of England, sometimes read as the noble quintessence of English landscape art, as sterile aestheticism devoid of content,[30] as truly decadent in a way which even the bitter and sensationalist garden at Bomarzo is not.

Late in the German *barochetto* come two works which seem genuinely decadent, genuinely disturbing. These are theatres built in the form of ruins, extraordinarily elaborate structural facsimiles of court summer-garden theatres as they might look after war, revolution or cataclysm had reduced them to a fragmentary condition. And yet the courts of the Margraves acted pastorals with music in them on summer evenings, thrilling deliciously to the imagination of their own destruction.[31] These theatres do seem disquieting in that they toy with the idea of what will be left when the revolutions have swept their owners, their courts, their *castrato* singers and their kappelmeisters away. That is very different from the contemplation of the *memento mori* and the contemplation of the passing of the glory of the world.

11 In the end 'Baroque' is used in much of Northern Europe and North America as a distancing term for a recurring mode of European culture

This is a crucial point for Eugenio d'Ors: his Baroque is recurrent, or perhaps remontant like the roses the Jesuits brought from China. Baroque in this sense is that which keeps coming round in alternation with the austerities of what are called Classicism or Enlightenment. Greek Alexandrianism and the Jewelled Style of late antiquity are both baroque phenomena. If Classicism is a cyclic phenomenon then Baroque is its cyclic alternative. In remotest antiquity, the Mausoleum of Halicarnassus is *already* baroque, by contrast with the paradigmatic Classicism of the Parthenon. Ancient synonyms, or near-synonyms, for Baroque are 'Asian', 'Persian' or 'African'. *Plus ça change* . . . Classicism often presents itself in the guise of the revival of ancient virtue, and a return to the values of a defined period of the past, always danger signals in European culture. They seem very visible at the moment.

Revolutionary enlightenment, of the political right or left indifferently, cannot tolerate Baroque, a mode which continually makes accommodations with the *status quo*, indeed continually offers strategies for living with the *status quo*. If one is looking for the origins of totalitarianism, in politics or in the arts, it is not to be found in the Baroque, however much the Baroque may have been the servant of absolutism. It is to be found in the civic pieties, national origin-myths and mystical nature-worship of the Enlightenment and the late eighteenth-century revolutions.

12 Baroque, despite all this, is still wholly valid as a descriptor of period
I have argued above that *Baroque* is *the* liberating word with which to
recognise the international cultural system of the early modern world.
It was certainly the case that the later sixteenth, seventeenth and most
of the eighteenth centuries saw a particularly long ascendancy of the
kinds of arts which we have identified as *Baroque*. Was the early sixteenth
century a great hinge in human history or was it not? There were many
who asserted that nothing had changed (often these were Protestants,
insisting that the Reformation was no more than a setting of the
Lord's house in order). The Jesuits, by contrast, asserted that everything
had changed, *and not irrecoverably for the worse.* 'Baroque realism'
sounds oxymoronic, but the more the phenomenon of the Baroque
is considered, the more it is possible to see it as the cultural mode of
those dealing with the world as it is, in its magnificence as well as its
melancholy and horror.

Baroque is an artistic mode for realists, beside which most 'realisms'
look mannered and contrived. If this assertion appears to contradict
the wide perception that the baroque arts occupy a dimension of out-
rageous fantasy and camp removed from reality, so much the better.
Baroque art always moves in parallel to reality, taking its cues from the
actual. Camp is not an escapist mode, it is a mode evolved for dealing
with reality using the high-baroque devices of ritualised and figurative
speech, paradoxical splendour and quotidian magnificence. The *correct*
response to many an allegorical painted ceiling in many a palace in
Rome or in many a Villa on the *terra firma* of the Veneto is to say 'in
your dreams', but not to say it with a twenty-first-century intonation.[32]

Having attempted, in however summary a way, to offer some ideas
about Baroque in the largest sense, it is time to conclude this introduction by indicating those aspects of Baroque which are especially the
subjects of this book: Baroque at the frontiers and on the margins. I
will not try to argue about the entire baroque world (no life would be
long enough) but will concentrate specifically on the phenomena of
baroque accommodation and baroque hybridity, phenomena found most
often at frontiers between cultures; so this book will concern itself mostly
with the frontiers of the Baroque. A series of such works from the
frontiers might serve to begin my newly proposed cartography of the
baroque world, by pinpointing widely scattered areas which look
peripheral on the cultural map of the world after the nineteenth
century, but which were then autonomous cultural centres, indeed
centres where an autocthonous culture interacted and hybridised with
what was international in the baroque mode.

So, in conclusion, which is also anticipation, let us list some of these triumphs from the frontiers of the Baroque:

*

The northern Scotsman Arthur Johnston's Latin verses on a clan feud which can be read *at once* as an Ovidian verse letter and as a traditional Highland *caointe* or lament for the dead.

*

The hybrid poetics of the 'Mestizo elegies' in honour of the Aztec ancestors by Don Fernando de Alva Ixtlilxóchitl which speak of Mexican kings in the style of Spanish medieval romance.

*

The paintings of the Cuzco school which show plumed and brocaded angels armed with firearms, figures which are both Inca wind-gods and apocryphal Christian archangels.

*

The poems of the Chinese savant and Jesuit convert Wu Li in Macao which combine Latin rhetoric and Chinese poetic diction, two balancing traditions of 'antiquity', two weighty sets of classical ancestors.

Notes

1 Eugenio d'Ors, *Du Baroque*, trans. Agathe Rouart-Valéry [1935] (Paris: nrf/Gallimard, 1968). The original Spanish version was published after the French version: a current Spanish edition which I have also consulted is *Lo Barocco*, ed. Ángel d'Ors and Alicia García Navaro de d'Ors (Madrid: Tecnos/Alianza, 2002). I refer to the French edition, but for occasional material not in that edition (added from d'Ors's papers after his death) I refer also to the Spanish text.
2 This is very approximately the use of the word made by the great Italian critic Benedetto Croce.
3 There are certain English academics who find themselves unable to use the word at all: I remember attending a colloquium initially titled 'European festivals of the Renaissance *and after*', my emphasis, naturally.
4 This summary account is based on Gauvin Alexander Bailey's nuanced history of these terms in *Between Renaissance and Baroque: Jesuit Art in Rome, 1565–1610* (Toronto: University of Toronto Press, 2003), pp. 22–30.
5 Michel de Montaigne, *The Essayes of Michael Lord of Montaigne*, trans. John Florio (London: Oxford University Press, 1910), p. 184.

6 Michel de Montaigne, *Essais* (I:XXVI), in *Oeuvres complètes*, ed. Albert Thibaudet and Maurice Rat (Paris: Gallimard, 1962) I, p. 160.

7 Benedetto Croce, *La storia di l'età barocca in Italia* (Bari: Laterza, 1957), pp. 34, 24.

8 *Ibid.*, p. 4.

9 d'Ors, *Du baroque*, p. 80.

10 Wallace Stephens, 'The Blue Guitar' in *The Collected Poems* (New York: Vintage, 1982), p. 165.

11 d'Ors, *Du baroque*, p. 83.

12 *Ibid.*, p. 170.

13 Robert Harbison, *Reflections on Baroque* (London: Reaktion, 2000), p. vii.

14 *Ibid.*, pp. 192 *et seq.*

15 *Ibid.*, p. 164.

16 *Ibid.*, pp. 165–6. My italics, I'm afraid.

17 Giovanni Careri, *Baroques* (Princeton: Princeton University Press, 2003), p. 7.

18 *Ibid.*, p. 24.

19 Gauvin Alexander Bailey, 'Le style jésuite n'existe pas', in *The Jesuits: Cultures, Sciences and the Arts*, ed. John W., O'Malley SJ, *et al.* (Toronto: University of Toronto Press, 1999), p. 39.

20 Anthony Blunt, *The Art and Architecture of France, 1500–1700* (London and Baltimore: Johns Hopkins University Press, 1953), p. 176.

21 A term widely used in architectural writing of the twentieth century to describe what any other European country would identify without hesitation as locally created Baroque.

22 These theses have been evolved with Dr Alison Shell: we are intending to publish a collaborative work, *Thirty-six Theses on the Baroque*, within the next few years.

23 For the Manila Galleon and for far-eastern artistic influences on baroque Ibero-America, see Gauvin Alexander Bailey, *Art of Colonial Latin America* (London: Phaidon, 2005), pp. 339, 344. Also at 344 see the extraordinary Brazilian church tower entirely ornamented with blue and white East Asian porcelain.

24 *Celebridad y Fiestas, con que la Insigne y nobilissima Ciudad de los Reyes Solemnizo la Beatificacion de la Bienaventura ROSA DE S. MARIA SU PATRONA Y DE TODOS LOS REYNOS Y PROVINCIAS DEL PERU, con Licencia en Lima el año de 1670.* The only copy of this rare work known to me is in the Victoria and Albert Museum, National Art Library, Piot 884B. This rose poem resonates with an English recusant Catholic example from a few decades earlier, a clinching piece of evidence *contra* anyone inclined to deny the existence of an English Baroque: 'O flower of flowers, rose of roses, o flower of roses, O rose of flowers, shore me up with flowers, because I languish for love of thy love, Jesus, the Bud of thee O rose, little in thy womb, greater in thine armes, And then fairest of all, when opened

throughly and displayed on the Crosse, by that precious blood of thine I beseech thee, and the shedding of his most precious blood, thou wouldest change my thornes into roses, and present as a rose of sweet odours to thy sonne and not as thornes for fewell for the fire of fierce Indignation, o grant mee this I beseech thee, and here doe I present in honour of thee, the misticall rose, and thy sonne, thy soveraigne budd, the hym that followes . . .' (Oxford, Bodleian Library, MS Eng Poet b. 5, p. 107).

25 Gauvin Alexander Bailey, *Art on the Jesuit Missions in Asia and Latin America, 1542–1773* (Toronto: University of Toronto Press, 1999), p. 155, quoting manuscript Archivium Romanum Societatis Jesu, Paraq. 8, f. 360*v*.

26 d'Ors, *Du baroque*, pp. 212–13.

27 St Ignatius of Loyola, *Personal Writings*, ed. and trans. Joseph A. Munitiz and Philip Endean (London: Penguin, 1996), pp. 307 *et seq.*

28 Careri, *Baroques*, pp. 124–8.

29 For the caricature heads representing extremes of emotion, made by the outsider artist Franz Xaver Messerschmidt, cf. Harbison, *Reflections on Baroque*, pp. 160–3.

30 A beautifully nuanced discussion of these gardens (which is not as laudatory as their greatest admirers might wish, nor as critical as my snide little hyperbole) is found in David R. Coffin, *The English Garden: Meditation and Memorial* (Princeton: Princeton University Press, 1994); see pp. 68–9 for a description of the extraordinary 1740s death garden of the proprietor of the London Vauxhall pleasure-gardens, Jonathan Tyers, a baroque survival if ever there was one.

31 Margurete Baur-Heinhold, *Baroque Theatre* (London: Thames and Hudson, 1967), pp. 155–6 for the ruin-theatres at Bayreuth and Berg Zwernitz.

32 Christopher Isherwood's interpretation is highly relevant: 'You can't camp about something you don't take seriously. You're not making fun of it, you're making fun out of it. You're expressing what is basically serious to you in terms of fun and artifice and elegance. Baroque art is largely camp about religion. The ballet is camp about love.' Quoted in Ian Gregson, 'Camp's Out', *Poetry Review*, 86:3 (Autumn 1996), p. 15.

I

British Baroque

The nation state is the enemy of the Baroque. More specifically, the traditions of historiography and cultural criticism fostered by the nation state are intensely hostile to those elements in the early modern world which clearly were supra-national and common to almost all territories. These elements (international Latin literature, an international language of symbol and image) are, habitually and indicatively, dismissed as 'foreign' to English cultural tradition by English-speaking critics. It is equally difficult to argue for Scottish or Irish participation in the baroque world, as their respective national histories have been developed (almost explicitly) to preclude this possibility.

The primary problem before us is the historical use of the word *Baroque* in English. It is hardly ever a neutral descriptor. Elsewhere, outside the English-speaking world, *Baroque* can be a neutral word, which has outlived most of the tensions which it generated in writers such as Benedetto Croce. It now identifies, relatively straightforwardly, a style in architecture, music and the visual arts which can be applied by simple extension to the literatures of the baroque centuries. English, for reasons which I will seek to disentangle in the course of this chapter, has always been structurally resistant to Baroque either as a word or a concept. In English, Baroque is commonly synonymous with the tortuous, the devious, the perverse. Anachronistically, it is identified as a manifestation of childish bad taste, hysterics, the bad form of varnished tears and sacred waxworks.

On the contrary, it is fruitful to think of the baroque arts as a single continuum which stretches (in literature and festival, in image and inscription) from Donne and Herbert in England to Crashaw in Cambridge, Paris or Loreto, to Marino in Naples, to Góngora in Madrid, to Huygens in the Hague, to the exiled and native Latinists of

Scotland, to Pierce Ferriter on the west coast of Ireland. And, crucially, this continuum fully embraces Sor Juana de la Cruz in her convent in Mexico City and the savant Carlos de Sigüenza y Góngora in the University of Mexico.

The Baroque in England

In the peculiar case of England, Shakespeare's immense posthumous prestige has distorted the whole picture of the literary arts in England in the sixteenth and seventeenth centuries. As has frequently been pointed out, he is the sole non-university graduate among the English playwrights; the only one who, as far as we know, preserved nothing composed in Latin. In much nineteenth- and even twentieth-century criticism, his anomalousness is loosely linked with his genius in an implicit argument that his relative lack of education is part of what makes him peculiarly English, a warbler of *native* wood-notes wild, and, for that very reason, better than any of his contemporaries.

British English and the academy in Britain are uneasy about *Baroque* as a neutral descriptor. Almost all definitions of *Baroque* offered by the *OED* are negative or disparaging, and there is a tradition both of thinking of the Baroque as Catholic and of perceiving the Catholic arts as the arts of the enemy, of that group of peoples against which Englishness defines itself by negation. This disjunction is maintained despite the fact that a vast sweep of British cultural activity falls squarely within even the most stringent definition of 'international Baroque'.

To name but a few: it would be difficult to assign any other descriptor than *Baroque* to phenomena such as these: controversies about British antiquity, especially the ancestral theories of Inigo Jones and Richard Verstegan;[1] much of the culture of the English court, especially the masques and pastorals of the reign of Charles I; most tombs and monuments of the seventeenth century throughout Britain, perhaps more unequivocally baroque the humbler and more remote they are, culminating in the series of tremendous grave-slabs with Latin inscriptions in the cathedral of Kirkwall; the tradition of portraiture stemming from Van Dyck and Dobson, particularly portraits depicting great ladies of equivocal reputation as personifications of the virtues; many of the most admired dramas of the London 'private' theatres of the seventeenth century, especially the pastorals of John Fletcher (we should perhaps add that these were admired extravagantly in their day, so much so that one of them was paid the baroque compliment of preservation in the imperishable amber of the Latin language);[2] the greater part of the poetry of Donne and Herbert, and, even more so, of Caroline poets such as William Strode, Clement Paman and Katherine Philips; the cabinets of curiosities of the Tradescants and of John Bargrave;[3] the extraordinary and, in the modern sense, queer, pavilion and grotto of Thomas Bushell at Enstone in Oxfordshire, complete, eventually, with an Egyptian mummy presented by Henrietta Maria; the moralised descriptions of gardens and galleries of Andrew Marvell; the process whereby Sir Kenelm Digby mourned and commemorated his dead wife; the gardens, buildings and opinions of John Evelyn; the magnificences of Wren and Hawksmoor in their idiosyncratic evocations of antiquity, particularly those moments where Hawksmoor's architecture evokes in the spectator melancholy, disquiet or panic; the tensions and formalities of the dramas of Dryden and Otway; the garden and grotto of Alexander Pope; and almost all the major architectural projects that were never realised, such as Inigo Jones's, Wren's and the Earl of Mar's rebuildings of London. Most of these manifestations of an English baroque culture will be discussed in the pages that follow.

Furthermore, England is not the only culture in the British Isles, which is perhaps the most important point of this opening chapter. There is as much evidence, indeed, for the arrival of high-renaissance Italian culture in Scotland (and its subsequent development into baroque culture) as in England, witnessed, for example, by the annotated Ficino in the possession of Hector Boece, first principal of the University of Aberdeen and friend of Erasmus, as well as by the programme of translations from modern European literature and the production and consumption of neo-Latin literature at the court of James VI.[4] Similarly, 'the Renaissance in Ireland' is far from the oxymoron that it seems in the eyes of conservative English historians. The brief period of respite which the indigenous Irish elite enjoyed in the 1640s, the time of the Confederacy, was also a moment for the flowering of a brief but real and accomplished international culture, expressing itself chiefly in Latin and Irish. In general, it would be accurate to assert that the arts in Britain and Ireland participated fully in international cultural systems and styles. But (I concede this) there was in England specifically a developed hostility to the foreign in general and the foreign arts in particular which ran alongside it: English use of 'foreign' to this day perpetuates an unusually pejorative perception of the trans-national, even in academic and educated discourse. Thus there arose a dichotomy which English cultural history has failed to resolve.

Early modern English culture moved in antithetic directions. The culture of Elizabethan England is *eccentric* in the sense of being oppositional to a clearly perceptible European mainstream, in a way which arose from sixteenth-century problems, but set the terms of political expression for the Queen's successors. Two impulses were at war in the circles immediately contiguous to Elizabeth, one of which represented English culture as stand-alone and autochthonous, while a contrary cultural impulse was eager to look civilised in continental terms. There was, as a background to this, the continual complication that the two European countries which contended for cultural primacy in the sixteenth century, France and Italy, had both, for political and religious reasons, to be defined as being in the hands of the enemy. This created a problem which dogs cultural history of the period to this day.

> Italie now, is not that *Italie*, that it was wont to be: and therfore now, not so fitte a place as some do count it, for yong men to fetch either wisedome or honestie from thence . . . I know diuerse noble personages . . . whom all the *Siren* songes of *Italie* could neuer untwyne from the maste of Gods word: no: no inchantement of vanitie, overturne them, from the feare of God, and love of honestie. But I know as manie, and some, sometyme my neare frendes, for whose sake I hate going into that countrey the more, who, partyng out of England feruent in the loue of Christes doctrine, and well furnished with the feare of God, returned out of Italie worse transformed, than euer was any in *Circes* Court.[5]

So there is, in sixteenth-century England, an insular culture, and an international culture. To generalise very broadly, the first of these tends to be expressed in English, the second, at least at first, in Latin. This divided mentality persists into the seventeenth century, fuelled to some degree by popular suspicion of the international cultures at the courts of successive foreign (and Catholic) Stuart queens.

The grounds on which early modern England consciously resisted some elements of international culture arose from perception of identity as well as religion: emotive, unstable and therefore dangerous territories. However, England was a participant in international culture to an infinitely greater degree than is generally thought, since the study of early modern England (this applies to visual art and architecture as much as it does to literature) has been focused on the vernacular to an extent which effectively precludes the discussion of how the culture functioned as a whole.

Although England was resistant to the international in some respects, at the same time English participation in international baroque modes in all the arts has, in retrospect, been underplayed very considerably. This is particularly the case with respect to the arts of the later seventeenth century. As we will see, this falsification expresses itself very much through terminology. The chief culprit is 'metaphysical', a term adopted in the eighteenth century, but revived in an atmosphere of nationalist anxiety as a deliberate attempt to suppress the degree of connection between the poetry of early modern England and that of the contemporary Continent.

False distinctions and falsified histories took hold in nineteenth-century England in the wake of the Oxford Movement, which was essentially a movement to Catholicise or re-Catholicise the Church of England, and the controversies which it subsequently engendered. In the context of the immense cultural self-confidence of late nineteenth-century England, Catholicism was very much seen as the Church of Rome: that is, an Italian, and therefore inimical, institution. Ultra-montanism, and its quietly baroque aesthetic reflections such as the Brompton Oratory in London, were seen as a threat to national religious integrity, and the academic backlash against the Baroque was therefore informed by anxieties which even the writers themselves may not all have consciously understood.

In nineteenth-century writing on the arts, Baroque is explicitly identified as Catholic and, consequently, of the enemy. This automatic English suspicion and dislike of foreignness, and Romanness in particular, was also exacerbated by an ideological hangover from the eighteenth century: the complication of the Jacobite cause, which inextricably linked Stuart absolutism with Catholicism, and combined religious with political alterity. Rome, the Catholic church, and the Latin language were thus further tainted by the association which they evoked: that of the Catholic shadow-court of the Pretender in the Palazzo Muti in Rome. The whole history of the subsequent misapprehension of the Laudian attempt to *Lutheranise* the observances and arts of the Church of England in the 1630s as an attempt to Romanise them has served greatly to complicate the issue.[6]

So, to summarise the histories of anti-baroque prejudice: acceptance of the international cultural mode is only partial in early modern England. The dichotomy between the Anglophone and insular party among England's artists and intellegentsia and the group which, conversely, participated fully in the international cultural life of the time hardened into a conscious opposition, as the first group identified itself in time with authentic Englishness, just governance and Reformed religion, a position which was partly achieved in opposition to the contemporary Catholic argument that authentic Englishness was by definition recusant. Thus internationalism is presented, at least by its opponents, as tainted by the absolutist innovations in church and state promulgated by the Stuarts which led to the civil war, and, in the eighteenth century, to the whole other dichotomy of the oppositional realities of Jacobites versus Hanoverians. It was only decades after the death of the last shadow-king at Rome in 1807 that the Oxford Movement, perceived as a foreign (and indeed baroque) assault on the religious identity of England, revived these polarisations at a time when the critical and historiographical vocabulary of the British nation state was developing the kinds of loaded terminology against which any positive anglophone use of the word *Baroque* is, to some small degree, still a challenge.

But early modern Baroque is, in fact, supra-confessional. There is Lutheran and Calvinist Baroque, as the flourishing baroque cultures of early modern Sweden and the Netherlands witness. Calvinist baroque art, architecture and poetry also flourished in Scotland. But, in the divided history of England, that element which was continuous with the Baroque of the Continent has by and large been elided from view.

However, to discuss early modern literary culture only in terms of vernacular literatures is to play an intellectual game as restricted and as divorced from early modern realities as any of the 'childish' games with anagrams or pattern-poems which have consistently drawn the wrath of English critics (except, of course, when they are the work of George Herbert). This is not to deny a demonstrable element of French and Italian influence on English writing. The point is that compared to the amount of intellectual activity which involved Latin, the quantity of early modern intellectual activity which involved individuals learning modern languages was comparatively modest, and the interface between vernacular cultures was correspondingly small. The polymath Constantijn Huygens in the Netherlands and the English diplomat Richard Fanshawe were both noted in their own day as prodigies simply because of their genuine command of a complete linguistic system in more than three modern languages. It might be noted, however, that both of them based their international cultural activities on their command of Latin, both being, even by the high standards of the seventeenth century, outstanding Latinists.[7]

There are two subsidiary points to be noted here – though there is no space to pursue either in detail. One is that the majority of Latinists could use their Latin as a means of at least passive access to the Romance languages (as readers, though not writers), the other is that early modern ritual assertions of the linguistic attainments of the elite must be treated with a considerable degree of caution. Ability to utter a few elegant sentences on a formal and ritualised occasion does not of necessity imply a command of the complete system of a language. There is a difference between greeting an ambassador and being able to compose verse in three languages. Elizabeth I's foreign languages were on exhibition in formal circumstances completely under her control, though there is considerable evidence that she worked hard on languages, and her grasp was frequently commended by relatively disinterested witnesses.[8] The miscellaneous ability of her cousin Mary Stuart to compose in French, Latin and Italian is attested by contemporary sources, but, it must be added, contemporary sources also attest that Mary's control of any Germanic language was confined (at least in writing) to a modest command of Scots.

The picture of cultural relations between Britain and Ireland and the Continent is enriched by locating vernacular writing as a part of an international cultural framework held together by the use of Latin as an international language. It is particularly important here that literary activity in Latin is crucial in both Scotland and Ireland (and in communities of exiles from Britain) and that this corpus of material is barely known, an absence which inevitably unbalances any understanding of the patterns of baroque culture in the British Isles.

Early modern England, Scotland, Wales and Ireland functioned as mutually distinct parts of an international literary world. European neo-Latin poets were read and printed in England, and the poetry of Scots and English writers was likewise read and printed abroad. Sir Thomas More's *Epigrams* were first printed in Basel; the Welsh John Owen's epigrams were appreciated throughout Europe and went through dozens of foreign editions; while many Scots writers, such as Arthur Johnston, Andrew and John Leech, George Buchanan and Patrick Adamson were printed in Europe.[9] Conversely, Latin schoolbooks of continental origin were printed in England, including the *Zodiacus Vitae* of Palengenius, which is the source for two of Shakespeare's most famous speeches, 'All the world's a stage . . .' in *As You Like It*, and 'Our revels are now ended . . .' in *The Tempest.* The circulation of texts flowed both ways, and it is impossible to arrive at an accurate idea of the culture of early modern Britain without taking this into account.

One foreign writer published in London who is worth pausing over is Matthias Casimir Sarbievius (Sarbiewski), a paradigmatic baroque figure, a twice-exiled Polish Jesuit whose poems set a standard for the Latinity of the seventeenth century. Among the many pleasures of the parallel-text *Odes of Casimire* (1643) is a poem on a friend's dead wife, glimpsed in the paradise garden;

> Aut vidi, aut vidisse putavi
> Errantem campo in magno, quem gemmea circum
> Perspicuis stant moenia portis:
> Auro prata virent; arbor crinitur in aurum;
> Crispantur violaria gemmis,
> Quae nec Apellaeus liquor, nec pulchra trigoni
> Assimulent mendacia vitri.
> Centum ibi formosis in vallibus Heroïnae
> Aeternam Paeana frequentant . . .[10]

> [I saw, or else me thoughts, I there had seene
> Her, wandring o're a spacious Greene,
> With walls of Diamond, gates of purest glasse,
> No Chrystall more transparent was:
> Each blade of grasse was gold, each tree was there,
> A golden Periwig did weare.
> The swelling banks of Violets did curle
> Themselves with Gems, and Orient Pearle;
> The glorious nothing, of the *Trigon* glasse –
> And all *Apelles* Art, which passe.
> Through the sweet vales a Quire of damsels sing
> Eternall Paeans to their King.]

It would be possible to assert that Andrew Marvell (whose command of Latin is attested by the fact that he was Cromwell's Latin secretary), to name but the most obvious, was utterly uninfluenced by, and unaware of, the poetics of Sarbievius, but such a stance is effectively a political statement about what one is willing to perceive.

That there are reasons for choosing not to engage with the challenge which Sarbievius offers to the view of English poetics as autochthonous (apart from, of course, a direct dependence on Petrarch's *dolce stil nuovo*), is suggested by a poem elsewhere in this volume, written to 'Paulus Jordanus Ursinus, Duke of Bracciano: he commends the pleasantnesse of the Countrey, where in the heats of September, he retyred from Rome'.[11] This is a classic country-house poem, a picture of an ideal Christian gentleman retired in a *locus amoenus* of temperate rural pleasures. But the Duke of Bracciano, of course, is more familiar to English readers as the lust-crazed, slavering monster in John Webster's *The White Devil*. Another of Sarbievius's poems, 'The voyce of Christe upon the Crosse. I Thirst', combining epigrammatic terseness with profound feeling, bears comparison with the religious verse of George Herbert.

Ah, sitio, clamas, Princeps pulcherrime rerum:
  Non habeo pro te dulcia vina, siti,
To tamen, ah sitio, clamas: dabo pocula, Sponse:
  Heu mihi! Sed misto pocula felle dabo.
Haec mi Sponse, bibe: quaeris cui fortè propines?
  Ad me pro mundi, *Christe,* salute bibi.[12]

[Alas I thirst, great King, thou loud dost grone;
  I have no pleasant Wine for Thee, thirst on.
Yet oh I thirst, thou cry'st: a Cup to thee
  Woes mee! I'le give: but mix'd with gall't must be.
Drink this, my Spouse: perhaps thou'lt ask to whom?
  To me, O Christ, to th'health o'th'world let't come.]

The difficulties in the way of acknowledging any kind of real interaction between continental writers such as Sarbievius and English poets are complicated by the fact that such interchanges normally occur in a language, Latin, which is not treated as a part of literary studies, and also arise from a somewhat naive assumption that, since Catholics in general, and the Jesuits in particular, were loathed, despised and execrated by English Protestant intellectuals, they therefore did not read Jesuit poets. English literary scholarship has seldom cared to look very hard at the reception history of foreign writers in England; though the fact that the seventeenth-century English reading public was devouring internationally best-selling writings by Catholics, such as Barclay's *Argenis* and the novels of Madeleine de Scudéry, both in the original and in translation, is obvious to anyone who looks at contemporary diaries and letters.

Another thing which obscures the picture of English relations with the Continent is English critics' traditional desire to see a direct line of literary influence on vernacular English writing from renaissance Italy, particularly from the admired tradition of vernacular poetry stemming from Petrarch, while simultaneously denying any influence from later Italian letters. At its simplest, this is a desire to demonstrate a cultural *translatio imperii* which vindicates the status of imperial England. The problem recurs, in the discussion of a later period, with the use of such terms as 'Augustan', in itself an arrogantly explicit claim for such a cultural *translatio.* 'Augustan' is, of course, yet another way of not saying 'baroque', while claiming neo-classical status for a cultural phenomenon only neo-classical in the same relative sense that much baroque literary and architectural activity is referential to the achievements of Roman antiquity.

The importance of Italian, and speakers of both Italian and English, in the reception of the new learning in England is negligible compared with the importance of Latin. As Michael Wyatt's recent study of Italian influence in Tudor England has demonstrated, the lines of transmission between renaissance Italy and England are much thinner and much more intermittent than has generally been held to be the case. His radically revisionist study painstakingly traces the limitations of Italian influence in England in the course of the sixteenth century, and the picture with which he concludes is one wholly at odds with the pieties and wishful thinking of mid-twentieth-century 'Renaissance Studies'.[13] What Wyatt successfully demonstrates is that Italian culture was received in England almost entirely through a small number of Waldensian refugees, and the Italian learned and spoken at Elizabeth's court was Waldensian dialect. It is as though (in an unimaginable reversal of roles) the Dukes of Tuscany or the Kings of Spain had wanted to know about English literature and culture and found that the only people available to tell them were a few recusant Catholic Highland and Lancastrian exiles. As far as is currently known, Elizabeth's court only ever received one really smart Italian visitor who was not on a formal embassy, Paolo Giordano Orsini, who lends his name to the duke in Shakespeare's *Twelfth Night.*[14]

This essential fact, that 'renaissance' or international ideas generally arrived in Britain through the medium of Latin, is one to which Britain seems still remarkably resistant. Again one can only assume the assumptions of the nation state have been anachronistically backdated; though, of course, it is also relevant to note that the fact that a knowledge of Latin has been a rare accomplishment among students of the humanities since the 1970s means that there is a considerable vested interest in the academy's *not* acknowledging it.

Enough assertions: it is time to move to facts and demonstrations. To appreciate the connectedness of Britain, rather than British isolation, requires some explanation of the degree to which the English intelligentsia, Protestant and Catholic, were in dialogue with Continental writers, mostly through the medium of Latin, and yet at the same time, paradoxically, a sense of England's parallel thread of insularity and xenophobia. At the beginning of the sixteenth century, Erasmus publicised the household of Sir Thomas More as an example of the new-style renaissance humanist household, rich in the study of Latin, Greek and mathematics. This English humanism survived the Reformation, but the Reformation shaped and limited the forms which it took.

The fact that many of the principal opinion-formers of the mid-sixteenth century were strongly Calvinist did not prevent them from being highly cultivated. Sir Philip Hoby was one of the very few Englishmen of the Henrician era to travel on the Continent, because he was perceived (accurately) as religiously sound and politically incorruptible. He is also one of relatively few points of interface between England and the Italian Renaissance, since he was acquainted with both Titian and Pietro Aretino. When the latter dedicated one of his books to Henry VIII in 1546, Hoby presented Aretino with a gratuity from the King. His half-brother Edward Hoby, who translated Castiglione's *The Courtier*, travelled extensively in Italy, but, rather more characteristically for an Englishman of his time, confined his acquaintance to religious reformers. In the 1550s and 1560s, such men formed a close-knit and much-intermarried circle of fiercely Calvinist intellectuals, men and women who were significant patrons of learning and culture in England.[15] Most of them could, and did, write Latin verse themselves; they also patronised various genres of new writing, including neo-Latin. For example, Phineas Fletcher presented his 'Querela collegii regali', the first Latin pastoral to be written in England, to Mildred Cecil, Lady Burleigh, herself a student of Latin and Greek and Edward Hoby's sister-in-law.[16]

The contrary, or nativist, movement in English culture is connected with the peculiarities of Elizabeth's position. In a purely legal sense, Elizabeth, defined as illegitimate by her father, had no more claim on the throne than her half-brother Henry Fitzroy would have had were he still alive in 1558. She was not in fact, queen by the grace of God, but by the grace of Parliament, a fact which explains much about her reign.[17] Moreover, there was an unequivocally legitimate claimant, supported by a major foreign power: Mary Stuart, the daughter of Elizabeth's father's sister, whose father-in-law, Henri II of France, began to speak of her as Queen of England as soon as he heard of the death of Queen Mary. The fact that the succession of Henry VIII's three surviving children seems according to common sense should not disguise from us that 'the lady Elizabeth' began in a far weaker position than either of her siblings. The additional fact that the shadow queen, Mary Queen of Scots, was Catholic, had two effects. It exacerbated anti-Catholic paranoia, which had already been given a considerable boost by Mary Tudor's unlucky attempt not so much to revive English Catholicism as to impose Spanish Catholicism. It also ensured attention to Elizabeth from other Protestant monarchs, and their writers.

Out of her weak position, Elizabeth created a kind of strength, built on fear of alternatives. As a result, her court culture was insular, capricious in its adoption of continental models, and not strongly intellectual. The insularity of Elizabeth's England is celebrated as a positive virtue by Robert Devereux, second Earl of Essex, one of the most adroit yet overweening of royal favourites, a man who absorbed nearly half of all the crown patronage dispensed by the Queen during the last decade of her reign.

> Seated betweene the olde world and the newe,
> A Land there is no other lande may touche,
> Where regnes a Queen in peace and honor true;
> Storyes or fables doe describe noe suche;
> Never did Atlas such a burthen beare
> As shee, in holding up the world opprest,
> Supplying with her vertue every where
> Weaknes of friends, errors of Servants best.
> No nation breeds a warmer bloud for warre,
> And yet She calmes them with her Majesty;
> No age hath ever witte refyned so farre,
> And yet she calmes them by her pollicie.
> To her thy sonne must make his sacrifice,
> If he will have the morning of his eyes.[18]

One aspect of Elizabethan court culture which does look forward to the Baroque is the tendency to produce images which are legible within more than one frame of reference. Roy Strong had made a case for reading a picture known as *The Persian lady*, now at Hampton Court, as a last-minute plea for reprieve from the gallows for this same Earl of Essex, and for identifying the Lady as Lady Essex, Frances Walsingham, who must therefore have commissioned the picture and presented it to Elizabeth in 1600 following the Essex rebellion.[19] Elizabeth would have read the picture in the same way that she was used to reading Accession Day emblems and other allegorical presentations by courtiers. The image of the lady in Persian dress standing beneath a tree with a tame stag is reinforced by a series of superimposed Latin mottoes and a sonnet in a fretwork cartouche. Superficially, it is a fantasy portrait of a great lady in exotic dress. It is also a plea for clemency in the light of that lady's symbolically articulated sorrow, melancholia and desperation. This type of mixed-media artwork is very common in the sixteenth century, and is strongly influenced by the emblem, an art form wholly acceptable to even the most Calvinist of Protestants (indeed, this painting effectively *is* an emblem, in which the purely pictorial element occupies an unusually prominent place with respect to the motto(es) and verses).

The humanist elite of the court was a very small one indeed. Burleigh and his wife were generous and systematic patrons,[20] and so was Leicester, whose activities as a patron have been discussed by Eleanor Rosenberg.[21] Thomas Drant's translation of Horace was dedicated to Lady Burleigh and Lady Bacon (her sister); while other Burleigh proteges included, apart from Drant, the translators Robinson and Golding, the chronicler Richard Grafton, Barnaby Googe and Thomas Wilson.[22] It is worth noting, however, that none of these people were seen as remarkable outside England itself. In 1563, the well-connected and well-informed Petrus Ramus confessed that he could not name a single English scholar.[23]

As Steven W. May has conclusively demonstrated, such verse as was produced at court in the first ten to fifteen years of Elizabeth's reign – and there was not a great deal – was almost entirely in Latin. Sir Philip Sidney's transformation of English poetry was only set in train in 1577, by which time Elizabeth had been reigning for nearly two decades.[24] The English-language literary culture of Elizabeth's court, as it developed in the second half of her reign, was an amalgam of renaissance elements (such as allegory, Petrarchanism and the imitation of Italian models, particularly Ariosto) with elements of the chivalric tradition and an indigenous English poetics looking back to the middle ages. At court, the chief manifestation of the medievalising backward glance was the chivalric metaphor which runs through so much of the verse directed to Elizabeth. This medievalism was partly a consequence of Elizabeth's weak financial position, which made the threadbare conventions of courtly love overwhelmingly useful to her. However, it risked appearing both quaint and inept to French, Spanish or Italian observers.

This paradox can be seen in all the Elizabethan arts. The grandeurs of the Elizabethan court were those that Elizabeth could persuade her courtiers to pay for themselves; their clothes, their tilting armour and fine horses, their receptions of the court on its progresses. There is no steady process of development in the assimilation of the new learning; indeed, there are aspects of the court culture of Henry VIII, or even of Henry VII, which are more patently 'renaissance' than those of Elizabeth, who could not afford to set up as a patron.[25] Everywhere in Europe, kings and their courts raised palaces influenced by ancient architecture, and in England, too, the second half of the sixteenth century was an age of passionate builders – in a style peculiar to themselves –

but the Queen of England herself built nothing. Similarly, she recruited no foreign artists or musicians of the first rank.[26] Though, in the field of music, both Thomas Tallis and William Byrd, members of the Chapel Royal, were admired abroad, English painting lagged behind the achievements of both the Low Countries and Italy in so far as it rose at all, or attempted to rise, from the static and the schematic. It is not without significance that the ability to portray expensive textiles was notably better developed in Elizabethan England than portraiture as such.

Moving to the seventeenth century, the grand century of the Baroque, it is similarly true that the Stuart court was not a centre of enlightened patronage. Ben Jonson and Inigo Jones were permitted to develop and elaborate the court's principal means of aesthetic expression, the masque. However, much of the court's patronage of the arts stemmed not from James I, but from Anne of Denmark. 'The Queen's household . . . was also a mainstay of literary and artistic patronage, and not just of court masques; the painter Isaac Oliver and the writers Samuel Daniel and John Florio were members of the Household.'[27]

The short-lived Crown Prince Henry seemed for a time likely to bring the renaissance arts more into the mainstream. The Earl of Arundel, one of the first great collectors, was a member of his household, and it was Arundel's participation in Prince Henry's court which brought Henry into contact with immigrant artists like Constaninio de Servi and Salomon de Caus, as well as other young aristocrats interested in continental European cultures. De Caus is a particularly interesting example of a baroque artist who worked both in England and abroad. His design for the Elector Frederick V's Hortus Palatinus at Heidelberg, an unusually complex and magnificent formal garden, is a prodigious early example of Protestant Baroque, based on two themes: the honouring of the natural elements and the representation of Frederick's rule. This is expressed directly in a statue of the Elector himself with a tablet bearing an inscription, and also allegorically, in the figures of Neptune, Hercules and Apollo. The statue of the gods of the rivers Rhine, Neckar and Main makes the garden itself a symbolic map of the Palatinate. They are represented within a strict hierarchy: Main and Neckar, tributaries of the Rhine, are on the lowest terrace, Rhine on the main terrace, Neptune with his trident on the upper level, and above even the god of the sea, Frederick. The overall message is that nature has been subjugated by art; the representation of political power is equated with power over nature, which has been vanquished and forced into obedience.[28]

Though the garden expresses, and represents, the Palatinate, it expresses beyond that a view of Frederick as a ruler on a considerably more grand scale than he in fact was, and hence encodes the political ambition which led to his disastrous attempt to make himself King of Bohemia in 1619. The garden was made visible beyond the immediate audience of the Palatinate and its relatively few visitors by an elaborate book of engraved views issued by Thedore de Bry (one of the great specialists in illustrated books of the period) in Frankfurt, which lays out the marvels, special effects and iconography of the Hortus in great detail. A case can be argued for this garden as 'The Garden' of Andrew Marvell's celebrated poem.[29]

The grotto-room on the ground floor of Woburn Abbey is consistently attributed to de Caus, and is thus his most certain work in England. It is an unequivocally baroque room, albeit baroque in a lesser mode usually associated with garden buildings and peripheral structures, usually dated to around 1630.[30] Originally it was a stone-paved loggia with a fountain, open to the garden. It partakes of the baroque ambiguities: partly room, partly cave, inside and outside. Furthermore, there is a sophisticated ambiguity about materials: the formal architecture of the ceiling is achieved with tightly organised shells, whereas the fantastical mermaids and sea-creatures who ornament the walls move in an element of illusionistic, glittering waves achieved by cleverly managed iridescent surfaces. The other ambiguity in the room is between land and water, solid and liquid, indeed – as in one of the most tremendous baroque rooms in England, Thornhill's painted hall at Greenwich, with its great ships on the ceiling – the thought inevitably arises that within the metaphor created by the decoration, the room has to be in some sense thought of as under water.

But to investigate further continental connections it is necessary to return to Heidelberg and to the marriage of James I's eldest daughter to the Elector Frederick, which was a proximate cause of the great garden works already discussed. The Arundels were part of the official entourage escorting the young Princess Elizabeth and her husband, the Elector Frederick, on their marriage journey. After a week's stay in Heidelberg, Arundel and his wife left with the Duke of Lennox for Strasbourg, then headed south through Basel to Milan. Their party included Prince Henry's former surveyor Inigo Jones, who had not yet distinguished himself as an architect but who did speak Italian and was already acquainted with northern Italy. Experiences shared on this trip, which were fundamental in educating both Jones and Arundel in Italian visual culture, cemented a lifelong relationship between them.

Arundel was outstanding among early Stuart collectors not only for the size and quality of his collection but for the depth of his intellectual interest in the arts, the range of his personal links with other collectors and artists, and the scale of his efforts to promote knowledge of visual culture. He almost certainly played a pivotal role in recruiting Anthony Van Dyck to England, both for his initial visit in 1620 and later in 1633. In Italy, Arundel gathered a library of treatises on painting and architecture surpassing any then available in England, and after returning home he patronised scholars who wrote on subjects relating to art. These included Henry Peacham, whose influential manual, *The Complete Gentleman*, helped to disseminate a revised ideal of gentility encompassing knowledge of art. Peacham also made numerous contributions to the dissemination of international symbolic languages of the Baroque with his emblem manuscripts.[31] John Selden was another member of the group: his *Marmora Arundeliana* (1628), analysing classical inscriptions in the earl's collection, deeply impressed Rubens.

Another antiquary who enjoyed Arundel's patronage was Franciscus Junius (François du Jon), who transferred to his household from that of Bishop Samuel Harsnett, and served him as a secretary responsible for correspondence with foreign scholars and collectors. Junius first acquired a scholarly reputation for his pioneering studies of Anglo-Saxon and ancient Germanic languages. The study of plural European antiquities was very much a baroque preoccupation. Questions of who owned the past, or how the past was to be understood, were lively issues, debated from Kilkenny in Ireland to Kiev in the Ukraine, though the disputants did not always assume the positions we would a priori tend to assign to them. The recusant Richard Verstegan's *Restitution of Decayed intelligence in Antiquities*, a pioneering work of Old English scholarship, presented the pre-Norman history of England as essentially Germanic, whereas the Protestant Inigo Jones, in his study of one of the most puzzling relics of antiquity, *The most notable Antiquity of Great Britain, vulgarly called Stone-Heng on Salisbury Plain* (1655), argued that, since it displayed 'elegancy and proportion', Stonehenge could only have been built by the Romans. Jones consquently reconstructed it as a circular, roofless structure, in what he argued was the Tuscan order, as a temple to the Roman god of the sky, Coelus, thus supporting the view that any form of complex culture must of necessity be of Roman origin. In the 1630s, with the encouragement of the Earl and Countess, Junius embarked on new studies of the arts in classical antiquity that culminated in the publication of *De pictura veterum*, translated as *The Paintings of the Ancients* (1638).

Peacham and Junius viewed painting as an extension of wider cultural and intellectual pursuits, including history, poetry, antiquarian research and the empirical study of nature. This attitude reflected Arundel's own outlook. Unlike collectors such as the Duke of Buckingham, who acquired works purely for purposes of display, the Earl valued even mutilated artefacts and rough sketches for what they revealed about the artistic process. He acquired fragments of ancient sculptures and what may have been the best collection of drawings by major renaissance artists ever assembled, including over 600 by Leonardo da Vinci.

In the mid-seventeenth century Protestantism continued to be no bar to the cultivation of international networks. A variety of Englishmen, and foreign residents in England, maintained a network of scientific connections (Francis Bacon, above all, and Samuel Hartlib). What is sometimes now regarded as the 'Hartlib circle' was, in reality, a diverse and self-selecting group of enthusiasts or 'ingenui', whose interests in the possibilities of technical change were supported by a shared viewpoint in which the potential of free and 'real' knowledge to benefit the commonwealth was contrasted with the greed of individual monopolists and the obfuscation of old institutions and learning.

One interface which was of particular importance as the century progressed was between intellectuals in England and the Protestant Netherlands. As early as 1571, there were over 3,000 Dutch living in London, by far the largest group of resident aliens in the city.[32] This connection was further encouraged by the political and military aid Elizabeth I gave to the United Provinces in 1585–86, which was enhanced and continued by a series of royal links in the seventeenth century. Many arts were cultivated in the Netherlands, for all that it was a Calvinist state, but the Dutch had an internationally acknowledged primacy in the cultivation of gardens and garden flowers, which was recognised even by the Italians; and the great Dutch painters were also internationally admired and collected. Another area which was something of a national specialty was emblematics.

It is thus absolutely possible to say that there is such a thing as Calvinist baroque art. One immensely important individual in this context is Constantijn Huygens (1596–1687), long-lived and learned secretary to the Stadhouder of Holland. Huygens both influenced, and was influenced by, English poetry: he was excited by the verse of John Donne, some of which he translated into Dutch; and his own long poem on his country house supplies whole sets of baroque images (such as tulips and trees as the guards of the garden, the green sea of the summer grass, the stormy waters of the trees) to Andrew Marvell's 'Upon Appleton House'.

Low Countries intellectuals also engaged in a variety of contacts with those of England (and, to a much greater extent and over a much longer time, Scotland). Caspar van Baerle, a well-connected Dutch neo-Latinist, brother-in-law of Constantijn Huygens, exchanged poems with Arthur Johnston (who had studied in Heidelberg, Sedan and Padua, and whose poems were published in Middelburg). The existence of neo-Latin is obviously central to this narrative of connection. Huygens spoke and wrote English prodigiously well, both prose and verse,[33] and Marvell, it seems, could read Dutch, but most such contact occurred through the medium of Latin.

Latin is a language in which poetry, not merely sterile academic exercises in versification, was composed from the fifteenth to the nineteenth centuries. It was also a language for imaginative literature, notably John Barclay's *Argenis* (1621), read all over Europe, and Ludvig Holberg's almost equally popular work of proto-science fiction, *N. Klimii Iter Subterraneum* (1741). There was a steady flow of Latin drama throughout the period, mostly Jesuit, though Protestant Oxford and Cambridge also produced enormous numbers of Latin plays. In the 1580s, Cambridge was staging two or three Latin plays every year, sometimes elaborately (costumes were borrowed from the Revels Office), utilising a fully formed literary language and poetic vocabulary far in advance of anything the popular stage could then offer. Some dramatists, notably Thomas Nashe, cut their teeth on Latin drama before essaying writing in English. It is perhaps worth observing in passing that Cambridge mounted an anonymous tragedy on a notable Oriental ruler, Suleiman the Magnificent, in 1581, when Marlowe was still a student there.[34] His own first play was of course *Tamburlaine the Great* (1587).

The cultural centrality of Latin is indicated by the variety of important vernacular works which were translated *into* that language: Chaucer's *Troilus and Criseyde*, Boccaccio's *Decameron*, Froissart's *Chronicles*, Marco Polo's *Travels*, Aretino's *Dialogues*, Machiavelli's *The Prince* and Guicciardini's *History of Italy*, among many others. Three Latin versions of Castiglione's *Courtier* were made in the sixteenth century. At least 166 vernacular texts were published in Latin translation in the course of the sixteenth century, and in the seventeenth at least 312 (many of which, inevitably, were theological). One late text translated was *Paradisus Amissus Johanni Miltonis.* As Peter Burke points out, the fact that we still call K'ung Fu Tzu 'Confucius' is a reminder that knowledge of his writings was spread by late seventeenth-century Jesuit Latin translations.[35] In an extraordinary testimony to the global importance of Latin, Josef Ijsewijn records that the treaty which was drawn up in

the seventeenth century between Russia and China was actually negotiated through the medium of Jesuit Latin.

In the sixteenth century, Latin still accounted for a significant,
though dwindling, proportion of what was printed. Italy was among the
most Latin-dependent: just over half (51.8%) of all sixteenth-century
Italian publications were still in that tongue, an unusually high figure.
The seventeenth century shows wide regional variation, from 21% of
output in Venice to 56% in Padua, the University town of the Veneto,
dropping below 30% for the country as a whole – which is still a very
high percentage compared with that in France or England.[36]

One of the most important international scholarly journals of the
baroque world was *Acta Eruditorum*, published in Leipzig from 1682,
which used Latin even when reviewing books in the vernacular. So did
the Swedish *Acta Literaria Sueciae* and the proceedings of the Academy
of St Petersburg, *Commentarii Academiae Scientiarum Imperialis Petropolitanae*;
they were thus accessible to an international audience, as they would
not have been had they been published in Swedish or Russian. Mathe-
maticians, an extreme case of a specialised international readership,
published in Latin well into the nineteenth century.

The Catholic church also remained dependent on Latin for purposes
of transnational communication, as well as for an international language
of the liturgy and of education; but the Reformers, though committed
to vernacular worship, were caught in a dilemma. To write in Latin was to
cut themselves off from ordinary people: to write in a vernacular was
to cut themselves off from the rest of Europe. Protestant reformers
tended towards a bilingual compromise, switching from vernacular to
Latin according to the topic and the audience, translating themselves
or having themselves translated where necessary. Their congregations
were addressed or exhorted in English, while formal refutations and
polemic were in Latin for the sake of an international readership – the
voluminous writings of the Independent John Owen are a case in point.
Reformers came to see the problems involved in abandoning Latin,
Catholics the problems entailed by retaining it.[37]

The Latin that the scholars of both confessions were using was consistently *referential* to Ciceronian or Virgilian Latinity, since after the
Renaissance the language of Cicero was taught afresh to each generation of students. However, in the seventeenth century, Latin actually
was a developed language for talking or writing about current concepts
in a mutually understandable vocabulary – and indeed, expansible at
all points for talking about completely *new* concepts (as, for instance,
in Newton's *Principia Mathematica*, or theological writing). It could thus

be Ciceronian only up to a point. Latin had to describe new technology, such as gunpowder or the printing press, new institutions, new religions, or parts of the world unknown to the Romans. Some writers solved the problem by classicising the modern. The Pope acquired the title of the pagan Roman high priest, *pontifex maximus.* Others invented new terminology to solve their problems.

The logic of 'correctness' requires Latin to be dead, that is, incapable of growth and development. However, far too much was being said in Latin for that to be altogether the case. As far as was practicable, vocabulary developed while syntax remained fixed; inevitably, however, there tended to be some degree of vernacular contamination. For example, there was a baroque tendency to use more prepositions than were used in classical Latin for the sake of clarity, rather than leaving datives and ablatives to explain themselves. Correcter writers inveighed against such tendencies, but since most students of Latin learned to speak as well as read it in early modern Europe, as far east as the Spiritual Academy of Kiev, their persistent reappearance was all but inevitable since they were aids to effective communication.

Exceptions to the rule of Latin can be found. Edward Browne, son of the learned doctor Sir Thomas Browne, went to Paris to hear Guy Patin in 1664 and was disappointed to find he lectured in French (which the young Englishman could not understand). In England, English was used as well as Latin in the lectures at Gresham College.[38] But such exceptions were relatively rare. It was in international relations that Latin, spoken and written, was least dispensable, remaining important all over Europe throughout the sixteenth and seventeenth centuries. The Swedish Chancellor, Axel Oxenstierna, explained to Bulstrode Whitlocke in 1653 (in Latin):

> Though he could, yet would not speak French, saying he knew no reason why that nation should be so much honoured more than others as to have their language used by strangers; but he thought the Latin more honourable and more copious, and fitter to be used, because the Romans had been masters of so great a part of the world, and yet at present that language was not peculiar to any people.[39]

It was above all in east central Europe that Latin came into its own as an essential lingua franca. When Henri d'Anjou, having been elected King of Poland in 1573, visited his kingdom, the Frenchmen in his suite were surprised to find that almost all the gentry and all sorts of people, even innkeepers, spoke Latin. The Duc de St-Simon noted that when the Poles entertained the Prince de Conti, 'they all spoke Latin, and very bad Latin at that' (*ils parlaient tous Latin, et fort mauvais Latin*).[40] Fluency and Ciceronianism were irreconcilable ends. Teachers and users of Latin were faced with the dilemma which faces modern language teachers today: should they concentrate on oral comprehension and fluency, or on the acquistion of formal grammar? For a Polish innkeeper, at least, the answer was obvious. For a Jesuit schoolmaster in the mission field, it was not.

Other places where Latin was of the first importance were the Scandinavian countries and Scotland. Christiern Pedersen (1480–1554) could fairly be regarded as the first great figure in the history of humanist learning in Denmark. He translated the Bible into Danish, for instance, and lent powerful support to the development of a vernacular literature: at the same time, he ardently advocated teaching in Latin so that young Danes could compete in an international arena.[41] In other Scandinavian countries, the situation was more extreme. In sixteenth-century Norway, for example, there was no university, no printing press and only two booksellers. From 1550 to 1600 about 200 Norwegians studied abroad, 134 of them in Rostock. For such boys, Latin was vital: it enabled them to think in terms of making a career abroad in the highly likely eventuality that there proved to be no opening at home.[42]

The Scots devotion to Latin illustrates the same point. The internal market for books was tiny, so scholars and writers needed to look to patronage for their support, and without a monarch on the throne, few pensions were to be had.[43] Early modern Scots who were not writing in Latin wrote in Scots, which nobody outside their own country could understand, not even the English: James Melville, for example, though he had taught in Paris, Poitiers and Geneva, and was reputed 'the best philosopher, poet, and Grecian, of anie young maister in the land', could not, as this fragment of his autobiography makes clear, write English.[44] The only ambitious sixteenth-century Scottish theocrat who could realistically look for an audience in England was John Knox, who spent many years there, and successfully mastered the crucial differences in vocabulary, syntax and pronunciation which divide the two languages.[45] Latin was the key to a personal future for ambitious young Scots, as it was for Norwegians. No wonder they took it seriously.

To understand the real cultural map of early modern Britain and Ireland, it is essential to concede this ubiquity of Latin. If Latin is taken into account, the circulation of information, ideas and energies becomes in some senses more scrutable, but in ways which are infinitely more pluralistic than many existing accounts of 'intellectual transmission' might allow. The problem is the drastic rethinking which has to be undertaken once the importance of Latin and (to some degree) the neutrality of Latin have been conceded. If the reception of writings from the British Isles by readers on the continent – that is, what the rest of the Western world perceived as its contribution to culture generally – is conceded as relevant to the question of what writing produced in the British Isles was 'important', the literary map of the three kingdoms of England, Scotland and Ireland in the early modern period reconfigures itself in a most extraordinary way.

The most significant change is that the three most internationally admired writers of these islands were two Scots and a Welshman: George Buchanan, John Barclay and John Owen. Shakespeare, by contrast, becomes a figure of purely local significance, while Buchanan's and Owen's names were known to virtually the entire reading public of Europe. Furthermore, one is also forced to perceive that there is a whole, immensely sophisticated and lively tradition of Latin drama (often using history to confront the present order of things) produced on the Continent by exiles from Britain. Since these were by and large produced as school plays and were offered as free entertainment to the towns in which schools were located, their view of English culture and history was rather more widely disseminated than any writings produced in English for internal consumption. Baroque historical drama, principally in Latin, was a Europe-wide phenomenon. As early as the seventeenth century, there were English intellectuals in the Established church and in the two universities, who felt threatened by the copiousness of the Latin writings of the Continent.

The academy is now in the process of finding a term for the 'Latin as a universal medium' of the baroque world. Indeed, the term 'Neo-Latin' (the banner under which much of the most scholarly and original research into the early modern world is currently being undertaken) is happily expanding its meaning year by year. It is ceasing implicitly to define a central thread of the imitation of the ancients, a neo-Classicism which can all too easily be taken as in some sense axiomatically opposed to the Baroque. The imitation of the ancients is clearly at the heart of all elite education from the fifteenth until the nineteenth centuries, but, often enough, writers of the baroque epoch thought they were imitating the ancients when they were actually doing something completely original, creating a bizarre and new figuration over a familiar ground.

What needs to be resisted here is the old idea that imitations of Horace or Cicero are the whole use of Latin (or the whole acceptable or important use of Latin) in the the early modern world. 'Neo-Latin', the new

Latin as overhauled by the humanists of the Renaissance, should remain a liberating term and not imply that its sole purpose is imitation. It should not be judged entirely in terms of its success or failure in translating the preoccupations and politics of the period in which the text was actually written into the language and cultural reference-system of 1,500 years before, a restrictive usage which employs works such as Buchanan's Horatian paraphrases of the psalms and strict Senecan dramas as a means to stigmatise the baroque epoch as a decadent falling-off from renaissance achievements.

One might say, mischievously, that it is in some degree a matter of choosing one's ancients. Much baroque Latin imitates late antique writers such as Claudian, whose flawlessly articulate panegyric of the inert and characterless Emperor Honorius is already baroque in its virtuosity, its magnificence and its ability to create an utterance of the highest quality to order, at once reflecting and disregarding the reality of circumstances. Claudian's achievement makes very good public poetry out of the celebration of a consulship which offered nothing to celebrate. Thus he is a true ancestor of the baroque poet, never at a loss, who could line up the river gods and the nymphs to celebrate, in harmonious song, the end of the term of duty of the captain of the fortress guarding an unimportant river at the margins of the Venetian territories. The Accademia of Saló applauds; the order of things has been preserved and adorned.[46] The baroque mode has yet again proved of the first utility. As I suggested in the Introduction, one of the defining factor of the baroque arts is never to be at a loss, to be able to produce an artefact for any occasion.

The most compendious account of the use of Latin throughout the world of the Renaissance and the Baroque is Ijsewijn's *Ancilla Neo Latina*.[47] Never has a revolutionary re-evaluation of the whole shape of an epoch in intellectual history appeared in a more modest, apparently conventional format. This work, remarkable in its modesty and its extraordinary achievement, covers every aspect of writing in Latin (its intellectual triumph is its inclusiveness) from five-act tragedies to herbals to novels to works on seashells or metalliferous mines.

To look again in the spirit of Ijsewijn at the cultural production of the British Isles is to discover that what seems the decorous study of a dead tradition is actually the key to finding the material with which to mount a direct and substantial challenge to perceptions of the shape of early modern culture which have drifted on unchallenged for far too long. Ijsewijn, for example, stresses that Scottish achievements in Latin are more than equal to those of England, and that much Scottish

Latin was composed and published on the Continent. Calvinist Latin developed over more than a century of intense intellectual contact between Scotland and the Netherlands.

It is not my purpose here to trace the rise and fall of Latin as the international language. This has been done by Françoise Waquet in her *Latin: The Empire of a Sign*. Her prodigious marshalling of facts gives us some sense of the real power and usefulness of Latin as a means of transmission and as a *medium* for the baroque world. As soon as we begin to realise that almost everyone capable of committing vernacular verse to paper was also capable of composing to some extent in Latin, all the maps and patterns apprehensibly shift and reconfigure before our eyes.[48]

When we include this universal language among the registers or media at the disposal of the international currency of the written word, we can begin to get some sense of the potential universality of early modern letters. Questions of centre and margin are radically realigned and the career of such an established cultural figure as John Milton begins to look very different. Distinction in Latin letters conferred genuine international celebrity, as in the case of John Barclay, a Scot born in Paris whose *Argenis* (1621) was, in its day, the most popular prose fiction in Europe – in an era when the Scots are still assumed to have lost all cultural initiative with the Union of the Crowns in 1603.

Much academic energy has been expended over the last decades in trying to discover where on the cultural map of early modern Britain 'subversion' and 'the subversive' might be located. Most of the groups advanced as posing a threat to the status quo (such as writers for the London professional theatre) seem, in historical fact, to have cost the ruling class remarkably little sleep. But as soon as we move into the consideration of British Latin, we are immediately brought up against a body of writings which were genuinely perceived as subversive, created by a group whose activities were monitored and whose writing and publication were controlled by censorship, by seizure of texts (not always very efficient), by fear engendered by exemplary and savage executions and by explicit legislation. These were the English Jesuits.

Here we have a clue to why there was this dividedness in English culture: Latin is not a secure system confined to the national elite; it is also the language of the enemy, a language which, particularly in an Irish context, might be troublingly accessible to native aristocrats and their priests.

The process of the capture and execution of English Catholic priests working in the mission to England as 'fugitives' and 'traitors' is complicated if captured mission-priests can claim not only common humanity but also access to the international language of the elite. Take, for example, the captured priest St John Ingram, who passed the period of his imprisonment in the Tower of London before his execution cutting Latin epigrams with a blunt knife in the sandstone of the walls. These are exactly the sort of elegant productions (as well as testimonies in equal measure to the religious fortitude and *sprezzatura* of the prisoner) which assert the internationally recognisable educated status of a man defined as an outlaw and traitor. These writings question the stability and authority of the English regime from two standpoints simultaneously.[49] The question of access to Latin in Ireland is even more vexed in the perceptions of the English establishment.

But the Latin writing of recusant Catholics is not only worthy of study because of its oppositional status. It is also a direct channel through which continental influence can be seen to be operating. The new, coherent and controversial organisation of the fresco-cycles in the Rome of the mid-sixteenth century novitiate of St Andrea al Quirinale has a demonstrable influence upon the superb devotional poetry of the Jesuit martyr St Robert Southwell.

I will only mention this subject briefly here, as it is treated at length in a recent monograph,[50] but it is a most telling and indicative instance: new, baroque Roman paintings (operating as a part of the coordinated cultural campaigns of post-Tridentine Catholicism) are being translated through the medium of words for a beleaguered English Catholic community, whose members, for the most part, will only ever see such works in prints or in the sacred visualisations which are part of baroque spirituality (visualisations which St Robert Southwell's poetry is often dedicated to sustaining).

The imaginative sweep of Southwell's Latin verse, with its remorseless representation of scenes of impossible, vertiginous grandeur and horror, is unremarkably Miltonic, Milton himself being one of the most baroque and most intensely Latinate poets of the seventeenth century. Death's council, for example, in Southwell's poem on the Assumption of the Virgin, should be set beside Milton's hellish Parliament:

> Est vastum scabris sinuosum anfractibus antrum,
> Solis inaccessum radiis, fundoque dehiscens,
> Et ruptas reserans immani horrore cavernas.
> Propatulo hic fluvius surgit Lethaeus hiatu,
> Ingentique ruens per concava saxa fragore,
> Precipitante rotat limosa volumina cursu,
> Et dirum aggeribus spumans fremit unda repertis.

Hinc atque hinc atrata patent fuligine tecta,
Et loca senta situ, varios spirantia morbos,
Aeternum spissae squalent caligine noctis.
In medio solium, nulla spectabile pompa,
Informi obductum limo, sanieque perunctum,
Eminet, exesis diuturna aerugine fulchris
Hic Annosa sedet canis mors horrida saetis,
Os macie, taboque genas confecta, cavisque
Immersos fossis oculos et livida circum
Dentes labra gerens turpique patentia rictu . . .
Excita turba ruit caecas furibunda per umbras . . .[51]

[There is a vast serpentine cave with rugged tortuous recesses, inaccessible to the rays of the sun, gaping from its lowest level and laying open riven caverns of monstrous horror. Here the river Lethe rises in an open cleft and, rushing through the concave rocks with tremendous crashing, it spins muddy whirlpools in its headlong course and makes a dire noise, foaming on encounter with obstacles. On this side and on that are seen dwellings black with soot and places bristling with squalor, exhaling diverse diseases, are filthy for eternity with the blackness of dense night. In the midst a throne, conspicuous despite there being no pomp, covered with unsightly mud and besmeared with gore, stands forth, its supports eaten away by the rust of ages.

Here sits the aged bitch Death, horridly bristled, her muzzle worn away with emaciation, her cheeks with wasting pestilence, displaying eyes sunk in hollow trenches, and livid lips around her teeth open in a repulsive grin . . . Roused, the throng, full of fury, rushes through the dark shadows . . .]

Recusant drama in particular offers a consistently oppositional version of British history and British identity, of considerable importance to how the English were perceived abroad, as has already been mentioned.[52] Despite the thread of influence from Rome, the most consistent continental influence on the British Counter-Reformation, especially in terms of visual culture, is overwhelmingly from Spain and the Spanish Netherlands, in particular from the exiled Jesuit colleges at Douai and from the Jesuit school for lay pupils at St Omer.

All these colleges put on large numbers of Latin plays. Out of the vast repertory which survives, many can, indeed must, be interpreted as directly political statements, such as the anonymous *Psyche et filii eius*, performed at Valladolid in 1615, an allegory of a family divided by religious and political faction; or *Leo Armenus*, performed at St Omer in the 1620s and revived at Rome in 1645, which applies the iconoclast controversies in ninth-century Byzantium allegorically, first to the desecration of English religious houses under Henry, Edward and Elizabeth, and (it may be conjectured), secondarily, in the 1645 revival, to the iconoclasm of the English Parliamentarians.

But I want to focus on a particularly fascinating example of the contemporary allegorical application of British antiquity: Joseph Simons's *Mercia*, first performed at St Omer in February 1624.[53] It is worth noting that Simons specifically acknowledges the antiquary William Camden as his source for this play set in the time of St Chad of Mercia (early seventh century). The Jesuits must have taken particular pleasure in making use of Camden, especially given the hostility with which Camden had written of the Jesuit Henry Garnet in the 1600s.

The play treats of the hellish deviousness of the pagan priests of Mercia, who lead the pagan king Ulferus to martyr his two Christian convert sons Ulfadus and Ruffinus. One fascinating aspect of this play is that the pagan religion of Mercia is imagined as full-blown Roman paganism: worship of Jove and Apollo, not the Saxon paganism documented by Bede and the antiquaries. There are indeed several scenes of the destruction of temples and the desecration of images, but the temples destroyed and the images desecrated are those of the pagan gods. The destroyers are the Christian heroes of the drama. The temples and ceremonies are imported aberrations (as Catholic apologists would argue that Calvinism and Lutheranism are imported aberrations) and the good ancient Catholic figure of St Chad has his being amidst pure lustral waters in the depths of the oak-woods of England. This almost druidic figure of pristine Catholicism is a surprise, a powerful counterweight to Milton's subsequent Papist enchanter Comus, also a dweller in the deep woods. Allegories and interpretations turn and evolve with the political and religious exigencies of the times.

So, to conclude this summary, if necessary, account of the place of Latin in integrating Britain, and especially England, within the international cultural systems of the baroque world, it is necessary to affirm that integration, while recognising also that there was a persistently inturned element within English culture which remained hostile to all such international phenomena.

Baroque in English vernacular literature

I turn now to examining that which was continuous with international culture in English vernacular literature of the early modern period. In Mario Praz's classic account of relations between Italian and English literature, his English-language *The Flaming Heart* of 1958, he provides an essential background by itemising the almost line-by-line correspondences between Crashaw and Donne and their international contemporaries.[54] This work is a summary (and, in some passages, a softening in deference to English sensibilities) of a startlingly original work which he had published in Italian at Florence in 1925, *Secentismo e Marinismo in Inghilterra (Baroque and the Style of the Cavaliere Marino in England)*. (Marino is the paradigmatic baroque poet of Italy, intricate, inventive and single-minded in his certainty that the purpose of poetry is primarily to astonish.).[55]

On the one hand, in both Italian and English, Praz treats the much-maligned Richard Crashaw with a scrupulous and scholarly fairness.[56] Regarding Crashaw from an international perspective, Praz sees him as an accomplished and unexceptional devotional poet of his time, and, crucially, a poet intensely connected to the poetic activities of continental contemporaries. Praz seems also to have a clear idea of those elements of Crashaw's writing which particularly elicit the hostility of English critics. It is wholly typical of his approach that he begins with a lengthy discussion of Crashaw's Latin poetry and its tissues of allusion and resemblance before he moves on to the discussion of the English material.

Donne is, admittedly, much more difficult for him to discuss in terms acceptable within England. In the quarter-century between his Italian publication of 1925 and the English version of 1958, Donne's status in the anglophone academy rose to an extent which placed him at the centre of the canon. As 'English literature' became a subject of study in its own right (all too often, a literature studied in contextual isolation) Donne's poetry became part of the essential standard by which all poets, not just his contemporaries, were to be judged. So the Praz of 1958 is cautious in drawing distinctions between Donne at his 'best' (his most idiosyncratic, his most English) and the Donne who wrote within the prevailing mode of his time, chiefly the (I use the word with studied neutrality) embarrassing Donne of the *Anniversaries*, of whom Praz says, 'Had Donne always written in the style of the *Anniversaries* he would not rank much higher than Marino or Góngora'.[57] He had been less circumspect in 1925, observing crisply (in Italian) that Donne's hyperbolic arguments in the *Anniversaries* not only compare unfavourably with Tasso or with Góngora at his most 'magnificent', but also in themselves 'go beyond any tolerable limit'; Donne's syllogism whereby the death of the paradigmatically beautiful and virtuous Elizabeth Drury is the death of all good and the death of the world itself is nothing more than the absurd or *baroque* syllogism itself.[58] Praz contrasts Donne's excesses with the right use of the marvellous and prodigious in baroque poetry, in this instance represented by the 'true and seemly beauty of the hyperboles of Crashaw'.[59] What he demonstrates in full in his long Italian essays on Crashaw and Donne is that this baroque poetry of England is inextricably part of the international system stretching from Marino in Naples to Góngora in Madrid to Vondel in Amsterdam. So why are these continuities of British culture and continental culture still overlooked or denied? Why, apart from the author's courtly good manners towards the country which was his second home, was *Secentismo e Marinismo* never translated in full?[60]

There is no space to fight once more the critical battles of the early twentieth century as to why the vernacular literature of England cannot be baroque, but has to be Elizabethan or metaphysical or Jacobean or Caroline or Cavalier or Augustan or something (or indeed *anything*) else. One can only glance back at those works from which the current terminology of style and periodisation is still drawn, and see that the extraordinary contortions of Sir Herbert Grierson and even the politic reticences of the foreigner within the gates, T.S. Eliot, when he wrote on cognate subjects, seem to stem from a reluctance to recognise the dividedness of English culture, the existence of two traditions, one inturned and exclusively vernacular, one permeable to external influence and therefore 'baroque' and international.

Grierson's view of the early modern world of letters was set forth in the celebrated essay of 1921 which formed the preface of his extraordinarily influential Oxford anthology, *The Metaphysical Poets*. There is almost no school or university course in the English-speaking world which does not in some sense reflect the way in which Grierson chose to select and describe the poets of the English seventeenth century. His revival of the term 'metaphysical' (a term he borrowed, not insignificantly, from the Italian, via Samuel Johnston, while rejecting any possible Italian influence) has proved crucial to the way in which almost the whole Anglophone world thinks of the poetry and arts of the seventeenth century. The extraordinary vigour and eloquence with which he argued into being a school of intellectually pyrotechnic and fantastical poets, operating exclusively within an Anglocentric universe, has had an almost uniformly destructive effect on the study of the arts and literatures of early modern Europe.[61]

Grierson's interpretation of the extraordinarily wide range of facts mustered in the introduction to his classic work is almost wholly wrong, albeit wrong in a way which tells us a great deal about the attitudes and fears of the British Isles in the first half of the twentieth century. The inclusions and exclusions he chooses to make doubtless seemed at the time the inevitable product of profound reflection. In his 1926 Clark lectures on the metaphysical poets, T.S. Eliot is himself clearly uneasy about some of Grierson's boundaries and assumptions.[62] He is clearly aware of a contrary or internationalist position, but is unwilling in many respects to challenge the isolationist view of post-Elizabethan letters: it seems that the radical wrench of perspective would have been too much at that cultural moment, given how invested the English establishment had become in the view represented by Grierson.

Grierson treats the poetry of seventeenth-century England as if it existed in a kind of intellectual void, barely connected with the poetry of Scotland or Ireland and (significantly) immune to all living foreign influence. London, Oxford and Cambridge constitute the only intellectual centres worthy of consideration within these islands. Despite the fact that he was a Scot and had begun his university career by teaching in Scotland, Scotland does not exist in the world he evokes, except for the isolated figure of the Anglophone Drummond of Hawthornden, a friend of Ben Jonson. He also goes out of his way to deny any living interchange between early modern Anglophone poets and their contemporaries on the continent of Europe. The influence of Dante on Donne can be allowed, but the influence of Marino, Góngora or Strada must be resisted as a matter of patriotic duty. To Grierson, if an Anglophone poet gets too near in manner to the poetry of his continental contemporaries, he forfeits his right to consideration as an English poet at all.

Hence the vexed case of poor Richard Crashaw, who became a Catholic, went into exile, wrote remarkable religious verse, and thereby resigned his right to be considered as an English poet. Grierson deliberately conceals the fact that much of Crashaw's most 'hectic' verse was written while he was still an Anglican fellow of Peterhouse, Cambridge. Grierson's dismissal of Crashaw is only one manifestation of a usage whereby 'baroque' means 'foreign' in all the wrong ways.[63] The root of Grierson's extraordinary definitions and exclusions lies in the sectarian conflicts which had so troubled the English religious establishment in the earlier nineteenth century, but they suggest that the anti-Catholic and anti-continental black legend seems to have been alive and well in the 1920s (the really extraordinary thing is that much the same attitude to Crashaw is manifested in Robert Harbison's *Reflections on Baroque*, published in 2000).[64]

The crux of the matter is Grierson's central piece of casuistry around Donne's religious poems, which asserts that they may be 'Anglo-Catholic' but that that, of course, necessarily means that they are medieval in so far as they are Catholic at all. Hence his citation of Dante. Praz, by contrast, in his 1925 Italian text, points out rather more relevantly that Donne had two uncles who were Jesuits. Why these contortions? Now we enter the realm of definitions. Donne, Grierson asserts, is notable for distinguished intellectual liveliness (as well as for being a forerunner of the poetic manner of Cowper whose style is that of 'an English gentleman of the best type'), and for eschewing the 'hectic' style of those who had the misfortune to be educated abroad. It goes without saying that he is in a different league from the hapless Crashaw.[65] Consider this peroration:

> there now hangs that *sacred Body* upon the *Crosse, rebaptized* in his owne *teares* and *sweat,* and *embalmed* in his *owne blood alive . . .* wee leave you in that *blessed dependancy,* to *hang* upon *him* that *hangs* upon the Crosse, there *bath* in his *teares,* there *suck* at his *woundes . . .*

This, of course, is Donne; the end of his sermon 'Death's Duell'. The firm, manly and truly English moderation of this is more obvious to Grierson than it is to me. It is hard to identify the basis for *contrasting* this writing with hectic, hysterically over-affective baroque piety on any other grounds than the religious confession of its author.[66]

But in Grierson's essay, Crashaw and Donne are opposed figures, on the grounds that Crashaw was too excited in his 'fireworks' which are 'in the confectionery manner of the Italians'. Grierson's word-choices suggest that he was propounding in all seriousness the view that on the day that the Council of Trent assembled, the Italians, who had been, until that moment, the virile and admirable protagonists of the Renaissance, became overnight a nation of hysterical pastry-cooks and castrato opera-singers. To Grierson, Crashaw, merely because he is a Catholic, is immune to 'spiritual conflict controlled and directed by Christian inhibitions, and mystical yearning'. Indeed, he is free from any 'diagnosis of his own emotional and spiritual condition'. He has instead only that which a Catholic poet can attain: a wholly impersonal and mindless 'thankfulness and adoration. It is this *opus operatum* which is the theme of all of Crashaw's ardent and coloured, sensuous and conceited odes.'

It is extraordinary enough that such assertions should have gained wide acceptance, despite their internal contradictions, but it is particularly remarkable in view of the lucid and scholarly exposition of the connections between early modern English culture and the baroque Continent in Praz's *Seicentismo e Marinismo* of 1925. It is refreshing to think of Donne as 'Marinistic', and certainly it is a more accurate estimation of Donne's place on the international literary map. The remarkable thing here is how little Praz's thesis has influenced the way that the Anglophone academy in general thinks about the 'metaphysicals'.

It would be possible and agreeable to multiply examples of the *meraviglia*, the baroque exciting of wonder, in English poetry of the seventeenth century, to find examples of Donne's countrymen and countrywomen producing verbal and imaginative fireworks to equal Góngora or Marino. It would certainly enrich our reading of Donne to consider the athletic hyperboles of his *Anniversaries* in comparison with the vertiginous wonders of the *Sueño* (the *Dream*) of the Mexican Sor Juana de la Cruz: they inhabit the same aesthetic.

What I am describing as a universal Baroque transcends confessional or religious divisions. Baroque cannot be identified exclusively with the Counter-Reformation. There is a telling example of the baroque mode transcending the most visible barriers of the early modern world, the war zones of the Netherlands. There is no doubt of the religious affiliation of Constantijn Huygens. His fine series of meditations on the events of the Christian year are the work of a poet secure in, and proud of, his achieved Calvinist spirituality. Yet he is beyond doubt using the meditative techniques of the *generalissimo* of the Counter-Reformation, St Ignatius, working across the baroque world, across boundaries of religious confession. His series of devotional sonnets, the *Heilighe Dagen* (*Holy Days*), although remaining within his own Calvinist con-fession, makes clear and profound use of the meditative techniques of the Spiritual Exercises of St Ignatius of Loyola.[67] The practice of sacred visualisation which is at the same time sensual imagination is not confined to the spirituality of the Counter-Reformation. It is worth emphasising this, given how much is usually made of this precise phenomenon as the marker of an uncrossable boundary.

When Huygens imagines himself as present in the stable at Bethlehem, he is following St Ignatius's composition of place:[68] the mental painting of a biblical scene within which the individual may place him- or herself.[69] All the elements of Huygens's poem are pre-sent in Ignatius: the instruction to the maker of the meditation to watch and contemplate the Holy Family in the place of the Nativity and 'make [her- or himself] into a poor and unworthy little servant', as an imaginative participant present in the scene. The third point of the meditation corresponds to Huygens's ll. 4–5: 'Daer schreidt wat in dit stroij/dat voor ons schreijen will' (He cries out in the straw/Who would cry out for all). 'Christ comes to be born in extreme poverty and, after so many labours . . . he dies on the cross and all of this for me', is the thought with which Ignatius wishes the devout mind to develop its perception of the Nativity.

> All is de herbergh voll, all light Gods Soon in'thooij,
> Mijn ziele mach'er in, en wild'er bij vernachten . . .

> [Though the inn is full, though God's son lies in hay my soul can enter watch by him till dawn . . .]

Huygens has the Ignatian emphasis on imagined sensual *presence* in meditative reconstruction: 'En nu te voete ligt. Hier ligt'[70] (Lies at her feet. Lies here). That 'here' is a Jesuit technique, available to one of the most senior and ideologically committed officials of a breakaway Calvinist state. This fact alone offers a counterbalance to the views of the early modern world promulgated in the twentieth century. The factual universality of the early modern style which we are calling Baroque inevitably transcends the confessional and religious divisions which gave birth to the endless wars of the *Grand Siècle*.

Critical vocabularies still work to prevent that perception gaining any wide acceptance. Some of George Herbert's poems are baroque in the wildest sense of the word, especially his Latin collections, *Passio discerpta* and *Lucus*. This is a characteristic epigram, 'On His Bloody Sweat':

> Quo fugies, sudor? Quamvis pars altera Christi
>   Nescia sit metae; venula, cella tua est.[71]

> [Where do you flee, O sweat? Although another part of Christ
>   Should not know bounds; your home is in the vein.]

In his vernacular pattern-poems, his use of paradoxes, lists and hyperboles, his considered but unfettered use of *devices* (in every sense of the word) are a full deployment of the armoury of the baroque devotional poet. For all that, he is most commonly perceived as quietly, plainly English, somehow adumbrated by the refined simplicities of his friend Nicholas Ferrars's community at Little Gidding.

We can see only the patterns in history revealed to our own age. I would like to propose a model which considers the majority of early modern English poets as part of an international movement, susceptible of infinite local variations, internationally identified as 'Baroque', using the term in a neutral sense.

How does this universality work: what do the developed cultures of the early modern world have, in all the arts, as common languages? As a means of communication and expression they have Latin, and as a common stock of knowledge, they have Christian scripture, and the mythologies of antiquity, and the fables and surviving works of the ancients. This descriptor is not exclusively confined to the European ancients, by any means: a consistent feature of the Baroque outside Europe is the creation of alternative ancients, a phenomenon of which Sigüenza y Góngora's Mexican histories form a distinguished example (see pp. 110–12 below).

The common past of the European Baroque, that territory to which a baroque artist may make a meaningful allusion, is not simply a matter of known instances from antiquity, from an international tradition of proverbs and emblems, from a tradition of Christian writings and their interpreters. Scriptural and antique material is infinitely susceptible of expression in an internationally shared symbolic visual language; the speaking pictures of *emblemata* and *imprese* relate to the elite vocabulary of heraldry, sacred as well as profane. But it also comprehends, and welcomes decisively, relatively new 'exotic knowledges' such as the Egyptological speculations of the Jesuit polymath Athanasius Kircher, or Sigüenza y Góngora's Aztec antiquity, his dreams that the apostle Thomas might have been the evangelist of the Americas. The kings of Spain quickly bestowed European coats of arms on the *cacique* elite of the Americas.[72] Sigüenza y Góngora equips the Aztec kings with *imprese*, expressive badges of picture and motto – this is simply part of how you understand an elite individual in any baroque culture. In her captivity, Mary Queen of Scots drew endlessly on books of *imprese* for the subject-matter of her encoded needlework.

Mary's emblematic embroideries, undertaken while under house arrest in England, spoke in an international symbolic language just poised between the late rennaisance *impresa* and the developed and universalising emblematics of the Baroque. More than once, Mary's emblematic needlework was produced before Elizabethan tribunals as evidence of treasonable intentions in herself or others, notably the Duke of Norfolk. Within months of her execution in 1586, the poet St Robert Southwell versified a succession of the images she had used in her lifetime into a baroque martyr-poem (beautiful, ingenious and allusive) to plead her case for admission to the English *martyrium* which was developing semi-officially in the English College's church of St Tomasso di Canterbury in Rome: 'S. Tommaso was . . . something quite unique for Cinquecento Rome – a pilgrimage site devoted to present-day and future martyrs, so that even living students were revered as walking relics with the greeting "Salvete Flores Martyrum" '.[73]

The pounded spice both tast and sent doth please
In fading smoke the force doth incense shewe
The perisht kernell springeth with encrease
The lopped tree doth best and soonest growe ...

Rue not my death rejoyce at my repose
It was no death to me but to my woe
The budd was opened to lett out the Rose
The cheynes unloo'sd to lett the captive goe[74]

One of the *imprese* the Queen embroidered on a panel was a hand with a pruning knife cutting down a barren vine, while another opposite it yields an abundant crop of grapes, with the motto, '*virescit vulnere virtus*', virtue flourishes by wounding. This conveys, on one level, the message that her trials have only strengthened her to yield abundant spiritual fruit. But this embroidery was sent to the Duke of Norfolk, implicated in a plot to release Mary and put her on the English throne, and it was used in evidence at his trial, since it held a second message: God will prune the unfruitful branch (the virgin Elizabeth) and cultivate the fruitful one (Mary, mother of a son). Elizabeth herself is said to have had this imagery in her mind some years earlier when, in the bitterness of hearing that Mary had been safely delivered of the future James I, she referred to herself as 'a barren stock'.[75]

In the face of international consensus and such patent evidence for the international circulation of ideas and energy, it is extraordinary that, in many of the English connotations of the word, *Baroque* is seen essentially as the sterile waste of human energy in the production of pointless marvels and grandeurs. This perception of the Baroque as the self-defeating and sterile sensibility of absolutism and repressive religion is perhaps the most difficult connotation to overcome for the speaker of English.

One might observe here that those Anglo-American scholars and writers who have ridden to the defence of the baroque arts of the Continent have sometimes done little to advance understanding of the international arts in the baroque period. Sacheverell Sitwell's *Southern Baroque Art*[76] was from the beginning intended to irritate the prevailing Anglophone consensus of the 1920s. It was a cult book for the contemporary aesthetes who employed Venetian giltwood furniture and Spanish ecclesiastical candlesticks to create rooms which were deliberately intended to produce shock and unease in their compatriots.[77] Another widely read author of the 1920s, Ronald Firbank, may similarly be a complicating factor, since he associates the baroque English thought of the period with homosexuality, flashiness and decadence. Sitwell and Firbank both tend to accept the unspoken English assumption that Baroque is both confessionally orientated and foreign to the sensibilities of northern Europe. The more they argue the merits of the Baroque of Weltenberg or Caserta, the more they imply that this art is utterly alien to anything in the English tradition.

It is in this context that one needs to consider that extraordinary baroque painter of the English twentieth century, Edward Burra (1905–76). Burra looked, above all, to that which was violent, excessive and indecorous in late baroque art, the works exhibited by the Sitwells and their circle at the Magnasco Society, for precedents for his own work. William Gaunt's *Bandits in a Landscape* (1937) is a manifestation of this concern – a book which Burra almost certainly owned. It draws attention to the eighteenth-century painters of ruins, mostly in Rome, portraying people moving among crumbling buildings; to *capriccios*, landscapes informed by personal psychology – Gaunt specifically observes that 'the method had something in common with the present-day "surrealism" '; and to the wild and crazy paintings of Monsù Desiderio and Alessandro Magnasco. (Exploding churches, their golden salomonic columns caught in falling fragments; the Virgin floating in the darkened air as *generalissima* of a squadron of animated corpses who are defending a cemetery chapel against sacrilegious robbers.)[78]

Burra embraced the baroque art of Mexico with comprehension and enthusiasm, and subsequently, without explanation or apology, painted a number of religious paintings in a mode influenced by Hispanic or Ibero-American Baroque, but with recognisable references to the visual culture of the mid-twentieth century – a group of shawled women glimpsed in a street in Galway, the bells of the trumpets of a swing band pointing skywards. If one thinks of Classical and Baroque as opposed tendencies in art rather than terms of periodisation, then much of what we think of as characteristic of 1930s art in England is classical: it uses a restricted, chalky palette, it is abstract or abstracting: an art built up on principles of exclusion. Burra's art, by contrast, is baroque, in the various senses that it was eclectic, that it mixed high and low cultural references, and that it was full of colour and incident.

If we return to the baroque culture of the court of Charles I, the early modern visual cultures of masque and festival in fact emphasise the continuity of British cultural production with that of the Continent and beyond. An international system had to be functional because it had to convey precisely nuanced political messages to a highly educated audience of ambassadors and courtiers, all of whom were trained from childhood to read an allegorical spectacle for a contemporary message. These spectacles transmitted royal messages, whether to the country at large, or to foreigners, or to the court – or in the case of the Stuart masques, between the King's and Queen's courts (a key example is *The Masque of Blackness,* which appears to be a public message sent from Anne of Denmark to James about her refusal to surrender her Catholicism).

The discourse of the masque has no option but to be baroque and international, since sending of coded messages to foreign ambassadors was no small part of its overall purpose; masques necessarily drew on an international discourse both verbally and imagistically.[79] In this, the masques are rather like contemporary garden design, a topic which has already come up in the context of the Palatine marriage. Just as in the Hortus Palatinus at Heidelberg, the programme of statuary at Versailles makes claims to universal dominion (a deliberate marshalling of everything on which the sun shines; thus a visual representation of an empire upon which the sun never sets). These are answered in the royal garden of Het Loo in the Netherlands by the golden fountain on the main axis. The subject is the infant Hercules strangling serpents while yet in his cradle: a clear allegory of the power of a comparatively new state to resist French aggression and to intervene in future in world politics.

The iconography of the masque had to use international visual languages. The allegorical figures at Caprarola near Rome which glorify the sack of the Netherlands by Farnese's troops can be identified by recourse to Cesare Ripa's universally popular handbook, the *Iconologia.* Similarly, the allegorical figures on the proscenium painting for the London court masque *Salmacidia Spolia* use the universal language of the Baroque to convey to the observing ambassadors the lie that the personal rule of Charles I is intact even in the shaken year of 1640–41:

> In a square niche on the right hand stood two figures of women, one of them expressing much majesty in her aspect, appareled in sky colour, with a crown of gold on her head and a bridle in her hand, representing Reason, the other embracing her was in changeable silk with wings at her shoulders, figured for Intellectual Appetite, who while she embraceth Reason, all the actions of man are rightly governed.[80]

Salmacidia Spolia is a particularly interesting case, because of the complexity of communication it makes to the French party, which included Marie de Médicis, mother of Queen Henrietta Maria and a considerable embarrassment, as well as to a divided court. In the way it discusses the barely discussable and addresses diverse audiences simultaneously, *Salmacidia Spolia* is an intensely baroque work of art. Most of the actual communication takes place through the visual language rather than the actual words, beginning with the highly conventional iconography of the proscenium, a neoplatonic scene of passions restrained by order and virtue to create harmony. The masque begins with a phantasmagoria of antimasques – an almost apotropaic asurvey of all the possible nightmares of disorder the baroque elite might ever have, from spagyrics to Scotsmen, to say nothing of 'the Invisible Lady, magical sister of the Rosicross' – but the real point is that the visual discourse of royal apotheosis with which the masque concludes is unmistakable and international, even if it goes beyond the usual extravagance of the Baroque in acclaiming a sovereign. Charles, attired as Philogenes (the king who loves his people), is disclosed sitting in a Throne of Honour, adorned with palm trees (which flourish despite oppression) between which stand statues of the ancient heroes, while Henrietta Maria appears in a cloud as Diana, chaste goddess of the moon. Charles hands her out of her cloud, whereupon the royal pair then move to their chairs of state, trailing their operatic divinity with them. In the final song, they are told,

> All that are harsh, all that are rude,
> Are by your harmony subdued;
> Yet so into obedience wrought,
> As if not forced to it, but taught.

The closing apotheosis is as extreme as that in Thomas Carew's 1634 *Coelum Britannicum,* in which Religion, Truth, Wisdom, Concord, Government and Reputation unite with Eternity, Right Worship, Truth, Wisdom, Harmony, Good Government and Eloquence to address the royal pair as virtual deities:

> *Eternity*
> This royal pair, for whom Fate will
> Make motion cease and time stand still,
> Since good is here so perfect as no worth
> Is left for after ages to bring forth.
>
> *Eusebeia*
> [*Right Worship*] Mortality can not with more
> Religious zeal the gods adore.

This deification of a monarch who is set amongst the stars (in a way which I suspect that a Catholic country would have found excessive) is more normally associable with the Sun King than with Charles I. Certainly, the claims Davenant and Carew made for Charles are at least as extravagant as any ever made for Louis XIV.

What this contemplation of Stuart court masques seems to lead to is the idea of camp as an element of British Baroque. In the 1630s and 1640s, the genre gradually moves to an extreme of self-dramatisation, which is reflected on a smaller scale by members of the elite who take an aesthetic of performance and spectacle to extremes.

A classic instance is Sir Kenelm Digby's reaction to the death of his wife, Venetia Stanley. He commissioned a portrait of his wife's waxen corpse – not laid out, but with her head still propped on her hand as she had died and a rose, its pale petals pulled from the flower, scattered on the sheet beside her. He had a death mask made, and casts of her hands, and cut and kept her beautiful hair.[81] On a less physical

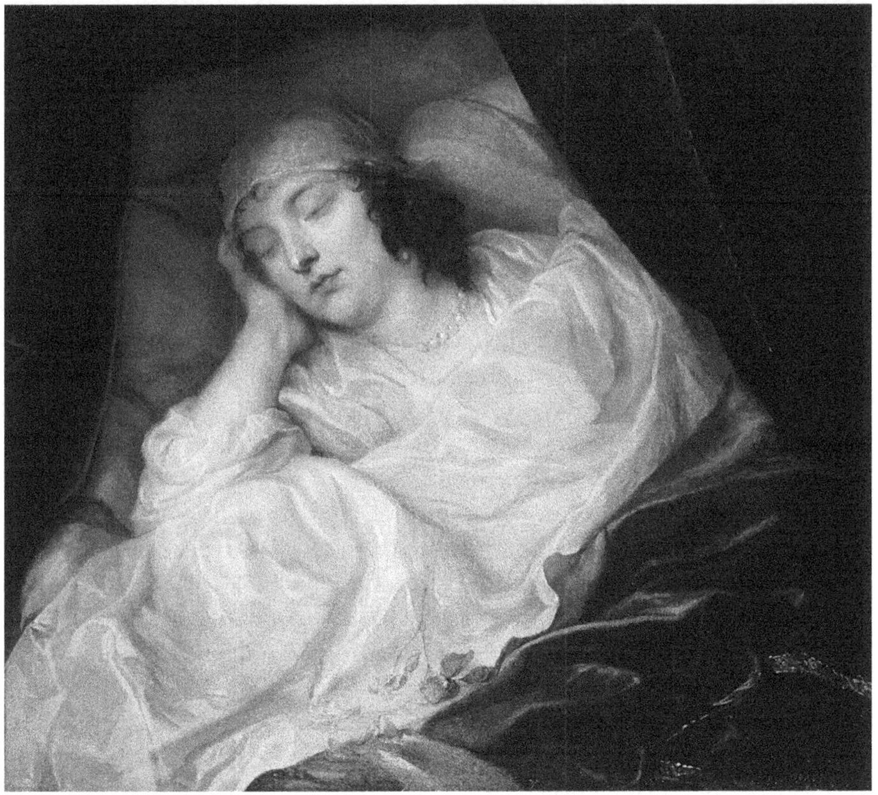

3 Sir Anthony van Dyck, *Posthumous portrait of Venetia Digby*, 1633.

plane, he put together a volume consisting of forty-five letters to the dead woman and five meditations, bound in a volume called *In Praise of Venetia.* This compulsive document analyses the fluctuations of his mourning, his bitter recollection of past infidelities, memories, weeping fits, guilt and an insistent evocation of his wife's body. Three weeks after her burial, his thoughts 'tumbled every corner of her grave', and dwelt on 'that fair body['s] putrefaction'; her lovely face, 'covered over with slime and worms'. To express his sorrow, he moved to the seclusion of Gresham College, and wore the dress of a melancholic, 'a long mourning cloke, a high crowned hatt, his beard unshorne, look't like a Hermite'.[82] Needless to say, he commissioned an elaborate tomb, which in style and materials reached for the universalising iconography of pagan Rome: Venetia appeared as a gilt-bronze demi-figure in Roman dress upon a black marble plinth with rams' heads and swags like a classical altar. This essentially pagan concept (consciously evoking the classical Roman tradition of memorialising the dead with life-sized statues representing the individual as in life) answered the problem of designing a monument to a Roman Catholic to be erected in a Protestant church, by going beyond the Protestant and Catholic iconographies of mourning to a universally acceptable set of formulae. This is one of the key functions of baroque art (this monument, sadly, was destroyed in the Great Fire of London).[83]

Considering the patterns of cultural exchange in early modern England, we are dealing with something complex and strange, rendered infinitely more difficult by the overlay of a series of anachronistic historical agendas. There is a genuine dividedness in the cultural life and activities of England, with two parallel streams of activity running from the later sixteenth into the eighteenth century. On the one hand, there is a tenacious adherence to the vernacular, stylistically as true of church monuments and portraits as it is of literature. On the other, substantial parts of the cultural life of the country are lived in terms of the international manner of their time. There are idiosyncratic hybridities, such as the Little Castle at Bolsover in Derbyshire, created for the Duke and Duchess of Newcastle,[84] which turns back to a kind of eclectic medievalism to produce a summer palace evocative of the chivalric romances which were the preferred reading of the international elite. Yet within the castle there are elements of painted decoration drawn (albeit hesitantly and without any great technical accomplishment) from contemporary continental prints, and even (in the green and gold decoration of the room known as the 'heaven closet') decorative motifs which appear to be copied from oriental lacquers.

Resistance

Britain has never been enthusiastic about describing its cultural production as a part of an international movement, an unease which extends to Modernism almost as thoroughly as it does to Baroque. However, the early modern arts defy categorisation by nation. The language of visual symbol, emblem and *impresa* is as supra-national as the Latin tongue itself. British determination to see Baroque as the style of the enemy has wrongly stereotyped the baroque mode in all the arts as the sad, empty, enforced style of religious and political absolutism, rather than acknowledging the flexibility and diversity (indeed the sheer *permeability*) of baroque cultural production worldwide.

A substantial part of my argument is for the permeability of the international Baroque: its ability to combine the vernacular with the international. This world-wide phenomenon can be found in many aspects of the cultural production of early modern England, especially in those aspects of culture, masques and festivals, which were compelled to use the international discourses of power and the celebration of power. Yet, it must be stressed, there are elements within the divided culture of early modern England which seem almost consciously resistant to hybridisation, a phenomenon as clearly demonstrated in architecture as in portraiture or literature. English culture is subject to a series of revisions, artistic as well as political and ideological 'returns' to the recent past, attempts to turn back the religious and political clock.

While the poets of the earlier seventeenth century are removed from any suspicion of contamination by continental baroque by the sleight-of-hand usage 'metaphysical', in the later seventeenth century, by a similar act of prestidigitation, the term 'Augustan' is used to withdraw English baroque artists such as Wren from the continuum of their continental contemporaries. Wren is in many respects a paradigmatic baroque artist in that he combines vernacular elements (English gothic survivals and the gothic inheritance of the Laudian architecture of the 1630s) with a sophisticated deployment of contemporary international developments of the architecture of Roman antiquity.[85] His successor Hawksmoor does so even more explicitly, as in the Venetian window which leads up into a gothic English spire at Christchurch, Spitalfields. Hawksmoor's work is especially baroque in that it combines monumentality (sometimes deliberately oppressive monumentality) with architectural elements which appear frozen in rotation.

It is interesting that Wren's most explicit work in the full continental baroque mode (coincidentally a Catholic work), his altarpiece for the brief ecclesiastical regime of James VII and II at Whitehall, undertaken in collaboration with Grinling Gibbons and Arnold Quellin, is barely mentioned in the tally of his production. It survives only as a set of dismantled figures, therefore removed from the symbolic context of their original arrangement. It has found a final home in a church in Somerset after having been moved around for several centuries as something between a prized curiosity and a national embarrassment.[86]

In its very dividedness, in fact, English culture remains something of an anomaly. But once that dividedness is recognised, there is at least a rational basis for the further discussion of international continuities rather than the simplistic reiteration of insular disjunctions.

Reading back the subsequent *political* history of the British Isles into the world of the fifteenth to seventeenth centuries, it has seemed obvious to literary historians that the culture of the islands as a whole is English, with subaltern and, so to say, dialectal variations in Scotland, Ireland and Wales. Actually early modern Scotland and Ireland (and to some extent Wales) engaged with the Continent consistently, but independently and in different ways. One could argue (with an element of deliberate mischief, but also with an element of truth) that the Latin cultural production of Scotland was equally, if not more, visible internationally as that of England.

Irish Baroque

Writings on early modern Ireland by defenders of English rule in Ireland have always tended to deny that the native Irish had anything which could be called a culture at all. Proponents of Irish independence, by contrast, have focused on the vitality, complexity and significance of Irish vernacular culture in the national language. However, somewhat awkwardly for defenders of either of these positions, there is an identifiable element within early modern Ireland which can be described as fully participant in the international Baroque.

There is Irish poetry in Irish which is to some extent influenced by the Baroque. Pierce Ferriter (*c.*1600–53), who has already been mentioned, is a case in point. He was a speaker of both English and Irish, whose surviving verse is entirely in the latter tongue, but perceptibly influenced from without: the love-poem 'Léig dhíot th'airm' ('Lay your Weapons Down') demonstrates his awareness of Petrarch and subsequent Italian poets, and plays with an almost Marinistic imagery of blazon and weaponry to describe his subject's hair, eyes and skin.[87]

Apart from the reflection of extraneous poetic traditions which is seen in Irish-language writers such as Ferriter, there is a much more straightforward involvement with baroque themes and methods in Irish writers who wrote in Latin. The quantity and quality of early modern Irish work in Latin is at last receiving the attention which is its due.[88] There are, for example, indications of the international culture of the west of Ireland in the Latin oration which Oliver Martin (*c.*1602–48) made to welcome the Earl of Ormonde to Galway. Martin was on the supreme council of the Confederate Catholics in the 1640s, and was Mayor of Galway from 1642–43: it is reasonable to conjecture that the oration was delivered during his period as Mayor. The Earl, for example, is informed that he exhibits a compendium of all the virtues of his ancestors, in just the same way as Zeuxis shaped the daughter of Tyndarus – famously, the ancient Greek painter Zeuxis portrayed Helen of Troy by bringing together the five most beautiful women he could find and taking the best features of each. Thus the compliment is a graceful one, but also one which bears direct witness to speaker and honorand's common immersion in the tropes of renaissance culture.[89]

This oration is preserved in a remarkable manuscript collection of poems and orations presented to James Butler (1616–88), Earl (later Duke) of Ormonde. The manuscript contains poems and addresses in Latin, Irish, French, Greek and English,[90] reflecting something of Ormonde's own ambiguous position in the Ireland of his time. Ormonde was a scion of a noble Catholic family of Norman descent ('Old English'), with many connections of kinship amongst those who became the Confederate Catholics. However, he was taken away from his family as a child and brought up as an English Protestant, with the intention that he should become the figurehead of Stuart rule in Ireland. Thus, though a member of an ancient Old English family, he was Viceroy in Dublin amongst their supplanters, the New English. The vicissitudes of the 1640s and the reverses and inconsistencies of Charles I's Irish policy further complicate his position. But what the Ormonde manuscript confirms is the internationalism of the troubled Ireland of the 1630s and 1640s, both in Dublin and Kilkenny, and the degree to which Latin functioned, as might be expected, as the language of negotiation at boundaries.

It should also not be forgotten that the Irish international diaspora of the early modern period included not only the noblemen turned soldiers of fortune known as the 'Wild Geese', but scholars and students in the Irish colleges abroad at Salamanca and Rome. One such, Roderick Lynch, who died in the later seventeenth century, received an epitaph from a classmate which is interpolated in a manuscript book of disputations and other texts by Manuel de Calatayud, with the ownership inscription 'es de la Libreria del Coll[egi]o R[ea]l de Salamanca', and turns neatly on a pun: Lynch in Latin comes out as 'Lyncus', which is also the name of a legendary king who was turned into a lynx, an animal noted since antiquity for the sharpness of its sight. The epitaph begins: 'The study of Logic is over, we now ask more subtle questions; Now we need the eyes of a lynx [or, of Lyncus, or Lynch] . . .'[91] The same confident grasp of the tropes of baroque Latin culture is found in the Latin poems prefixed to the works of exiled Irish scholars, such as the verses which adorn Barnabas Keirney's *Heliotropon* by a Jesuit colleague and a theology student of Kilkenny, both of whom offer a graceful descant on the notion of the sunflower following the sun, a common emblem motif.[92] The signature of the second writer, Bartholomew Archer, 'Theologus Kilkeniensis', also reminds us of the presence of a Jesuit college in Kilkenny and the extent to which this college participated in the international culture of the Jesuits. The Kilkenny college was the principal Jesuit school in Ireland, and its staff offered instruction in the classical languages, grammar, poetry, rhetoric and philosophy. Like all Jesuit colleges, it put on Latin plays, since the Jesuits, like many more recent educationalists, believed that drama achieved a variety of pedagogic desiderata simultaneously. The college was quite ambitious in this respect: a specific Father, Stephen Callous SJ (1613–78), was appointed Master of Dramatic Poetry in or around 1649, and was the first person in Ireland ever to produce plays with scenery. Fr William St Leger SJ sent a report on the Kilkenny college to his superiors in Rome, which stresses this aspect of its activity:

> In the schools, plays and tragedies were splendidly presented as well as other scholastic exercises which drew great crowds of spectators and earned their applause.[93]

It was normal for the masters and pupils of a Jesuit school to produce at least one play a year, usually more. The only surviving witness to the dramatic culture of Kilkenny is not a play, but merely the argument for one, called *Titus or the Palme of Christian Courage.* This was printed at Waterford in 1644, and presumably distributed in Kilkenny for the convenience of spectators who had trouble following spoken Latin. A single copy has survived.[94] The plot is based on an incident from the Jesuit mission in Japan which was reported in a Jesuit history, in which the courage and resolution of a Japanese convert, Titus, and his family was tested to the utmost by the local ruler, who threatened to execute Titus's wife and children if he refused to recant. However, the fortitude of all members of the family amazed the oppressive king so greatly that ultimately he allowed them to go free. The narrative has a clear allegorical application of a recent but geographically distant event to present circumstances, since Irish Catholics, like those of Japan, faced tremendous pressure to abjure their religion.

Even though all we can know of *Titus* is from a summary on a single bifolium, this is revealing in a number of respects. The cast of characters includes not only the resolute Japanese Christians and their opponents, but also a variety of allegorical personifications: Divine Love, Faith and Fortitude, Idolatrie and the militant Church, among others. It seems likely that some at least of these characters were singing roles: music was much cultivated in Jesuit colleges. Even if this were not the case, the texture of the drama was clearly of considerable variety; to relieve the high drama of Titus's defiance of the King of Bungo, there were scenes of comedic intrigue involving a 'Countrey Clowne' and an unreliable soldier, and exalted passages of religious expression. The key series of scenes, in which '*Titus* his wife and familie voweth loyaltie to God before the Crucifix, the militant Church doth comfort them', and '*S. Francis Xaverius* appeares & encourages them' quite strongly argues for the use of scenery and perhaps even some stage machinery: contemporary Jesuit drama produced elsewhere routinely brought saints down from the clouds. Thus the Kilkenny elite were being given the same sort of drama as the elite of any city worldwide with a Jesuit college; they were exposed not only to a well-developed tradition of highly affective drama, but to poised and sophisticated comment on the present troubles of Ireland, and, since the shape of the narrative equates the English with the Japanese, to implicit criticism of the English as mindlessly oppressive barbarians.

Another aspect of the Catholic Confederation which demonstrates its genuine claim to be considered part of the international baroque world is its ability to mount a festal culture. The Confederate Irish reception of the Papal Nuncio to the Catholic Confederation, Giovanni Battista Rinuccini, Bishop of Fermo, when he entered Kilkenny on 12 November 1645, was a formal *adventus* such as he would have received from any court of Europe.[95] Even as late as September in the crisis year of 1648, the reception given to Ormonde on his desperate last-ditch visit to Ireland with offers of peace to the Confederate Catholics at Kilkenny, on behalf of a master already powerless and in captivity, is in

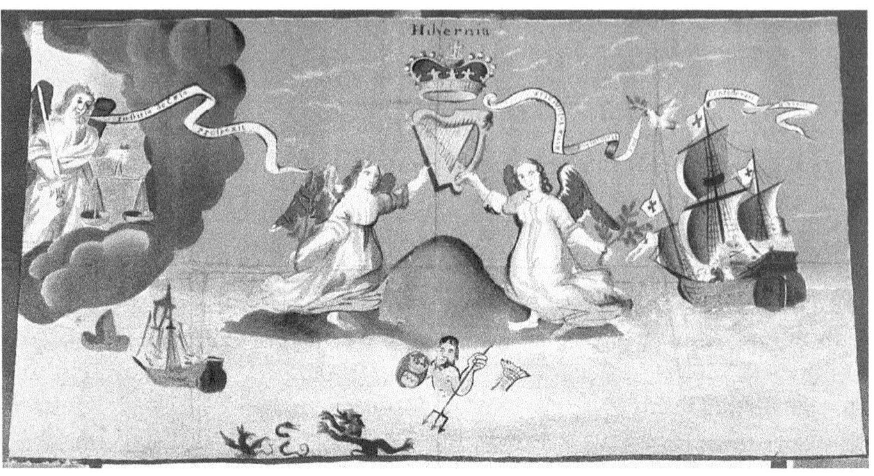

4 Walter Lawles, *Illuminated address to the Earl of Ormonde*, Kilkenny, 1648.

the international language, Latin, and uses the international codes of emblem and *imprese* to convey political points.

> Excellentissimo Nobilissimoque Domino D. Jacobo Marchioni Ormoniae &c. Serenissimi Regis nostri Caroli in Regno Hiberniae locum tenenti, Regii exercitus praefecto Generali, nec non totius Regni Hiberniae Gubernatori Generali Kilkeniam suam ingredienti Patrono suo plurimum colendo humilimus Cliens Walterus Lawles foelicitatem & prosperitatem adprecatur.

> Turbida Noeas agitant dum flumina puppes,
>   Impulsae irato flectere vela Deo.
> Gens humana solo depulsa per ardua Ponti,
>   Natales iterum visere quaerit agros.
> Atque ducem votis, submissa et voce fatigat,
>   Ut reduces tandem Patria terra tegat.
> Audiit, et niveam mittit de puppe columbam,
>   Quae refereat, num sit terra habitanda prius:
> Illa volat, rostroque novas deportat olivas,
>   Nuncia puppi vagis grata, probata *Noe.*
> Magne *Jacobe*, tuis quadrant successibus ist haec,
>   Fluctuat in mediis dum tua terra malis.
> Scala *Jacob[i]* divum coelestia nuncia portat,
>   Deque solo, alternas transtulit illa preces.
> Scalaque tu *Jacob*, dum Regi nostra reportas,
>   Quaeque gravare queant, quaeque levare queant.

Dum fera septenis fremitat Bellona procellis;
  Tu vigil es Patriae Syndicus usque tuae.
Aversum emollis Regem, similisque Columbae,
  Promissa *Hibernis* pacis oliva, tua eat.
Alta procellosi fugiens modo Littoro belli,
  Te duce, desertum quaerit *Hibernus* humum.
Quaerit, et inveniet, promittunt sydera pacem,
  Ore omni foelix pacis oliva tuae:
Crescat in aeternum, semperque virescat *Hibernis*,
  Ut plaudant pacis tempora fausta tuae:
Pacifici sic fidus eris provisor et actor,
  Antiquam firmans pacis honore fidem.
Concordesque tuos reddes Regique Deoque;
  Unio fortis amor, Arx sacra pacis amor.

[To the most noble Lord, James Marquis of Ormonde . . . his humble servant Walter Lawles wishes happiness and prosperity.

While the turbid waters toss the ark of Noah, its sails are filled and it is driven forward by an angry God. A human people, cast forth on the harsh soil of Pontus, begs to see once more its native fields. And it wearies the duke with prayers in submissive voice, 'Lead us back, so that at last their ancestral lands will nurture us'. He heard, and sent forth a snow-white dove from the ark, which he asked whether the land they had before was habitable. She flew off, and brought new olives in her beak, a welcome messenger to the wandering ark, approved by Noah. Great James, these same things accord with your successes; since your land is tossed in the middle of evils. Jacob's ladder carried a heavenly messenger from the gods downwards to the earth, and carried up prayers from there by turns. And it is your ladder, James, since you carry back our affairs to the King, they can give weight to some things, and make light of others. While fierce Bellona snarls with sevenfold tempests, you are constantly wakeful, the Representative of your Fatherland. You soothe down a contrary King, and like the Dove your promised olive of peace may go about among the *Irish*. Fleeing from the steep shores of stormy war with you as leader, the *Irishman* sought his deserted land. He sought, and he found it, and the stars promised peace, the happy olive of peace in your mouth for everyone it grows in eternity, and always flourishes with the *Irish*, so that the happy times may applaud your peace: thus you will be faithful provider and actor of peace-making confirming the ancient pact of peace with honour. You bring back your agreements between the King and God, a union of strength and love, a sacred Ark of the love of peace.]

Seldom have thirty-two lines of elegiac couplets contrived to say less, and nobody, neither writer nor addressee, was required to believe a word of it. But the important point is that the conventions are being duly observed. In context, the sentiments are less insanely sanguine than simply apposite and courteous; there is a desperate wishfulness in the way that the word 'peace' occurs in every other line. The basic metaphoric structure of the poem casts Ormonde as Noah: the ark is a common emblem deployed in contexts to do with personal or national security. It is interesting, and characteristic of renaissance Latin verse, that the land where the ark comes to rest is identified not as Ararat, but as Pontus, Ovid's loathed place of exile. Part of the problem faced by the Old English, of course, was their dispossession by the New English. The additional presence of Jacob's ladder is in compliment to Ormonde's given name of James (Jacobus in Latin).

The presentation copy of the poem has illustrated borders left, right and top, which place it as securely within international representational conventions as a Stuart court masque. At the top, two angels hold up the crowned harp of Ireland above an island in the sea. On the left, Justice with sword and balance looks from the clouds with a banderole stating *Justicia de Caelo Prospexit*. On the right is a ship with three banners of a cross on a white ground and the banderole *Confederati Hiberni*, above the ship, a dove with olive branch and the banderole *Pax hominibus bonae voluntatis* (peace to men of goodwill). Also on the left is Jacob's ladder with angels and the motto, *Scala Jacobi*; on the right is a palm tree, with the motto, *Cresco sub pondere* (I grow beneath my burden), a complex visual statement of the essential righteousness and justice of the Confederate cause.

The Kilkenny Confederacy was brought to an end by Oliver Cromwell; there after there is no further context in which any of the Irish lords could deploy this vocabulary of tropes and images. There is, however, an epilogue to this brief glimpse of baroque high culture in Ireland in a ballad-poem by Luke Waddinge, Bishop of Fearns, written when yet another reversal of fortune for the Catholics of the three kingdoms – the 'Popish Plot' invented by the unbalanced Titus Oates – had once more closed the Latin schools: 'The Lamentation of the Schollers presented to their Master . . . at the dissolveing of the schooles in Ross'.

> Must our Apollo from us now begon?
> And all our Muses leave their Hellicon
> Must they forsake their new Parnasses hill
> And leave no taste of Aganippeas well . . .
> When they Are gon, then must we feare, that we
> (by Ovid's rule) must Metamorphos'd be
> And that our soules by transmigration pass
> Unto the bodies, of an Oxe, or Ass.

Without them, we can onely feed and feast
And sleep, and rest, and live as doth the beast.[96]

The scholars are made to say that if learning is removed, they will be reduced to the condition of brutes – a condition which the English, in any case, perceived them to inhabit. Waddinge's poem, however, stresses the obduracy with which international high culture, Aganippean wells and all, was maintained in the most extraordinarily difficult circumstances. In the eighteenth century, the so-called 'hedge schools' carried the flame as best they could. Inevitably, the quality of instruction varied wildly, but some masters, at least, continued to teach classical Latin as well as, or instead of, classical Irish.[97]

Bishop Waddinge, author of these simple verses, belonged to one of the principal Anglo-Norman families of County Wexford. Among his connections were the Waddings of Waterford, who included his profoundly learned namesake, the historian Luke Wadding, the theologian Michael Wadding SJ, better known as Miguel Godinez, and Peter Wadding, Chancellor of the University of Prague – a group far from untypical of the learned diaspora of Catholic Ireland. The other Luke Wadding had, in his day, been one of the Confederacy's most ardent supporters, and was instrumental in Innocent X's decision to send Rinuccini as nuncio. It is characteristic of the sheer obduracy of Irish learned culture that some thirty-five years after the Confederacy's collapse, a member of the Wadding family is still to be found doggedly maintaining the right, and duty, of young Celts to become members of the greater confederacy which is the *respublica litterarum.*

A remarkable instance of the survival of Irish Latinity is an epitaph produced in the 1790s by an alumnus of the hedge school of Sliabh gCua (and briefly of the Irish College in Rome), Donnchadh Ruadh Mac Con Mara (Denis Macnamara the red-haired), who lived from 1715–1810. This perfectly balanced epitaph on the poet Tadgh Gaedhealach Ó Súilleabháin is also an illustration of the doubleness of the life of the highly educated Irish poet: it is at the same time an epitaph made by one desperately poor man for another, and the utterance of one admired poet at the grave of a fellow poet of distinguished ancestry. Seldom has the bizarre duality created by penal laws and the truculence of Anglophone culture in Ireland been more movingly displayed.

Thaddeus hic situs est, oculos huc flecte viator,
    Illustrem vatem parvula terra tegit!
Heu! Jacet exanimis, fatum irrevocabile vicit

> Spiritus e terra sidera summa petit . . .
> Pacem optavit pace igitur versatur in alto
>   Ad superi tendit regna beata Patri

> Thady is buried here, weep, traveller: this little grave encloses the distinguished poet. Alas he lies lifeless, overcome by conquering fate, his spirit is gone form earth seeking the heights of the stars . . . He desired peace, therefore he sought the peace of the heavens above in the blessed kingdom of the Father.[98]

O'Sullivan and Macnamara by these words assert their absolute claim to membership of the international republic of letters.

Scottish Baroque

The history of the Baroque in Scotland is overwhelmingly a history of Scottish Neo-Latin literature, though there are also distinct baroque manifestations in architecture and the visual arts. The best known, most widely read poet to emerge from the British Isles in the sixteenth century was George Buchanan (1506–82), who was, to the Parisian humanist printer Henri Estienne, '*poetarum nostri saeculi facile princeps*' (easily the best poet of our age).[99] His education and early career took him to and fro between Scotland and France and Italy; the fact that ultimately he decided to go home to Calvinist Scotland after extensive experience of the universities of continental Europe is a reminder of the Latinate internationalism of lowland Scotland – the qualification 'lowland' is important, since early modern Scotland was very far from being a unified culture. Even at the simplest, it is necessary to distinguish lowland, northern and Gaelic-speaking Scotland as separate culture-provinces.

A very clear instance of lowland Scottish participation in the modes and the sensibility of the continental baroque is the extravagant mourning of the Ayrshire landowner Robert Montgomerie of Skelmorlie, which recalls that of Sir Kenelm Digby already discussed. In 1636, Montgomerie constructed for himself a theatre of death comparable to the manifestations with which Digby mourned his Venetia: he built an aisle on to the parish church of Largs, with an elaborate painted ceiling, to contain a monument to his recently deceased wife Margaret Douglas and eventually to receive his own remains. The monument itself is a finely cut triumphal arch, stylistically not far removed from the monuments to Mary Stuart and Elizabeth Tudor which James VI and I had erected in Westminster Abbey not long after his accession to the English throne. Below the central part of the tripartite arch, stairs descend to a sunken crypt which contains the coffins of Montgomerie and his wife.

The inscription on the window side of the monument itself is in the voice of Montgomerie's wife and emphasises that she has moved from a devout life on earth to absorption into God.

> Bis duo bisque decem transegi virginis annos
> Ter duo tres decem consociata viro . . .
> Clara genus generosa animi speciosa decore
> Chara deo vixi nunc mihi cuncta deus.[100]
>
> [I lived for twenty-four years unmarried, and thirty-six years as a wife with my husband. I was of a good family, with a noble spirit, and beautiful. I lived dear to God, and now God is everything to me.]

The epitaph is thus unexceptional, but the imagery on the painted wooden vault above the tomb presents, by contrast, a number of enigmas. There are representations of the seasons, of the signs of the zodiac, of the arms of the twelve tribes of Israel, and panels of grotesque-work as well as the arms of Montgomerie and his wife and families closely allied to them. But two large panels still elude precise analysis: the first shows a richly dressed woman with the fruits of the earth at her feet apparently taming a wild horse, while the other shows a woman with a flaming heart in a chalice on the seashore with ships behind. The painted ceiling, with its seasons and zodiac, is concerned with time and the occupations of life and the years of the world continuing. All this is opposed to the contemplation of death in the vault below the monument.

It is the use which Montgomerie appears to have made of this structure which compels our interest in its baroque intensity. The inscription on his own coffin reads:

> Ipse mihi praemortuus fui, fato funera
> Praeripui, unicum idque Caesareum,
> Exemplar, inter tot mortales secutus.
>
> [I anticipated my death and forestalled my fate, as I followed the unique example among men of Caesar.]

He means that he followed the example of the Emperor Charles V, who rehearsed his own funeral shortly before his death in 1558, after he had already abdicated to spend the last years of his life in monastic prayer and contemplation. After a youth in which he had energetically feuded with his neighbours, and especially after the death of his wife, Montgomerie performed many acts of expiation (he was almost certainly a discreet Catholic) and was in the habit of coming to the tomb to spend the night in prayer by the coffin of his wife and (in the manner of John Donne), presumably, by his own waiting coffin. It is the recording of this fact on the coffin plate which adds the touch of performance to the complex of acts of commemoration and meditation, and relates Montgomerie to Digby.

The Latinate and festival productions of the early modern Celtic countries are hardly known. Many texts are still accessible only in very rare printed books or in manuscript. Yet it could be argued that the culture of early modern Scotland, with its wholehearted embracing of Latin as its literary medium, is less ambiguously connected to the international cultures of its day than is England. The Celtic countries are cultures which are themselves divided, most obviously by religion and language, but along different lines from English culture. Celtic-speakers in Scotland and Ireland had a very considerable degree of access to contemporary international culture, infinitely more than metropolitan historiography would allow, even today.

In the fifteenth century, and up until the Reformation, Scots doctors of medicine, theologians and jurists almost invariably took at least one of their degrees abroad. Buchanan's career is a characteristic one: Scots swarmed in the French universities, notably in Paris, Orléans and Montpellier. But, unlike the English, they continued to study abroad after the Reformation, though the seats of learning sought out naturally changed in deference to religious considerations. The contacts of the English elite with the Continent, the travels of a Sidney, a Digby or a Milton, were numerically insignificant compared to the flood of lowland Scots studying at the Protestant academies of the Netherlands, most particularly the universities of Leiden and Utrecht, right through the sixteenth, seventeenth and eighteenth centuries.

The sheer numbers of students involved should not be underestimated. From about the 1640s until the 1740s, a Netherlandic influence is apprehensible in every aspect of Scottish life from architecture to music, to gardening, medicine and the study of antiquity, particularly in the lowlands. The paradigmatic figure here is Sir John Clerk of Penicuik (1676–1755), an early patron of William Adam, who built his own house in the Lothians very much in the style of Pieter Post.[101] Beyond this, Clerk brought home from the Continent sophisticated training in musicial composition, initially deployed on ambitious cantatas in the style (and with some of the accomplishment) of his teacher Corelli; but he turned later to a manner of composition which combined indigenous elements with the metropolitan Baroque. Clerk also maintained a lifelong correspondence with the medical innovator Hermann

Boerhaaven. This correspondence is in a supple, unclassical Latin which clearly records the language used by the international community in Leiden as a medium of everyday communication.

In addition to these specifically Calvinist networks, there is the whole further set of contacts and influences of exiled Catholics, or Catholics who risked the severities of the Penal Laws by temporary exile to obtain on the Continent the education legally denied them at home. Northern Scotland was less securely in the grip of the Kirk than were the lowlands; and this gives northern Scottish links with the Continent a characteristic, somewhat alternative, flavour. If George Buchanan is a paradigmatic figure for internationalist lowland Scottish culture, his equivalent in the north is John Barclay (1582–1621), equally well known as an author for his Latin romance *Argenis,* an allegorical treatment of contemporary politics. Barclay was not born in the ancestral castle, Towie Barclay in Aberdeenshire, because his father had exiled himself from Scotland on account of his religion. French by cultural formation, Barclay nonetheless maintained a sense of his Scottish roots and an attachment to James VI.

After the death of James IV and Scotland's entry into a dire sixteenth century of long minorities (James V, Mary and James VI all came to the throne as infants), Scottish poetic energies were increasingly channelled into Latin. There was a lull, or St Martin's summer, in the early Scottish reign of James VI, in which the vernacular cultural life of Scotland was invigorated by his 'Castalian Band', poets immersed in contemporary French culture who also undertook translations from Italian into Scots with royal encouragement. There was also a profound engagement with continental Baroque in the vernacular poetry of Alexander Montgomerie (*c.*1556–1610), whose long allegorical poem *The Cherry and the Slae* was, in turn, rendered into Latin by the Scottish historian and professor at Bologna, Thomas Dempster.[102] But on the departure of the court for England in 1603, and with the absence of any magnates able to sustain a court level of patronage, Scots as a language of expression for learning and literature virtually ceased to exist.

A curious misapprehension still circulates that Scotland therefore ceased to have a developed literary culture when the court went south. This is not the case, but since almost all Scottish literary energy in the seventeenth century is expressed in Latin, much of it was for an international audience and much of it was published abroad, it has been invisible, or when visible, embarrassing, to a national culture which has chosen to define itself as impoverished and vernacular, and, in so far as it looks beyond national boundaries at all, as struggling to withstand

the cultural hegemony of its over-mighty neighbour south of Hadrian's
Wall. The name of Mark Alexander Boyd will always be held in respect
in Scotland for his one surviving, unmatchable, sonnet in Scots, but
we would do well to remember that we have still two volumes of his
Latin poetry in which the same quality is apparent on virtually every
page. As Principal Geddes wrote, in seventeenth-century Scotland, Latin
verse was 'the normal and recognised vehicle of poetic expression'.[103]

The depth of the Scottish Catholic response to the continental
Baroque is illustrated in other media than Latin verse. The extraordinary emblematic room of Chancellor Seton at Pinkie House, East
Lothian, is one of the most Italianate spaces in Britain: its whole iconography and layout is formed by Seton's Jesuit education in Rome.
By the use of prudential emblems and their subscriptions, aligned with
a series of prose apophthegms, the whole room – from the crane as
emblem of vigilance painted over the oriel window, to the feigned domes
populated by angels – is a self-portrait, and an externalisation of the
Jesuit 'contemplation to attain discernment'. It is at the same time a
set of exhortations to self-control and self-reliance, and a place of retreat
and refreshment for a man of considerable intellectual gifts holding
high office who was attempting to guide Scotland through a period of
drift towards fanatic theocracy and civil war.

Perhaps the most important of the baroque Scottish poets is George
Strachan (*fl.* 1592–1634), a product of the same distinctive northern
Scottish culture as John Barclay and Arthur Johnston, and, like Seton,
a product of the colleges of Rome. He was a Latin poet of breathtak-
ing accomplishment, and also the most accomplished linguist of the
first generation of Europeans to live in and study the Arabic world. He
was a product of the Aberdeen region, which, as Hill Burton pointed
out, was culturally as well as geographically remote from the rest of
Scotland, and, owing to the power of the Earls of Huntly, the most powerful magnates in Scotland (most of whom were Catholics), something
of a state within a state. 'The map shows the district to be naturally
separate from the rest of Scotland, stretching far eastward into the
German Ocean. It had thus the means of uninterrupted communication with the European continent by sea.'[104]

Strachan's story is so remarkable and so little known that it is worth
recounting. Self-exiled from Scotland because of his Catholicism, he
studied at Pont-à-Musson (where John Barclay was brought up) and Paris,
as well as at the newly founded Scots College in Rome. His *Album amicorum,* covering the years 1599–1609,[105] permits us to reconstruct both
the sophistication of the circles in which he moved on the Continent

and his travels as an undercover agent in Scotland acting on behalf of the Jesuits. He left Paris for the east in 1613, and in 1616–18 travelled with the nomadic court of the Emir Feyyad. In this period, he married and converted to Islam, while becoming more deeply knowledgeable in Arabic and in Islamic theology and philosophy than any European contemporary. In 1619, he secured a position in Isphahan as translator and physician to the English merchants of the East India Company, which he left the following year in spectacular circumstances when a mentally disturbed colleague denounced him as a traitor, murderer and embezzler.

He then went to live in the Carmelite house in Isphahan and taught Arabic. His will of 26 September 1621, witnessed by the Italian traveller Pietro della Valle, bequeathed his books to the Discalced Carmelites of Rome, although there are indications that it was not made on his deathbed and he lived for some time afterwards. Not the least important aspect of Strachan in the context of the present narrative is that his life begs the question of why such colossal achievements, evidenced by sixty oriental manuscripts with interlinear translations, letters and poems, are so little known. His biographer, G. L. Della Vida, estimates that his knowledge of Arabic was far beyond that of any other Western European of his time, and exceeded even that of the famous Dutch Arabist Thomasus Erpenius, who has, by contrast, received his due measure of learned attention.[106] Strachan's translations of literary and philosophical texts constitute a vital, almost wholly unexplored, body of early translation from Arabic, and a monument of early modern reception and understanding of Islam. But because the target language of his translations is Latin, not a vernacular, and his life and work fit neither with an English view of Scotland, nor with the Scots' view of themselves, he has disappeared from the historiography of East–West contact.

Strachan's elegy for a young relative called Patrick Seton was printed in the *Delitiae poetarum Scotorum*, edited by Arthur Johnston. It was much admired by contemporaries such as William Barclay,[107] and is comparable in both theme and range to Milton's *Epitaphium Damonis*, with its evocation of friendship, the beauty and charm of the lost youth and moments of shared danger and hardship, set against the cruel irony of his family's hopeful thoughts:

> Nonne ergo te, lacerae cum naufraga membra carinae
>> Gallica saxoso littore fregit hiems,
> Nocte manu trepidum scopulosa per aequora traxi,
>> Colla mihi premeret cum tremebunda nepos?

O utinam paribus licuisset cedere fatis
  Tunc, et in amplexu pectora cara mori. (47–52)

[When a storm in France smashed on a rocky shore the sinking timbers
of a wrecked ship, did I not carry you, trembling as you were, through
the reefy sea by night, my nephew, hanging round my shivering neck? If
only we had been permitted to yield to an equal fate at that moment,
and to die, in the embrace of a loved body.]

nunc ignara parat redituro mater honores,
  Emptaque Patricio nomine villa iacet.
Forte etiam votis expectant scripta sorores,
  Eque peregrinis dona remissa locis. (77–80)

[now his mother, unaware, prepares a reception in honour of the
expected one, and a country house, bought in Patrick's name, lies
empty; perhaps his sisters too are looking forward to letters, and gifts
from far countries.]

This is an extraordinary poem by any standards and could only have come
out of a complex and achieved Latinate and internationalist culture.

The question of finding the most useful way of thinking about the
status of Scottish culture in the early modern period, with its extraordinary blending of that which is international and universal with that
which is truly local, is a question which still ought to be under discussion. Perhaps a useful interim definition might be that the Scottish
culture of the seventeenth century is composed of a series of hybrid
cultures, each blending, to a different degree, the vernacular with the
international.

What is so beguiling about the idea of the world of Latin letters and
of shared emblems and images is that it makes us consider the local
and the international in a different, fruitful and convincing way.
Strachan's evocation of Patrick Seton's mother waiting hopefully at home
for her dead son can be juxtaposed with a far better known verse from
the ballad of Sir Patrick Spens,

Lang, lang, may thair ladies sit
  Wi' their fans into their hand,
Or eir they se Sir Patrick Spence
  Cum sailing to the land.[108]

Arthur Johnston, perhaps the most accomplished of the Aberdonian
Latinists of the seventeenth century other than Strachan, provides a
wonderful example of the international interacting with the local. His
vastly sophisticated command of Latin style allowed him to produce a

series of elegant Latin versions of the highest level Caroline lyric poetry, including Thomas Carew's 'Ask Me No More' and William Davenant's 'Go Hunt the Whiter Ermine' (*'Armeniam venare feram, pretiosaque terga / Endymioneae munera mitte Deae'*).[109] At the same time, he was still able easily to take the local as his subject matter.

The tone of eighteenth-, even nineteenth-century writers who lay claim to Scottish roots tends to carry an implicit, or sometimes explicit, apology for hailing from somewhere provincial or quaint: Johnston, by contrast, seems entirely clear in his own mind that it is possible to be an internationally celebrated poet from Aberdeenshire. His work emphasises his rootedness on one specific point of the globe, notably in his idyllic poem on his place of origin, Caskieben, just under the jagged peak of Bennachie:

> Mille per ambages nitidis argenteus undis
>   Hic trepidat laetos Urius inter agros.
> Explicat haec seras ingens Bennachius umbras,
>   Nox ubi libratur lance diesque pari. (3–6)[110]

[Where with the thousand glimmering sequins of her waters the Urie trembles between her happy fields, and where the great mass of Bennachie spreads all around the shadows of evening, where night is weighed in the balance, and equals the day.]

He evokes, both explicitly and implicitly, the classical Latin tradition: Ovid's lines on his equivalently provincial birthplace, Sulmo; Mantua's claim to fame as the birthplace of Virgil; ending with the modest claim that by contrast with Virgil, 'it is my native soil which sheds lustre upon me'.

Another interesting poem is called 'On his Garden' – many upper-class Scots of his generation were devoted gardeners, expending much money and ingenuity on cosseting exotic fruit, but Johnston, it seems, was not among them. His garden is patently his library room, perhaps painted with the garlands of oranges and pomegranates which formed part of the basic repertory of Northern European decorative painting, like the garlands of fruit and flowers which were painted on the ceilings of Northfield House, near Edinburgh, early in the seventeenth century.

> Hic tristis dum saevit hiems, quae Punica tellus
>   Quaeque ferax mittit Media, poma lego . . . (3–4)
> Aureus est hortus nobis, hunc protulit aetas
>   Aurea, qua fructus sponte ferebat humus. (7–8)[111]

[Even while gloomy winter is raging, I cull the fruits which the Punic land produces, and that which fierce Media sends (pomegranates and oranges) . . . Mine is a golden garden, the age of gold produced it, when fruit came spontaneously from the ground.]

Johnston demonstrates that the snows of the remote Cabrach, one of the most rugged and snowbound upland valleys in the country, can be brought within the compass of baroque Latin verse – and interestingly, the lord of so remote a mountain castle is both a scholar and a gentleman, capable of appreciating verse which sparkles with wit, even if it is not wholly tactful towards his friend's demesne:

> Siccine, Gordoni, Cabriis affixus ericis,
>   Urbe procul, rupes inter et antra lates?
> Quid iuvant ingenio genium vicisse Minervae,
>   Ingenii dotes si sinis usque premi? . . . (1–4)
> Hic ubi tu latitas, nil, praeter lustra ferarum
>   Et caeli volucres, saxaque surda, vides.
> Nullum hic, qui doctas haurire aut reddere voces,
>   Aut a te quidquam discere possit, habes.
> Barbara gens tota est, et inhospita terra, pruinis
>   Semper, et aestivo sub Cane, mersa nive. (9–16)[112]

[Why, O Gordon, are you thus glued to the Cabrach's heather, hiding away far from the city, among rocks and caves? What good is it to have conquered Minerva in wit, if thus you allow your gifts of the mind to rust unused? You have lurked there nearly five years, seeing nothing but wild animals, deaf rocks, the birds of the air. You have nobody who can utter or answer an educated voice, or who is able to learn anything from you. The people are entirely barbarian, the land is stark, it is always raining, and even in the dog-days, it is mired in snow . . .]

One of Johnston's most compelling poems is concerned with the feud of the Gordons and the Crichtons which culminated in the Fire of Frendraught. Two noble sons of the house of Gordon were the guests of the Crichtons at their tower of Frendraught on the night of 8 October, 1630. By two in the morning, the tower was on fire, and the Gordons both perished. Contemporary balance of opinion favoured arson rather than accident as the cause of the blaze, and suspicion attached to their Crichton hosts, particularly to Elizabeth Gordon, wife of Crichton of Frendraught, who was a cousin to the Gordons of Huntly.

The way in which Johnston articulates this tragedy in verse is well within the international conventions and frame of reference of Latin. The diction and atmosphere and versification are immediately apprehensible as Ovidian. The mind of a contemporary would immediately have gone to the *Heroides* of Ovid, that series of imaginary complaints of the heroines of mythology, imitated in every Latinate country since the middle ages, especially to 'Penelope to Ulysses'. Johnston is speaking at once with two voices: the local, which moves effortlessly in the mental world of the ballads, and also, in this linguistically transitional region, of highland laments; and the international voice, which places a local tragedy in the history of the universal *respublica litterarum*. As Patrick Kavanagh reminds, in 'Epic': 'Homer's ghost came whispering to my mind. He said: I made the *Iliad* from such / A local row. Gods make their own importance.'

The first of Johnston's poems is spoken by the widow of one of the victims, Sophia Hay, Lady Meglum. In putting a speech in elegaic couplets into her mouth he is ultimately following the example of Ovid. But as she relates her wrongs and casts the gravest suspicions on Elizabeth Gordon (referred to only as 'Lupa': 'she-wolf') we see in operation one of the most compelling possibilities of the baroque arts. The stance and the method of telling the story are quite different, but the sentiment marches precisely with the ballad of the Fire of Frendraught: while turns of phrase continually remind us of the Celtic ritual lament for the dead, the *caointe*.

> When he stood at the wire-window
>   Most doleful to be seen,
> He did espy her, Lady Frendraught,
>   Who stood upon the green.
>
> Cried, Mercy, mercy, Lady Frendraucht,
>   Will ye not sink with sin?
> For first your husband killed my father
>   And now you burn his son.[113]

('He' is Viscount Meglum; a wire-window is a window with defensive bars.) The ballad, furthermore, ends with Sophia Hay wringing her hands and tearing her hair.

Johnston's lament is differently structured: Sophia visualises her husband settling down to what proved to be his last night on earth:

> Nox erat, et coniunx tradebat lumina somno,
>   Lumina post roseo non fruitura die.
>
> [It was night, and my husband was closing his eyes in sleep; eyes which would not rejoice in the sight of rosy dawn.]

She does not imagine him desperately pleading with his murderer through the impassable window; her vision is dramatic in a different mode, a specific visualising of malicious arson, with combustibles piling up around her innocently slumbering husband in his bed.

> Ecce faces circum volitant, circum omnia fumus,
>   Omnia pix, sulphur, naphta, bitumen, erant . . .
> Cetera Di norunt, et nox, et conscia turris,
>   Saxaque, quae tantum nunc superesse vides.
> Scire quod heu nollem, mors solum mariti est,
>   Et comitum, quibus haec nox sine fine fuit.

> [Look! Firebrands are flying around, there is smoke all about; everywhere there is pitch, sulphur, naphtha, bitumen . . . The rest God knows, and the night, and the guilty stones of the tower such of them as still stand today. All I know is what I do not want to know: the death of my husband and his friend, for whom that night had no end.]

A particularly Celtic aspect of her grievance is her affront at the disrespect shown to the corpses, which were unceremoniously laid out in the stables and not treated with the honour they were owed: funeral honours are a subject on which early modern Europe in general was extraordinarily sensitive, but the focus on the actual body rather than the *arredamento* around it is reminiscent of that of other anguished widows such as Eileen Dubh O'Connell, whose husband, Art O'Leary, was shot dead on the Inch of Carriganimmy on 24 May 1773:

> I foud you dead before me by a little low furze-bush, without bishop, without cleric, without priest to read the psalm over you, but an ancient worn old woman who had spread the end of her cloak on you; your blood was streaming from you, and I did not stop to wipe it, but drank it up from my palms.[114]

Johnston's poem is, as it were, intensely local and universal at the same time. At the same time we have an international elegy in the tradition of Ovid, and a lament (particularly when it touches on the lack of respect paid to the bodies of the dead Gordons) which is existing in an emotional continuum with the highly ritualised keens or laments of the Scottish and Irish traditions, which were often made by, or put in the mouth of, the widow. Here is the opening of another such poem of lament from the sixteenth century, made by the daughter of Campbell of Glenlyon after her father had murdered her lover in 1570:

> Moch madainn air latha Lùnasd'
>   Bha mi sùgradh mar ri m'ghràdh,
> Ach mun tàinig meadhon latha
>   Bha mo chridhe air a'chràdh.

Ochain, ochain, ochain uiridh
  Is goirt mo chridhe, a laoigh,
Ochain, ochain, ochain uiridh
  Cha chluinn t' athair ar caoidh.

[Early on Lammas morning I was sporting with my love, but before noon came upon us my heart had been crushed.

Alas, alas, alas and alack, sore is my heart, my child, alas, alas, alas and alack your father won't hear our cries.]

Many points of confluence can be found: the question of who is to support the fatherless children, the vowing of revenge, the calling for divine justice on the murderers.

Cetera mortales castigent crimina, solos
  Haec habet ultores carnificina Deos.

[Mortals punish other crimes, but this act of butchery will have only the gods for its avengers.]

The voices of Ovid and of Eileen Dubh O'Connell speak simultaneously in these words.

*

This first chapter comes to rest on the main theme of the book, its chief thesis. The same work of baroque art functions simultaneously within two cultural systems. The portrait of the Jacobite Sir Stuart Thriepland is a case in point from Scotland's visual culture. It appears at first to be a 'fancy' portrait – a meditating figure in highland dress, with an *amorino* leaning on his shield and a troop of soldiers marching away behind the hill. We might think for a moment that it represents a moment in a stage play, or an allegorical or 'fancy' portrayal of the metaphorical battles of love of which Pierce Ferriter wrote in his baroque Irish a century earlier. But the picture is in earnest, and requires in fact another system of reading to unlock its purpose – it is an *ex voto* or miracle painting in a mode far more familiar from continental Catholic countries. Sir Stuart is rendering thanks to the operation of God through his guardian angel (the *amorino*), who brought him his shield and protected him from the English troops in the genocidal bloodbath which followed the battle of Culloden in 1745. Jacobite Aberdeenshire and Moray had a profoundly complex culture in which one individual necessarily moved between, or within, competing frames of reference. Traditional and national simplicities cannot account for a double-faced work such as this, any more than they can be applied to Johnston's Ovidian epistle which is also a Celtic lament for the dead.

Such works in all the baroque arts are functioning simultaneously within two cultural systems, one indigenous, one global. All the baroque arts become more interesting, and their accomplishments greater, at what are conventionally thought of as margins. As we are beginning to see, they are at their most compelling at their frontiers.

Notes

1 Inigo Jones, *The most notable Antiquity of Great Britain, vulgarly called Stone-Heng* (London, 1655); Richard Verstegan, *Restitution of Decayed intelligence in Antiquities* (Antwerp: Robert Bruney, 1605).

2 Richard Fanshawe's *Fida Pastora*, in *The Poems and Translations of Sir Richard Fanshawe*, ed. Peter Davidson, 2 vols. (Oxford: Clarendon, 1997–99), vol. 1, pp. 237–315.

3 A full account of whose collection can be found in Stephen Bann's *Under the Sign: John Bargrave as Collector, Traveler and Witness* (Ann Arbor: University of Michigan, 1994).

4 See Helena Mennie Shire, *Song, Dance and Poetry of the Court of Scotland under King James VI* (Cambridge: Cambridge University Press, 1969), also Ian Dalrymple McFarlane, *Buchanan* (London: Duckworth, 1981).

5 Roger Ascham, *The Scholemaster, or plaine and perfite way of teachyng children, to vnderstand, write, and speake, the Latin tong* (London: John Day, 1570), ff. 23*v*–24*v*.

6 I am much indebted to Dr Arnold Hunt for this simple but crucial distinction.

7 For Fanshawe, see Davidson (ed.), *Poems and Translations of Sir Richard Fanshawe*, vol. 2, pp. 335–6, for Huygens, Peter Davidson and Adriaan van der Weel (eds), *A Selection of the Poems of Sir Constantijn Huygens* (Amsterdam: Amsterdam University Press, 1996), pp. 214–15.

8 See Victor von Klarwill (ed.), *Queen Elizabeth and some Foreigners: being a Series of Hitherto Unpublished Letters from the Archives of the Hapsburg Family* (London: John Lane the Bodley Head Ltd, 1928), pp. 25–6; Latin letter from Elizabeth to Ferdinand I in her own hand, 28 Nov. 1558, and a letter from the ambassador George von Helffenstein to Ferdinand, 16 March 1559, p. 48, in which he notes, 'the queen during our walk [in the garden] further told me that if I had any further commission of your Imperial Majesty's to communicate, I might do it freely then, as the maid of honour on duty did not understand Latin'. See also Dana F. Sutton, 'The Queen's Latin', *Neulateinische Jahrbuch/Journal of Neo-Latin Language and Literature*, 2 (2000), pp. 233–40.

9 James Wallace Binns, *Intellectual Culture in Elizabethan and Jacobean England* (Leeds: Francis Cairns, 1990), pp. 109–14. Binns also notes London editions of other continental Latin texts for the use of schools. These

included Baptista Mantuanus, *Eclogues*: 'Mantuanus seems to have been taught well-nigh universally, and is often quoted in English vernacular literature'. There were also English editions of Hugo Grotius's *Poemata*, several of which are of English interest, and of the religious verse of Theodore Beza.

10 Mathias Casimir Sarbiewski, *The Odes of Casimire, Translated by G. H[il]* (London: Humphrey Mosley, 1646), pp. 89–95.

11 Sarbiewski, *Odes of Casimire*, pp. 105–21.

12 Sarbiewski, *Odes of Casimire*, p. 141.

13 Michael Wyatt, *The Italian Encounter with Tudor England: A Cultural Politics of Translation* (Cambridge: Cambridge University Press, 2005).

14 *Ibid.*, pp. 130–4.

15 Franklin B. Williams, 'The Literary Patronesses of Renaissance England', *Notes and Queries*, 9:10 (1962), p. 366. John N. King, 'Patronage and Piety: The Influence of Catherine Parr', in *Silent but for the Word*, ed. Margaret P. Hannay (Kent, OH: Kent State University Press, 1985), pp. 43–60.

16 *A Calendar of the Manuscripts of the Most Hon. The Marquess of Salisbury, KG, &c., Preserved at Hatfield House, Hertfordshire* (London: Historical Manuscripts Commission, 1888–1973), vol. 13, p. 103.

17 Howard Nenner, *The Right to be King: The Succession to the Crown of England, 1603–1714* (Chapel Hill: University of North Carolina Press, 1995), p. 4, observes that what Elizabeth leaned on as the validation for her position was not so much her birthright, but her right by act of Parliament – Henry VIII's third Act of Succession of 1544.

18 Lawrence Stone, *The Crisis of the Aristocracy, 1558–1641* (London: Oxford University Press, 1967), p. 473. For the poem, see Steven W. May, *The Elizabethan Courtier Poets: The Poems and their Contexts* (Columbia: University of Missouri Press, 1991), pp. 251–2, and London, National Archives, SP 12/254/67.

19 Roy Strong, ' "My Weeping Stag I Crowne": The Persian Lady Reconsidered', in Michael Bath, John Manning Alan R. Young, (eds), *Art of the Emblem* (New York: AMS Press, 1993), pp. 103–42.

20 Jan van Dorsten, 'Mr Secretary Cecil: Patron of Letters', in *The Anglo-Dutch Renaissance: Seven Essays* (Leiden: Leiden University Press and London: Oxford University Press, 1988), pp. 28–37, p. 31. Both William and Mildred Cecil clearly acted as the patrons of a variety of humanist poets and intellectuals, including foreigners such as Utenhove, Franciscus Junius and Daniel Rogers, as well as Anglo-Latin poets such as John Herd, Giles and Phineas Fletcher, and Christopher Ockland.

21 Eleanor Rosenberg, *Leicester, Patron of Letters* (New York: Columbia University Press, 1955).

22 Jan van Dorsten, *The Radical Arts*, (Leiden: Leiden University Press and London: Oxford University Press, 1970), pp. 62–3.

23 *Ibid.*, p. 12.

24 May, *Elizabethan Courtier Poets*, pp. 41–52.

25 On which see Timothy Mowl, *Elizabethan and Jacobean Style* (London: Phaidon, 1993). Mowl makes a strong, if idiosyncratic, argument in favour of an Elizabethan aesthetic of abundance which was not in any sense a failure to absorb classical models, but a rejection of them: 'Classicism can act as the controlling factor in a building's design or as a mere decorative trim. In the years of Elizabeth and James, it usually functioned as the latter.' Elizabeth's favourite palace was her father's wholly unclassical building, Nonsuch (p. 72): Mowl also notes the Earl of Leicester's rejection of classical models in his reconstruction of Kenilworth as a palace (p. 74), and suggests that this rejection was strongly influential on subsequent Elizabethan palace architecture.

26 R. Malcolm Smuts, *Court Culture and the Origins of Royalist Tradition in Early Stuart England* (Philadelphia University of Pennsylvania Press, 1987), p. 16.

27 Linda Levy Peck, 'Women as Court Brokers: Queen Anne's Household', in *Court Patronage and Corruption in Early Stuart England* (London: Routledge, 1993), pp. 68–74, p. 70.

28 Monique Mosser and George Teyssot (eds), *The History of Garden Design: The Western Tradition from the Renaissance to the Present Day* (London: Thames & Hudson, 1991), pp. 158–9. See also the facsimile edition of Theodore de Bry's 1620 book of plates, *Hortus Palatinus: die Entwürfe zum Heidelberger Schlossgarten von Salomon de Caus, 1620* (Worms: Werner'sche Verlags Gesellschaft, 1980).

29 Peter Davidson, 'Marvellian Questions', *TLS* (3 December 1999), pp. 14–15.

30 Barbara Jones, *Follies and Grottoes* (London: Constable, 1974), pp. 145–7.

31 *Henry Peacham's Manuscript Emblem Books*, ed. Alan R. Young (Toronto: University of Toronto Press, 1998).

32 Wyatt, *Italian Encounter*, pp. 137–8.

33 See Davidson and van der Weel (eds), *A Selection of the Poems of Sir Constantijn Huygens*, pp. 195–200.

34 Binns, *Intellectual Culture in Elizabethan and Jacobean England*, p. 123.

35 Peter Burke, *The Art of Conversation* (Cambridge: Polity Press, 1993), pp. 41–2.

36 Françoise Waquet, *Latin, or the Empire of a Sign*, trans. John Howe (London and New York: Verso, 2000), p. 82.

37 Burke, *Art of Conversation*, pp. 39–40.

38 *Ibid.*, pp. 46–7.

39 *Ibid.*, p. 52.

40 *Ibid.*, pp. 53–4.

41 Minna Skafte Jensen (ed.), *A History of Nordic Neo-Latin Literature* (Odense: Odense University Press, 1995), p. 19.

42 *Ibid.*, p. 69.

43 Some Scottish writers received patronage from major magnates, but there were few such who could afford anything very extensive.

44 *The Autobiography and Diary of Mr James Melvill*, ed. R. Pitcairn (Edinburgh: Wodrow Society, 1842), p. 39. His writings aimed outside Scotland are therefore in Latin, for example, *Ad Serenissumum Jacobum Primum . . . ecclesiae scoticae libellus supplex* (London: George Thomason & Octavian Pullen, 1645).

45 Much of Knox's oeuvre is in English, for example, *An Answer to a Letter of a Jesuit called Tyrie*, though it was printed in St Andrews by Robert Lekpreuik (1570). Somewhat later, William Drummond of Hawthornden could also (and almost always did) write English (e.g. *Forth Feasting: a panegyrike to the King's most excellent maiestie* (Edinburgh: Andro Hart, 1617), but this was not a common accomplishment – Drummond, again, had spent time in England.

46 This is not an invented or symbolic example: the Accademia of Saló produced a most elegant copy of a pamphlet for the retirement of the Venetian Captain of the River. There is a copy in the Biblioteca Communale at Padua.

47 Jozef Ijsewijn, *Companion to Neo-Latin Studies*, 2 vols. (Leuven: Leuven University Press and Peeters, 1990, 1998).

48 Some readers may object at this point that this excludes women, who were not taught Latin. In fact, though there are important early women writers who did not know Latin, a surprising number of them did: see Jane Stevenson, *Women Latin Poets* (Oxford: Oxford University Press, 2005).

49 J. Hungerford Pollen (ed.), *Unpublished Documents Relating to the English Martyrs* (London: Catholic Record Society, 1908).

50 Anne Sweeney, *Robert Southwell, Snow in Arcadia: Redrawing the English Lyric Landscape, 1586–95* (Manchester: Manchester University Press, 2006), especially pp. 45–50.

51 Stonyhurst College, Clitheroe, Lancashire, MS Anglia.v. IV. Edition and translation in Peter Davidson and Anne Sweeney (eds), *The Collected Poems of St Robert Southwell SJ* (Manchester: Carcanet, 2007).

52 This subject has been touched upon in William H. McCabe SJ's *An Introduction to the Jesuit Theater* (St Louis: Institute of Jesuit Sources, 1983). The political and allegorical aspects of Jesuit drama and the degree to which it represented a decisive means of argument in the confessional battle for history have been brilliantly discussed in Alison Shell's *Catholicism, Controversy and the English Literary Imagination* (Cambridge: Cambridge University Press, 1999).

53 A useful translation by R.F. Grady SJ can be found in *Jesuit Theater Englished*, ed. Louis J. Oldani SJ and Philip C. Fisher SJ (St Louis: Institute of Jesuit Sources, 1989), pp. 79–159. For all this material I am, as ever, heavily indebted to Dr Alison Shell of Durham.

54 Mario Praz, *The Flaming Heart* (New York: Norton, 1973 [1958]).

55 ' *"Chi non sa far stupire" lasci di fare il poeta e "vada a la striglia", vade a fare il mozzo di stalla*' – 'the poet who cannot astonish is fit only to be a stable boy'. Croce, *Storia dell'etá barocca in Italia*, p. 26.

56 *Ibid.*, pp. 204–63.
57 *Ibid.*, pp. 199–200.
58 Mario Praz, *Secentismo e Marinismo in Inghilterra* (Florence: La Voce, 1925), pp. 52–5.
59 *Ibid.*, p. 54.
60 There is an anthropologically significant footnote to the history of Mario Praz and the study of the 'metaphysical' poets. Praz, whose name is seldom to this day mentioned in his native land unaccompanied by apotropaic gestures or words, was celebrated for his possession of psychokinetic powers (the kind known locally as *mal occhio*) which, many strands of academic *legenda metropolitana* affirm, were once employed to precipitate the late Dame Helen Gardner down the Spanish Steps.
61 Sir Herbert Grierson (ed.), *Metaphysical Lyrics and Poems of the Seventeenth Century* (Oxford: Clarendon, 1921), pp. xiii–lviii. Strangely, Grierson was, earlier in the century, the author of a comprehensive guide to the literatures of continental Europe, *The First Half of the Seventeenth Century* (Edinburgh: Blackwood, 1906), a volume in George Saintsbury's Periods of European Literature series. Indeed, the introduction to the *Metaphysical Poets* volume makes reference to Marino and Vondel. This previous history, wholly at one with a Scottish tradition of internationalism, makes the denials and refusals of Grierson's crucially influential 1921 essay more mysterious, and even less attractive.
62 T.S. Eliot, *The Varieties of Metaphysical Poetry* (London: Faber, 1993 [1926]).
63 English perceptions of the baroque Continent are greatly complicated by the imaginative creation of an evil Italy in the English drama of the earlier seventeenth century. The most lurid creations of the tragedians of revenge have as their *dramatis personae* real people from the highest families of the nobility of Italy, particularly the families of the 'black nobility' of the Papal States. The problem, and I am not the first to recognise this, is that the southern Baroque is thereby defined as the art of the enemy, the medium and the delight of the evil dukes of Websterian drama.
64 Harbison, *Reflections on Baroque*, pp. 31–2.
65 John Donne, *Selected Prose*, ed. Neil Rhodes (Harmondsworth: Penguin, 1987), 'Death's Duell', pp. 310–26.
66 Contrast St Robert Southwell's poem on 'Christs bloody sweate' discussed at the end of Chapter 3, pp. 117–19 below.
67 Constantijn Huygens, *Heilighe Dagen*, ed. L. Strengholt (Amsterdam: Buijten and Schipperheijn, 1974); some translations in Davidson and van der Weel (eds), *A Selection of the Poems of Sir Constantijn Huygens*, pp. 114–25.
68 St Ignatius of Loyola, *Personal Writings*, pp. 306–7.
69 For the Ignatian meditation on the Incarnation, see St Ignatius of Loyola, *Personal Writings*, pp. 305–7.

70 Davidson and van der Weel (eds), *A Selection of the Poems of Sir Constantijn Huygens*, pp. 122–3.

71 'In sudorem sanguinem', from *Passio Discerpta* in F.E. Hutchinson (ed.), *The Works of George Herbert* (Oxford: Clarendon, 1945), p. 404.

72 Cf. Joaquín Bérchez (ed.), *Los siglos de oro en los virreinatos de America* (exhibition catalogue, Madrid: Museo de América, 1999), pp. 216–17: '*Escudo de los descendientes del Inca Tupa Yupanqui*'.

73 Bailey, *Between Renaissance and Baroque*, pp. 153–65, p. 156.

74 St Robert Southwell, 'Decease, release: dum morior orior', text from Stonyhurst MS Anglia. v.27, edition by Sweeney and Davidson, in *The Collected Poems of St Robert Southwell SJ*.

75 Margaret Swain, *The Needlework of Mary, Queen of Scots* (Carlton: Ruth Bean, 1987), pp. 75, 77.

76 Sacheverell Sitwell, *Southern Baroque Art* (London: Grant Richards, 1924).

77 Cf. Francis Wheen, *Tom Driberg* (London: Chatto & Windus, 1990), p. 39.

78 William Gaunt, *Bandits in a Landscape* (London and New York: The Studio, 1937), p. 73.

79 In the chapter on baroque hybridity below I will consider how, despite the inevitably international discourse in which the arguments are conveyed, English court masques in fact present a summary and dismissive view of the newly contacted inhabitants of the Americas.

80 Stephen Orgel and Roy Strong, *Inigo Jones and the Theatre of the Stuart Court*, 2 vols., (London: University of California Press, for Sotheby's, 1973), vol. 2, p. 730.

81 Nigel Llewellyn, *Death, Passion and Politics* (London: Dulwich Picture Gallery, 1995), p. 56.

82 *Ibid.*, p. 64.

83 *Ibid.*, p. 111.

84 Built by the Smythson family, from 1613, for Sir Charles Cavendish.

85 For this phenomenon, see Graham Parry, *The Arts of the Anglican Counter-Reformation* (Woodbridge: Boydell, 2006).

86 See the description of the surviving fragments at Burnham on Sea in Nicolaus Pevsner, *The Buildings of England: South and West Somerset* (Harmondsworth: Penguin, 1958) p. 110 and fig. 31.

87 Seán Ó Tuama and Thomas Kinsella (eds), *An Duanaire 1600–1900* (Portlaoise: Dolmen Press, 1981), pp. 96–101.

88 A development which owes much to the efforts of Prof. Keith Sidwell and other members of the Centre for Neo-Latin Studies at the University of Cork: see now www.ucc.ie/acad/classics/CNLS.

89 Yale University, Beinecke Library, MS Osborn Shelves fb 228, p. 29 (original pagination).

90 This manuscript is described in *The Manuscripts of the Marquis of Ormonde, preserved at the Castle, Kilkenny* (London: Historical Manuscripts Commission,

1895) pp. 105–18. The greater part of this collection (with some losses) now forms Yale University, Beinecke Library, MS Osborn shelves fb 228.

91 Salamanca University Library, MS 1343, p. 238.

92 (Paris: Cramoisi, 1633), sig. Aijjj4*r* and sig. Aijjj 4*v*.

93 '*In scholis splendide, et concinne exhibeantur drammata, tragoedia, aliaeque scholasticae exercitationes, summo concursu et applausu*': Dublin, Jesuit Archives, 36 Lower Leeson Street, no shelfmark, p. 58. See Alan J. Fletcher, *Drama and the Performing Arts in Pre-Cromwellian Ireland* (Cambridge: D.S. Brewer, 2001), p. 374; Peter V. Farrelly, *600 Years of Theatre in Kilkenny, 1366–1966* (Kilkenny: P.V. Publications, nd), pp. 28–9.

94 Cambridge University Library, Bradshaw collection 5311, Hib. 7.664.33. Fletcher, *Drama*, pp. 489–91.

95 Giovanni Battista Rinuccini, *Commentarius Rinuccinianus* (Dublin: Irish Mansucripts Commission, 1932–49), vol. 2, pp. 25–8.

96 *A Smale Garland of Pious and Godly Songs, composed by a devout Man, for the Solace of his Freinds and neighbours in their afflictions* (Ghent, 1684), p. 45.

97 Patrick Dowling, *The Hedge Schools of Ireland* (London: Longmans, Green & Co., 1935).

98 Daniel Corkery, *The Hidden Ireland* (Dublin: M.H. Gill and Son, 1925), pp. 263–5.

99 William Duguid Geddes, *Musa Latina Aberdonensis*, 3 vols. (Aberdeen: New Spalding Club, 1892–1910), vol. 3, p. 278.

100 This monument, its decoration and the use which Montgomerie may have made of it is discussed at some length in Michael Bath's *Renaissance Decorative Painting in Scotland* (Edinburgh: National Museums of Scotland, 2003), pp. 128–45.

101 See James Macaulay, *The Classical Country House in Scotland, 1660–1800* (London: Faber & Faber, 1987), pp. 55–86.

102 See Roderick J. Lyall, *Alexander Montgomerie, Poetry, Politics and Cultural Change in Jacobean Scotland* (Tempe, Arizona: ACMRS, 2005); Dempster's translation, as *Cerasum et Sylvestre Prunum, opus poematicum,* was twice published ('Aretauni Francorum', 1613; Edinburgh, 1696).

103 *Geddes, Musa Latina,* vol. 1, p. vii.

104 John Hill Burton, *The History of Scotland from Agricola's Invasion to the Extinction of the Last Jacobite Rebellion,* 8 vols. (Edinburgh: William Blackwood & Sons, 1897), vol. 6, pp. 206–7.

105 Strachan's manuscript *Album amicorum* is currently in the Scottish Catholic archives, Columba House, Drummond Place, Edinburgh.

106 Giorgio Levi Della Vida, *George Strachan, Memorials of a Wandering Scottish Scholar of the Seventeenth Century* (Aberdeen: Third Spalding Club, 1956), especially p. 72.

107 *Delitiae Poetarum Scotorum,* ed. Arthur Johnston (Amsterdam: Johann Bleau, 1637), vol. 2, pp. 504–9. Barclay's two poems in praise of *Lacrymae* are in vol. 1, p. 141.

108 James Kinsley (ed.), *The Oxford Book of Ballads* (Oxford and New York: Oxford University Press, 1989), p. 312.

109 Geddes, *Musa Latina*, vol. 1, pp. 201–4.

110 *Ibid.*, vol. 1, p. 21.

111 Bath, *Renaissance Decorative Painting*, p. 20. Geddes, *Musa Latina*, vol. 1, p. 41.

112 Geddes, *Musa Latina*, vol. 2, p. 305.

113 Kinsley (ed.), *Oxford Book of Ballads*, pp. 610–14.

114 Kenneth Hurlstone Jackson, *A Celtic Miscellany* (Harmondsworth: Penguin, 1971), pp. 268–74 and p. 321 (Eileen Dubh was, incidentally, the aunt of Daniel O'Connell, 'the Liberator').

II

Hybridity; mestizaje; cultural bilinguality

This chapter will have to proceed selectively, even symbolically. The phenomena of hybridity and cultural bilinguality which it discusses are universal, but space in these pages is finite. Ibero-America will appear as a constant point of reference, but standing *pars pro toto* as a representative of analogous phenomena taking place world-wide.

Baroque internationalism was very much a two-way traffic. Knowledge and energies, things and ideas travelled and circulated between continents. To begin to form an idea of this swirling, complex traffic, let us focus on two strands within it which are symbolic of many more.

Baroque traffic: feather cloaks and magic lanterns

The feather-work of the Americas elicited amazement throughout Europe; optical devices, including the magic lantern, were one of the chief wonders of the age internationally.

Optical instruments for the manipulation of light were one of the things which delighted the baroque appetite for *meraviglie*, from the court of the Quinglong emperor to the viceregal courts of America. The magic lantern, that is, the projection through a lens of an image painted on a glass slide by means of a mirrored light placed behind it, seems to have been an invention of the Collegio Romano and the polymath Athanasius Kircher SJ.[1]

This device of light was only one of his many inventions and investigations: hieroglyphics, the world below the earth, music, mirrors and acoustics were all part of the intellectual activity of this paradigmatic baroque scholar. Paradigmatic not only because of his restless energy, his attempts to encompass everything, but also because of his consciousness of his own position at the centre of the Jesuit system of international communications as an unique scholarly opportunity to study and collect the world. He thought in global terms and his celebrated museum in Rome echoed in its layout and iconography his intention that it should function as a microcosm of all that was and all that had been. If there is such a phenomenon as 'baroque knowledge', even 'baroque wisdom', it centres on the museum, on the collection of marvels which is in itself a first step to the apprehension of the virtuosity of God refracted through the world and its peoples.[2]

As Kircher discovered, a moving light projected through the painted slide in a magic lantern even projected a moving image. The purpose of this device, apart from the eliciting of wonder, was use in the mission-fields of the Jesuits. Thus the images were often catechetic: the two which are illustrated in Kircher's *Ars Magnae Lucis et Umbrae* (1671) are a personification of death and of a soul in the flames of Purgatory. There would also seem to have been a set of slides circulated by the Jesuits world-wide showing the wonders of the city of Rome.

We have surviving responses to Kircher's device from both sides of the world: from Mexico and from China, both territories in which the Jesuits were active. In Mexico, the poet and scholar Sor Juana de la Cruz (1648–95) used the magic lantern as a simile for the clearing of the last smoky vestiges of sleep and dream:

> Así lanterna mágica, pintadas
> representa fingidas
> en la blanca pared varias figuras,
> de la sombra no menos ayudada
> que de la luz . . .

> [And as a magic lantern throws feigned painted pictures on a white wall, assisted no less by shadow than light . . .]

The dream of which she writes seems, for a moment, a reality in the instant of its dissolution.[3] This image is part of a vast, complex poem of dream and waking and the movement of the light, a poem in scope and feeling, as I have suggested (p. 56 above) not unlike John Donne's *Anniversaries*.

The other response to the magic lantern comes from the other side of the world, as the Chinese painter, poet and savant Wu Li (1632–1718) – who eventually became a Jesuit convert to Christianity and wrote remarkable Christian poems in traditional Chinese forms – responds to a magic lantern with slides of Rome and a written commentary on them. He dates his poem within the Chinese year by saying that the lantern which works the device has been lit from the fires of the spring Cold Food festival:

> This lantern from distant parts is strange:
> its flame has been lit from Cold Food fires
> I try viewing the scenes of Rome;
> horizontally reading the Latin characters.
> Moths flit about the light but can't approach;
> a rat peers out, his shadow all alone[4] . . .

Parallel to this high-status export from Europe is the Mexican feather-work which found its way into the treasuries of the courts and cathedrals of the world. Anne of Denmark was reputed to have had a Mexican feather picture of St Francis in her private oratory at Oatlands.[5] As well as a Mexican turquoise mask, obviously considered a great treasure from the elaboration of its European gold setting which incorporates the heraldic oaks of the Della Rovere of Urbino (from whom it passed to the Medici), the Medici collections contained at least five feather garments and six feather shields, as well as six feather cloaks ('and horse-trappings of the same' – *forniture da cavallo al medesimo*) adapted with green taffeta to serve the Medici dukes as masquerade costumes for the carnival.[6] There is also a little-known set of episcopal feather-work vestments (mitre and cope) in the rooms of St Philip Neri at the Chiesa Nuova in Rome, sent to the Oratorians as a gift from the New World.

Symbolic and emblematic readings of the plants of the New World

It was not only artefacts which came from the 'new' worlds, but also plants and creatures. The Medici collected paintings of American birds and animals. Some are incorporated into the *grotteschi* decoration of the Uffizi in Florence. Given the intellectual habits and genius of the baroque world, it is inevitable that these things and creatures should have been subjected to the most intense *reading* as elements in a new chapter in the unfolding of the symbolic creation.

In retrospect, the great baroque-revival writer of the twentieth century Alejo Carpentier, contemplating the arts of his native Ibero-America and Caribbean, said that it required the splendours and extravagances of the Baroque to express the stupendous nature of the Creation in the New World with its unknown trees, extraordinary plants and immense rivers.[7] It is my purpose here to chart one early modern response to that stupendous Creation newly contacted by Europeans: the way in which some of the plants of the New World were brought into the international discourse of baroque imagery and, specifically, baroque emblematics.

It can be argued that emblematics in its widest sense (going beyond the construction of the classic three-part emblem or two-part *impresa* to a wider imaginative enterprise of interpreting Creation as it unfolds, seeing the symbolic potential in things) lies at the heart of the baroque arts. It is also the case, I would argue further, that the baroque arts are far from being the rigid servants of absolutism in church and state, the ministers of European domination. On the contrary, what is remarkable about the baroque arts is their *permeability*, their ability to engage in dialogue, particularly at cultural frontiers, their openness to the incorporation of the new into the international symbolic and imaginative world.

The baroque arts form a universal system, easily embracing all the known world and capable of comprehending (in every sense) the peoples, customs, plants, animals and things of any newly discovered place. This is an important point in any consideration of the arts of the baroque epoch world-wide. The baroque age was also, proverbially, the age of great voyages and of many first contacts with lands and peoples of the Americas and the East. But it is important to remember that the traffic in energies, creativity and ideas did not flow in one direction only.

Indeed, it would be possible to maintain that to talk of 'colonial' Baroque at all is to simplify the intricacies of the two-way circulation of energies and ideas. There is certainly baroque visual art, music and literature produced in the territories which were colonies of the European powers, but it can be argued that that art (a hybrid art which is the true production and possession of those territories) is no servile echo or imitation of the arts of Europe.

As long ago as 1931, this perception was voiced by the Spanish critic Eugenio D'Ors, in the essay on Portuguese art appended to his definitive study *Lo barocco*. Naturally he voiced it in the terms of the decade in which he wrote. D'Ors questions the primacy of Europe even in classical antiquity. He perceives an element in the art and thought of the baroque world which has only very recently been once more the focus of critical attention: the universality capable of learning from the 'new worlds' and of honouring them by assuming that the civilisations of the whole world are based on plural and parallel 'antiquities', all of weight, dignity and authority.

> The coloniser is colonised, the conqueror conquered. Alexander the Great subdued the Orient: mark how he returned an emperor, bearing on his forehead the tiara of the emperors of Asia.[8]

We might note also that d'Ors, perhaps unconsciously, echoes a famous line from Horace about cultural hybridity, 'Graecia capta ferum victorem cepit et artes intulit agresti Latio'[9] ('Captive Greece captured her fierce captor and brought the arts into uncultured Latium'), The possibilities raised by these perceptions are vast, and I would like to focus here on only one of them – the way in which poets, scholars and emblematists embraced the plants of the New World and how they made an imaginative reading of the 'vegetaciones increíbles' of the Americas. This kind of baroque consideration of the unity of Creation centres inevitably on the most internationalist religious and cultural force within baroque society: the Society of Jesus. Increasingly, the Jesuits come to be seen as internationalists and the great interpreters between cultures in the baroque world.[10] The assessment of such mid-twentieth-century scholars as Benedetto Croce, quoted in my Introduction to this book, are increasingly being called into question. Croce, not atypically, thought of the baroque era as tainted by association with the Jesuits and the Counter-Reformation,[11] and with the Inquisition's suppression of free thought and free speech.

An increasing body of recent critics, however, perceives the consciously internationalist Society of Jesus, rather, as instrumental in the complex process of cultural exchange – leaders in the international circulation of energies, things and ideas throughout the world of the long seventeenth century. Perhaps one way in which Jesuit baroque art can still usefully be defined is by its very universality, its maintenance of dialogues with the peoples, ideas and things of the new worlds.[12]

There is a sacred *impresa* carved in the Jesuit church of Córdoba in Argentina, far into the interior, which expresses this. The image is of the Pillars of Hercules – that is, the straits of Gibraltar, gateway from the Mediterranean sea to the New World, to everything unknown beyond the Mediterranean. The motto is *cura est Antipodium* ('our love/concern is the Antipodes'). The love of the Jesuits is directed to the peoples of the New World. The Pillars of Hercules, the gateway to unknown worlds, were also the personal badge or *impresa* of the Emperor Charles V, the first European ruler to possess vast territories in the Americas.

My focus will be deliberately precise. One of the areas of the greatest creative energy in the baroque system was the emblematic interpretation of reality, so I want to dwell on the emblematic interpretation of the plants of the new worlds. Emblematics (taken in its widest sense) was the most honest and acceptable form of imaginative endeavour. The question was not so much whether moral messages derivable from the natural world were divinely installed, but rather, once they had been read as such, what followed? This process of emblematisation of the New World shows us how the discovery of a plant was not only reported for its potential medicinal or culinary application, but also assessed for its intellectual (indeed spiritual) application as a crucial part of piecing together the progressive revelation of Creation.

John Prest has written about the importance of the botanic gardens of the late sixteenth and seventeenth centuries and how,

> Contemporaries interpreted the foundation of these encyclopaedic gardens in a context of a re-creation of the earthly Paradise . . . when it turned out that neither East nor West Indies contained the Garden of Eden, men began to think instead of bringing the scattered pieces of Creation together into a Botanic garden or new Garden of Eden.[13]

The Jesuit poet St Robert Southwell expresses this when he writes of the prelapsarian Earthly Paradise in his *Poema de Assumptione Beatae Mariae Virginis*, implicitly suggesting that a leading part of the work of reuniting scattered Paradise has fallen to the Society:

> Quicquid in immenso pulchri diffunditur orbe,
> Et sparsum solumque alias aliasque per oras
> Cernitur, hoc uno totum concluditur horto.[14]

> [Whatsoever of beauty is spread over the immense globe and is seen, scattered and solitary, throughout region after region: all this is enclosed in one garden.]

In his treatise on meditation on daily things and surroundings, *Le Peinture Spirituelle*, first published at Lyons in 1611, equally a treatise on the emblematising habit of mind and on the symbolic reading of experience from moment to moment, the Jesuit Louis Richeome provides a detailed and moralised tour of the Jesuit novitiate house of St Andrea al Quirinale in Rome. The last book is a very detailed description of the gardens of that house, including descriptions and emblematic interpretations of plants from both Asia and the Americas.

As well as providing documentation of a real Jesuit garden (complete with sundials and symbolic obelisk contributing an extra layer of meaning to the layout), Richeome's text offers a clear insight into a process of mental training in the right perception of the world. Nothing is allowed to pass without being at once supplied with a spiritual reading, an interpretation concerned with the virtuosity and mercy of the Creator as well as with the perceptions and spiritual growth of the observer.

It is not necessary to follow his progression from the garden gate on the top terrace to pyramid and obelisk on the lowest, but it is useful to give some indication of the nature of the complex process of education which Richeome lays out for the walk through these gardens. They are a symbolic representation of the continents of the world in their flora, as well as a reconstruction-in-progress of the Earthly Paradise where all flowers once grew together.

The central position of the fountain on the upper terrace at once evokes Eden. This symbolic positioning is common to the recorded layouts of many early modern botanical gardens: four quadrants for the continents with a central fountain to recall the fountain whence flowed the four rivers of Paradise. At least one plant, in this case the myrrh bush, seems to have been provided with an actual inscription from the Song of Songs, so that it becomes a living *impresa*, with the motto 'my love has come into my garden'.[15]

Richeome turns almost immediately to the interpretations of exotic plants. His text makes clear that some of these were not physically present, but it is not unreasonable to conjecture that the others were. The Jesuits of mid-seventeenth-century Rome had a developed garden culture: botanical curiosities sent from the mission-fields were among the sophisticated cultural currencies with which they maintained good relations with the urban elite.[16]

Richeome connects the physical garden with the interior garden of the memory and soul:

> Or mes bien-aymez, ces herbes ne croissent pas en vostre jardin, ie vous les ay portées des mers, & païs estrangers, afin de les planter, & domestiquer en la terre de vostre memoire, où elles pourront prendre racine, viure, & verdoyer eternellement pour vous.[17]

> [Although, my dear friends, these plants do not grow in your garden, I have brought them to you from beyond the seas and from strange lands, with the intention of planting them and naturalising them in the soil of your memory, where they can take root, live and grow eternally green for you.]

The first New World plant is the sensitive plant (*Mimosa pudica*), so called because its leaves shrink away from a touch. This was known to him as '*l'herbe vive de Brazil*'. He emblematises it as the image of the pious man, constant in the ice of adversity or the warmth of prosperity:

> Le Bresil donne vne herbe qui a sentiment: Car elle referre ses feuilles, si quelqu'vn s'approche elle, et les dilate apres quand ils s'en est allé; les Brasiliens l'apellent L'HERBE VIVE pour ce sentiment, par ce aussi qu'elle est toujours verdoyante, ne craignant plus le chaud que le froid, portant en ceste qualité la semblance de l'homme pieux, & juste, dont

la feuille, & belles oeuures sont toujours en verdeur aussi bien en la glace de l'adversité, qu'en la chaleur de la prosperité.[18]

[Brazil gives a plant which has feeling: as it draws back its leaves if anyone comes near and spreads them again when they go away. Also, it is always green, fearing neither heat nor cold, having in this respect a resemblance to the just and pious man whose good works like leaves are always growing, just the same in the ice of adversity as in the warmth of prosperity.]

He goes on to a tree from the Jesuit station in Goa, at the other side of the world, home of the shrine of St Francis Xavier, 'Apostle of the Indies', one of the first companions of St Ignatius, founder of the Society.

L'arbre triste de Goa, & lieux voisins croit l'arbre appellé Triste, parce qu'il ne fleurit que la nuict, & aussitot que le Soleil leve, les fleurs luy tombent, comme s'il quittoit ses beaux habits pour entrer en dueil, & continuë ceste façon de fairetout l'an ses fleurs sont d'une odeur tressoaveuse, & n'y en a point des pareilles en l'Orient . . . c'est un symbole d'un vray Chrestien, d'vn homme penitent ou Religieux, qui fuit le Soleil & splendeur des biens & honneurs de ceste vie, & se resiouyt en la nuict des afflictions d'icelle, triomphant en sa penitence, & donnant l'odeur de ses sainctes oeuures.[19]

[The sad tree of Goa, and neighbouring places is so called because it only flowers at night, and as soon as the sun rises, its flowers fall, as if leaving off fine clothes to go into mourning, and continues in this way all year. Its flowers have a pleasant smell, there is nothing to equal them in the East . . . it is a symbol of a true Christian, of a penitent or a Religious, who flees from the sun and splendour of the good and honours of this world, and takes himself to the night of affliction, triumphing in his penitence, and giving forth the sweet scent of his good works.]

Crossing the world again, like the Society, he contemplates the tinder tree of New Spain, with its,

bois si massif et si dur, que si on frotte vivement vne piece contre l'autre, les estincelles sortent comme d'vn caillon frappé du fusil, & se brusle quelquefois de son feu, symbole de gens fort coleriques, qui s'entre-chocquans ensemble produisent le feu, duquel par apres ils sont tourmentez & bruslez.[20]

[hard, bulky wood, from which, when one piece is rubbed vigorously against another, the sparks come forth like powder in a gun when the flint strikes and sometimes burn with their fire. This is a symbol of people of a choleric temperament, who jar against each other producing fire, and afterwards they are burnt and tormented in fire.]

Lastly, he writes of a tree in one of the Fortunate Isles, l'Isle d'Ombrion, presumably the 'Travellers' Tree', which gathers water from the clouds of morning (in the natural reservoirs where the leaves join the trunk), so men and animals can drink from it during the day. Here we have not only an instance of the providence of God but also an emblem of the operation of divine grace:

> Que la faveur celeste de sa grace, peut arrouser les feuilles & tronc de nostre secheresse, & fournir eau de soulas, pour nostre rafraischissement.[21]

> [That the celestial favour of his grace and might water the leaves and trunk of our dryness and give us consoling water for our refreshment.]

As Richeome moves, meditating, through the garden of the Jesuit novitiate house in Rome, he is almost unconsciously himself an epitome of the Jesuits' 'way of proceeding' as brokers of meaning between the 'old' and 'new' worlds. The naturalist and proto-anthropologist Juan Eusebio Nieremberg was another Jesuit who dedicated his best work to the exposition of the New World, determined to view Creation as a unity embracing the Americas.

The culmination of Nieremberg's reading of the New World is his recognition of the *arma Christi* in the flowers, petals and stamens of the Peruvian *grenadilla*. The Indies could instruct Europe and furnish further and more marvellous subjects to the emblematists of both worlds. The Passion Flower crowns the disclosure of the American creation, an unequivocal hieroglyphic placed by God in the distant mountains of Peru. A Christian sign placed in the American landscape, it affirms the rightness of Christianity as the adopted religion of those territories. His reading of the signs of the flower is not only Christian, but specifically Catholic.

His accompanying wood-engraving makes clear that the bud of the Passion Flower is read as the Eucharistic chalice. The flower itself is described at length in a piece of (anonymous, but presumably Jesuit) Latin verse: the Five Wounds of Christ are the outer petals, and the Column of the Flagellation the central infloresence. The inner filaments of the flower are read as the Crown of Thorns. The three prominent stamens borne above the flower are read as the three nails. The illustration to Nieremberg arranges these precisely as they are depicted in the Jesuit badge, so the hieroglyphic on the Andean landscape not only anticipates the arrival of Catholic Christianity, but the arrival of the Society of Jesus.[22]

The visionary Spanish nun Maria de Ágreda was popularly supposed to have travelled miraculously to the Americas in the 1620s, converting indigenous peoples of what is now Texas and New Mexico to Christianity, speaking to them in their own language. Her legend relates that when eventually the first Spanish Franciscan arrived in the territories of the Jumanos, they came forth with a cross garlanded with the flowers of America to greet him as he made the 'first contact'. They said that they had been instructed to do this by the miraculously manifested Spanish nun and that she had helped to fashion the garlands with her own hands. The story of Maria de Ágreda expresses the longings and ambitions of early modern Spain that the vast Spanish possessions in the Americas could become spontaneously assimilated to the religion of Spain.[23]

In Nieremberg's account of the Arbre Triste of Goa, already mentioned in 1611 by Richeome and described in much the same terms, there is also a fascinating indication that the flora of the New World were one of the subjects set for the poetic competitions and emblematic exhibitions which marked festival days at Jesuit Colleges world-wide.[24] Nieremberg quotes three epigrams on the flower and its associations, introducing these 'Gnomoglyphics' as the recreation of 'our people', presumably the students of the Jesuit college in Madrid. The interpretation of the discovered Creation was made a part of the Jesuit educational system.

The contemplative reading of exotic trees appears in its most developed form in the 1660s in *Ashrea: or, the Grove of Beatitudes*, a book of emblems and meditations published at London. These are extremely Jesuit in their tone.[25] The author is identified only by the initials 'E.M.' and may have been the English Jesuit Edward Mico (*c.*1628–78) educated in St Omer and Rome and admitted to the novitiate there. He presumably therefore knew the novitiate house and garden which is the subject of the loving and detailed meditations of Richeome's *Peinture Spirituelle*. He died of a fever in prison during the anti-Catholic scare of 1678. The Lady 'M.B.' to whom the book is dedicated can plausibly be identified with the recusant Catholic Lady Margaret Bedingfield. The author's epistle prefixed to the work described concisely the complex meditations which the book sets forth:

> Eight Trees . . . representing to you the Eight great Lessons of Christian Resignation, and those again exemplifi'd upon that Tree, wheron the great work of Man's Redemption receiv'd its period.[26]

So descriptions of the eight trees of the imaginary Grove[27] are mapped on to the beatitudes and on to eight contemplations of the condition of Christ crucified. The complex of ideas is meant as the starting point for meditations for Lent. It also fixes the sequence of contemplations and devotions in the reader's mind by the techniques of the *ars memorativa*. The imagined place, a grove of trees, is also Christ's body and attaches to particular locations within that place (specific trees, specific parts of the body) the particular virtues expressed in each of the Beatitudes.

The reading of the Indian fig tree is typical of the way in which the book develops each of its eight meditations. The picture of the banyan, *Ficus indica*, bending its branches down to the ground where they take root as new trees, thus forming an ever-expanding grove of concentric circles, has the motto *sic iuvat esse tenacem* ('Thus steadfastness is rewarded'). The connection with 'the meek shall inherit the earth' is made through the tree's habit of bowing its branches to the ground to root in the earth. The process of progressive rooting is compared to one virtue leading to another,

> Behold, how like this *Indian Fig-Tree*, the devout soul makes her progress, and advances forward, still taking new root, still laying faster hold, never accounting herself secure, or that she hath done enough . . . A man must not therefore fix a *Ne plus ultra* ['no further'] to his better thoughts and Actions, but go on, like this Tree.[28]

The contemplation comes round to the Passion by the introduction of Christ's head bowed on the Cross as a silent sign enjoining the virtue of meekness, just as the habit of growth of the Indian fig tree enacts that virtue. Just as Richeome interpreted the trees of the Americas and Asia to furnish the meditations of the Jesuit novices walking in the gardens of St Andrea al Quirinale, so the author of *Ashrea* instructs a lay person in meditation. The purpose and method of both texts are similar. They form a unity with the interpretations advanced in the descriptions of the plants of Asia and the Americas in the works of the naturalists. Creation is alive with God's signs. It is the business of the emblematic arts of the Baroque to advance the art of reading them.

There is a delightful epilogue from the eighteenth century to this enterprise of interpreting the plants of the 'new worlds'. By this time the colleges and universities of the Americas (many of them Jesuit foundations) had produced generations of poets who viewed the Creation as a unity, but from the perspective of the Americas. In book twenty-three of his epic *De Deo Deoque homine heroica*, which was finished in 1780 in European exile after the suppression of the Jesuits in 1773, the Mexican Jesuit Didacus Abad writes about the flowers which are brought to the Stable of Bethlehem as offerings from the Shepherds.[29] This leads him to consider the Passion Flower, the American flower which Nieremberg read as containing the hieroglyphics of the Passion. Then he says, in a wonderful baroque moment which re-unites the scattered Creations of the Old and New Worlds in the vertiginous transformation wrought by the Incarnation – '*Floss equidem Puero gratissimus hic est*'— that it was this American flower which pleased the Christ child above all others.

Representations of peoples of the Americas

Representations of the Americas and their peoples vary sharply: most English representations of the inhabitants of the New World offer simple exotic fantasy or allegorical vagueness. Aurelian Townshend's anti-masques to *Florimène* of 1635 offer just the adjectives 'rough and rude' to describe the inhabitants of Canada. In the *Masque of Flowers* written by Thomas Bushell (later maker of the grotto at Enstone) America is simply personified by a commodity, 'Kawasha the god of Tobacco'. In Chapman's *The Memorable Masque* of 1613, the Virginians and their priests are sun-worshipping ciphers: the important thing about their country is its gold. They are easily converted, at a European word, from the worship of the sun to the worship of James VI and I. Marc Lescarbot's *Les Muses de la Nouvelle France* offers an altogether more complex representation. His water-masque *Le Theatre de Neptune*, was presented in 1606 for Le Sieur de Poutrincourt on his return to Port-Royal in Canada after a visit to the Armouchiquois people. This text is highly specific about the indigenous people of New France, some of whom appear with speaking roles. Even the mythological figure of Neptune, who opens the masque, addresses the governor with the indigenous honorific 'Sagamos', the local word for leader or chieftain:

> Arrete, *Sagamos*, arrête toy ice
> Et regardes un Dieu qui a de toy souci . . .[30]

> [Halt here, *Sagamos*, and see a god who has some care for you.]

Later in the masque four native people speak, admittedly in French, and offer the governor gifts of the country: game, beaver skins, woven ribbons and bracelets identified by their indigenous name of *matachiaz*, and the promise of fish.[31] Thomas Gage reports similar spectacles later in the century from the Mexican town of Chiapas.[32] This contrasts sharply with the display of captive Brazilians to Henri II of France as a mute spectacle observed as specimens in a 'Brazilian village',[33] and even more so with the articulate Brazilians presented in Lisbon (perhaps impersonated by elite European performers) in 1619.

In the allegorical play *La real Tragicomedia,* described by João Sardinha Mimoso and written by António de Sousa SJ, presented before King Philip III of Spain in the Jesuit College in Lisbon, there is a representation of a wide variety of languages (and indeed of creole dialects incorporating elements of more than one, the languages between languages in which dialogue developed), but what is remarkable here is that the singers of the *Chorus Brasilicus* sing in Tupí to the honour of King Philip:

Tiaçò o pacatù Egué
Dádiarà repiáca Egué
Nhéaraíbmagaratù Egué
Paracéabè opacatù Egué[34]

[Let us all go together to greet our good King with great rejoicing . . .]

However terrible the conquest, however repressive and exploitative the regimes that followed it, terror and exploitation were not the whole of the narrative of Ibero-America. It has, of course, suited many Anglophone historians to represent Ibero-America as a desert (geographic and cultural) from which gold and silver were extracted regardless of the human cost. This is the misapprehension of the Iberian empires expressed in eighteenth-century England by Alexander Pope,

Oh stretch thy reign, fair Peace! From shore to shore,
Till conquest cease and slav'ry be no more:
Till the freed *Indians* in their native groves
Reap their own fruits, and wooe their sable Loves,
Peru once more a race of Kings behold,
And other *Mexico*'s be roof'd with gold.[35]

But the more we investigate the Iberian Americas of the baroque centuries, the more complicated, at the very least, the picture becomes. One thing is certain: colonial Latin America produced, in all the arts, works of extraordinary interest and beauty, which are only now coming to be widely appreciated.

Hybrid festivals in Mexico: the elegies of Ixtlilxóchitl

A particular nexus of energy in arts which have become specifically American existed in Mexico City in the 1680s in the circle of Sor Juana Iñes de la Cruz and Carlos de Sigüenza y Góngora. The first of these writers is widely studied, but her work and that of her circle are most happily considered within a world-wide discourse addressing simultaneously the local and the international. Sor Juana's elegant combinations of the different cultural (and literal) languages of Mexico is remarkable. In one *villancico* (saint's day carol) she writes with true baroque ingenuity in a language which is simultaneously Spanish and Latin:

> Divina Maria
> rubicunda Aurora,
> matutina Lux,
> purissima Rosa . . .

> Tristes te invocamus:
> Concede, gloriosa,
> Gratias quae te illustrant,
> Dotes quae te adornant.[36]

[Divine Mary, blushing Aurora, light of dawn, purest rose . . . sadly we invoke you, give to us most glorious one, the graces which make you glorious, the gifts which adorn you.]

The *villancico*, the one vernacular element within the otherwise Latin music of the Iberian church, offered considerable scope for popular hybridity and local expression, including (in some places) dancing and the use of indigenous American instruments.

Most of Sor Juana's verses for this purpose are in Castilian, but some are in Latin, several mocking the shaky Latinity of sextons and minor clerics. In another, for the feast of St Pedro Nolasco in 1677, she invokes a black Puerto Rican visiting the church and improvising a stanza on an African refrain – *tumba, la-lá-a; tumba, la-lé-le* – followed by a dialogue in Latin and (popular) Spanish, and ends the piece with an indigenous Mexican dance sung in a macaronic of Spanish and the indigenous Nahuatl:

> Los Padres bendito
> Tiene on redentor;
> *Amo nic neltoca*
> *quimati no Dios*

> Sólo Dios *Pilzintli*
> *del Cielo bajó,*
> y nuestro *tlatácol*
> nos lo perdono . . .

[The blessed fathers have a redeemer, I do not believe they know my God. Only the little son of God came down from the sky and he will forgive us our sins.]

These are festive works, demonstrations of virtuosity, but they emphasise the worth of indigenous culture in a popular medium, as it is set
forth in a more formal register in the festal texts of Sigüenza y
Góngora and the hybrid poetics of the 'mestizo elegies' of Sigüenza
y Góngora's friend the indigenous aristocrat Don Fernando de Alva
Ixtlilxóchitl.

Don Fernando de Alva Ixtlilxóchitl (*c.*1568–1648) was himself the
descendant of one of the kings commemorated in the festival of
Querétaro (see below, p. 110) and, as his name suggests, was poised
between worlds. He was aware of his distinguished American ancestry,
but committed to the belief that the events which brought Christianity
to Mexico were of necessity benign. He could be seriously compared
to St Bede of Jarrow in the first millennium, who was proudly aware
of his Saxon forbears, but convinced that the providential development
of English history which had made him and his people Christians was
necessary and good.

Two of Ixtlilxóchitl's elegies survive, as well as a fragmentary romance about Spanish history. Beautiful and nostalgic as these 'mestizo
elegies' are, with their lament for the glories of the old order in
Téxcoco and Mexico, they do not express the slightest desire that
history should be other than it is. He speaks the last words of commemoration for a royal line, for the poet-king Netzahualcóyotl and his
famous gardens, but he is not in any sense pleading for their revival.

It is possible that Ixtlilxóchitl's surviving poetry is based on poems
from the court of Netzahualcóyotl, the ruler of Téxcoco who died
in 1472. Certainly in Ixtlilxóchitl's *Historia Chichimeca* he cites what
appear to be the Nahuatl words opening one of Netzahualcóyotl's poems,
in a genre of spring songs called *Xompancuicatl*, with a Spanish prose
version following.

> *Tlacxoconcaquican hami Nezahualcoyotzin* etc. que traducidas á nuestro vul-
> gar castellano . . . quieren decir 'oíd lo que dice el rey Nezahualcoyotzin
> con sus lamentaciones . . .'[37]

> [*Tlacxoconcaquican hami Nezahualcoyotzin* etc., which translated into our
> Spanish vernacular . . . would say 'Hear that which was said by the king
> Nezahualcoyotzin, with his lamentations . . .']

The matter of this poem is of the same order as the pieces which
Ixtlilxóchitl put into Spanish verse, except that Ixtlilxóchitl's verses
have a sense of finality as much as regret: the implied answer to the
rhetorical *ubi sunt* of his elegies is that all is indeed over and done with.
He re-uses elements from earlier poets, but the context in which he

translates their work is altered. The mention of the disposing force of God also suggests that, like many who surveyed the alterations of society and religion of the sixteenth century, Ixtlilxóchitl concludes that all has changed irrecoverably, but not absolutely for the worse. The recollection of the famous American rulers of the past is balanced by a sense of divine providence shaping history:

> En México famosa,
> Moctezuma, valor de pecho indiano;
> a Acolhuacán dichosa,
> de Netzahualcóyotl rigió la mano;
> a Tlacopan la fuerte,
> Totoquihuatzin le salió por suerte.
>   Ningún olvido temo
>   de lo bien que tu reino dispusiste,
> estando en el supremo
> lugar que de la mano recibiste
> del gran Señor del Mundo
> Factor de aquestas cosas sin segundo.

[At Mexico, Montezuma the famous and valorous Indian, at Acolhuacàn the fortunate Netzahualcóyotl, and at the stronghold of Tlacopan, Totoquilhuatzin. I fear no forgetting of the just deeds of your reign, being in the high place appointed to you, by the Supreme Lord of the World, who governs all things.]

He goes on to speak of the need to seize the moment in the context of the certainty of death and the uncertainty of the future. One of the most conventional tropes of elegiac poetry is rendered extraordinary by the litany of American names which compose the *ubi sunt*.

> Goza, pues, muy gustoso,
> oh Netzahualcóyotl, lo que ahora tienes;
> conflores de este hermoso
> jardín, corona tus illustres sienes;
> oye mi canto y lira
> que a darte gustos y placeres tira . . .
> ¿ Qué es de Cihuapatzin
> y Cuauhtzontecomatzin el valiente
> y de Acolnahuacatzin?
> ¿ Qué es de toda esta gente?
> ¿ Sus voces oigo acaso?
> Ya estan en la otra vida; éste es el caso
>   Ojalá los que ahora
> juntos nos tiene del amor el hilo

que amistad atesora,
i viéramos de la muerte el duro filo!
Porque no hay bien seguro:
Que siempre trae mudanza lo futuro.[38]

[Therefore, O Netzahualcóyotl, rejoice in what you have today, crown your noble brow with flowers of this beautiful garden, hear my song and lyre which aim to give you pleasure . . . What has become of Cihuapatzin? and the brave Cuauhtzontecomatzin? And of Acolnahuacatzin? What has become of all of these? Perhaps I hear their voices? They are indeed in the other life. Would that we who are now united by the ties of love and friendship could foresee the harsh blade of death, for nothing is certain, the future always brings changes.]

The double perspective of this poem reflects one aspect of the hybrid mentality of the Americas. Given that Ixtlilxóchitl is in part apparently translating material two hundred years old from the court of Netzahualcóyotl, the Spanish voice which he invents to do it in is appositely retrospective and elegiac. The tone which he adopts is reminiscent of the romances of the medieval Iberian kings. The third poem of Ixtlilxóchitl's which survives is a fragmentary romance about the early King of Castile, Don Sancho.[39] This confirms that he is performing an intricate act of translation, reading the culture which he inherits through the glass of the language and culture which he inhabits, thereby creating a third term.[40]

*

Now we need to consider public manifestations of cultural hybridity and the religious syncretism (albeit carefullly monitored) displayed in the festal life of the Ibero-Americas. Such wholly hybrid festivals as the mascarada in honour of the Virgin at Querétaro recorded by Sigüenza y Góngora[41] emphasise the degree to which, in the *barroco de las Indias*, 'images are both stratified and joined, at the level of both form and content, in such a way that in the end a third term appears, neither European nor indigenous, and outside the categories of either.'[42] Here elements from the universal language of festival and religious procession have been overlaid, rather as they are in Sigüenza y Góngora's own festival for the entry of the Viceroy to Mexico City in 1680 (see below pp. 114–16) with the representations of the American ancestors. Following the Conquistador Diego de Tapia are the six Chichimecas rulers including Ixtlilxóchitl, whose descendant was Sigüenza y Góngora's friend the poet and historian who was the author of the elegiac poem just discussed. Then come representations of the Aztec rulers of Querétaro, the kings of Téxcoco including the Netzahualcóyotl also commemorated in the elegy of Don Fernando – all these monarchs crowned with turquoise and with the plumes of the Quetzal bird and draped in featherwork cloaks – and following them a figure representing Charles V as the successor of the American kings and emperors. Then comes a float or carriage combining metropolitan and indigenous elements. There is a great ship riding on waves of blue and silver gauze; in the stern of the ship is a canopied throne in the shape of a shell at the top of a flight of steps covered with silk carpets. Within the shell is the image of the *Guadalupana*, Our Lady of the Americas, attended by angels, streamers of taffeta and bouquets of flowers.[43] Sigüenza y Góngora compares the appearance of this float to the paradise-gardens of the Virgin where it is always spring, and describes a child kneeling in adoration on the steps of the throne, dressed in 'Indian' clothes, to represent the Americas. The child holds a heart in one hand[44] and a censer in the other. Around this triumphal float the Indians are dancing one of the royal *toncontines* of the ancient Mexicans. The final part of the procession is made up of old men chanting the praises of the Virgin to the accompaniment of indigenous instruments: tlalpan-huetuetl, teponaztli, omichicahuztil, ayaycaztli and cuauhtlapitzalli.

In this hybrid context, it is worth considering the signification of the ship – is it the ship of faith, the state, the church, the ship between the new worlds and the old? It is all of these things. It is also bearing the Queen of the Americas like a marine goddess, accompanied by the indigenous dances of the Americas. The heart and censer held by the child are emblems of devotion and prayer, as international as the child's dress is local. Human hearts, however, played a significant part in the religious rituals of pre-conquest, pagan Mexico, as well as being one of the most universal of baroque hieroglyphics.

Such sequences of indigenous kings were not confined to Mexico, nor indeed to the ephemeral medium of festival. The iconography of festivals elsewhere feeds our knowledge of the context for the viceregal celebrations at Mexico City in 1680, which we will consider shortly.

At the festivals in Cuzco for the beatification of St Ignatius Loyola in 1610, perhaps moved by his connections by marriage with the Inca royal family, the native Andeans carried in the processions figures of the eleven monarchs of the Inca dynasty from Manco Capac to Huáscar, prefiguring the images of Aztec monarchs displayed on Sigüenza's arch for the 1680 Mexican festival.[45]

The engraved title-page of Antonio de Herrera's *Historia General de los Hechos de los Castillanos*, published at Madrid in 1615, has, in medallions surrounding the title, the earliest surviving representation of the monarchs of the Incas. The iconography of Sigüenza y Góngora's arch is paralleled also in a print by Alonso de la Cueva, issued at Lima in 1724–28, which shows the series of Inca monarchs succeeded by the Spanish kings.[46] In 1725, the coronation celebrations of Luís Fernando I in the mining town of Potosí included an elaborate festival in the main square, in which, among various allegorical and geographical representations sculpted on the main triumphal car were the images of the Inca kings of Peru from Manco to Atahualpa, bearing lamps.[47] An elaborate engraving of 1748 represents the dynasty of the Incas and the kings of Spain in a series of portrait medallions suspended in a complex architectural setting, highly reminiscent of the festival and ephemeral architecture of the late Baroque. The end of this iconographic tradition is equally fascinating, representing as it does a return of sovereignty from Spain to the Americas, in that the central medallion, sustained by an allegorical figure with the attributes of Faith, is that of the liberator Simón Bolívar.[48]

All this iconography is tending to the legitimisation of Spanish rule, certainly, but also to the commemoration of indigenous rulers. It is stating that the Spanish kings and viceroys rule as successors to what were already legitimate monarchs (indeed themselves conquerors of earlier indigenous inhabitants). The sense is conveyed also that there is a valid *American* antiquity to be taken into account. This, as has been indicated (pp. 12 and 27 above) was part of the way that the Egyptian past functioned for the Baroque: to make a place for a parallel antiquity still obscured in the medium of an undeciphered language beside the known anti-quities of Greece and Rome, and thus to prepare for the idea of Mexican just as much as Britannic antiquity.

Popular festivals at San Gregorio and Sucre

The Jesuit College of St Gregorio in Mexico City was the institution dedicated to the education of the children of indigenous Americans. It also functioned as a centre for confraternities and devotional gatherings of adults from the same community. In his long account of the evangelisation of New Spain, Andrés Pérez de Ribas SJ, a chronicler who makes a very sharp distinction between civil society and the 'ferocious and barbarous' people dwelling in the remote regions of New Spain, ends with some account of the indigenous culture which flourished with Jesuit encouragement at San Gregorio in Mexico City.

On festal days the pupils of the College presented sacred dialogues in the Nahuatl language, accompanied by music and dancing. More remarkably, Perez de Ribas records calmly that the dances of the court of Moctezuma were carried on by the seminarians, except that now the honours and obeisances were directed to the Sacrament of the Altar rather than to the living emperor.[49] Otherwise, in costume, music and gesture, the strewing of flowers and the ritual sweeping of the ground with feather fans, the *mitote* of the emperor carried on as before. In the new order, at the invitation to the dance, the participants now sang 'Come out, Mexica, and dance the *tocotín*, we have the King of Glory here'. He adds that this Aztec court dance is imitated by the sons of the *criollo* elites.

He also records that processions of the Sacrament are greeted on their arrival in the main square of the city by the 'flying dancers' of the former imperial entourage:

> Flyers who come flying down through the air. When the float of the Most Holy Sacrament reaches the plaza, they come flying down in a very unusual manner, sustained on cords tied to a pole that is like the mast of a ship, with some of them shaking rattles or playing other instruments.[50]

*

If we now consider a 1718 vernacular festival from Sucre in present-day Bolivia, we see the same fusion of the American and the international. The intellectual driving-force is the interpretation of imagery, the making of emblems. The reconstruction of this sequence of festal *villancicos* in honour of Our Lady of Guadalupe is the work of Bernardo Illari, the distinguished scholar of American music.[51] These festal carols would have formed part of a festival composed also of plays, dances, bullfights and sung services in the cathedral, with the Marian texts of the *Salve Regina* and the Litany of Loreto at their centre. All these *villancicos* were composed by a mestizo priest, Roque Jacinto de Chavarria (1688–1719), whose music is preserved in the cathedral service books.

There are aspects of the local to the texts of the *villancicos*: the Virgin is greeted as the Queen of Sucre, under its old name of 'La Plata':

> A la flor de Alba
> De la Plata Reina
> Damos parabienes . . .
> Sea bienvenida
> Bienvenida sea

> A ser de la Plata
> La flor y la perla[52]

[To the flower of the dawn, Queen of Sucre, we pay our compliments
. . . how welcome you are to be the flower and the pearl of Sucre.]

The most distinctive aspect of this sequence of texts is the bullfight *villancico*, whose text, in Spanish with interjections in the indigenous language, Quechua, compares the Virgin of Guadalupe to the successful bullfighter. The forces of evil are represented as a series of bulls named for their characteristics – *el Barroso, el Pintado, el Damasceno*. A perfect example of cultural hybridity and of the emblematic genius of the baroque, the bullfight is the *pictura*, and the *villancico* itself is the moralisation and explanation. '¡Guachi, guachi toro, hao!' [Beaten bull, spent bull, hey!], an interjection in Quechua, confirms the absolute localisation of the work. The piece ends with the celebration of the triumphant Virgin:

> ¡Viva la Infanta Maria!
> Pues en las fiestas
> Triunfa del pecado.

[Praise the Princess Maria, since in the bullfights she has triumphed over sin.]

There is a *villancico* of equal audacity and baroque ingenuity by Sor Juana, sung in the persona of a roaring boy, extolling the virtues of St Peter as exemplary fencing-master and fighter.[53]

Mexico City: the viceregal entry of 1680

The most complex and magnificent expression of the past of the Americas is the festival text of Carlos de Sigüenza y Góngora: *Teatro de Virtudes Politicas* – the *Theatre of the Political Virtues*.[54] This formed the first part of the 1680 viceregal festival in Mexico City, the second part of which was devised by Sor Juana de la Cruz.

One of the glories of this 1680 festival is the way in which Sigüenza y Góngora applies the full visual and verbal splendours of the international Baroque to the local laudation of the Aztec monarchs who had preceded the *conquistadores*. This is a triumphant example of that baroque flexibility which can accommodate the indigenous and the locally idiosyncratic. The festivals in Mexico City in 1680 were a manifestation of an international and supra-national phenomenon, a work which can be decoded simultaneously through more than one system of representation, by the perceptions of more than one culture.

Sor Juana Inés de la Cruz is a writer paradigmatically capable of stating the universal and the local in the same work. Her festival arch for the new Viceroy of Mexico in 1680 is filled with the specific: along with emblem material, classical myth and the pseudo-hieroglyphics which the Baroque derived from the incomplete evidence then available about ancient Egypt, there are references to local custom, traditions and history.

Sigüenza y Góngora's arch for the same 1680 festival glorifies the kings of the Aztecs, seeing the kings of Spain and their viceroys as their natural successors in the western paradise. The Baroque of Mexico is, in this context, especially distinct from the Baroque of metropolitan Spain: it is a local use of international modes and conventions, but the result is as specific (and as international) as any metropolitan event.

Depictions of past monarchs, the line which an honorand is joining, are a regular feature of the baroque festival entry. Paintings of the duchesses and statues of the dukes of Urbino welcomed the Medici Princess Claudia to that city in 1621 on her marriage to the heir to the dukedom; Scottish kings welcomed (if that is the right word) Charles I to Edinburgh in 1633.[55]

The 1680 Mexican festival represents and emphasises the indigenous sovereigns while asserting that the Spanish rulers are their legitimate successors. Nothing could be further from the stereotype of colonial cultural policy which rejects all aspects of the indigenous civilisation as primitive or inferior. It is necessary to remember that, in the Spanish viceroyalties, the indigenous elite were admitted to many of the central rituals which distinguish the European elite, specifically the grants of arms in the European style – an admission of the former outsider into the crucial visual language of power.

Sigüenza y Góngora goes further in endowing the Americas with an ancient Christian tradition: while St Thomas had been asserted by the Mexican Franciscan chronicler Baltazar de Medina to have preached in that country at Anáhuac, Sigüenza asserts the Christian antiquity of his beloved Mexico. (He advertised, but never published, a tract entitled 'Phoenix of the West: St Thomas found with the name of Quetzalcoatl'.)[56] His acts of imaginative assimilation extended to secular history: in his 1680 text he derived the descent of the Aztecs from Misraim, founder and ruler of Egypt, partaking of their hieroglyphic wisdom in their pre-Columbian codices, such as the manuscripts which he inherited from his close friend the poet and historian Ixtlilxóchitl (see pp. 108–10 above) as part of a collection of Mexican antiquities.[57]

What the 1680 festival achieves is a genuine synthesis, a *criollo* revision of hierarchy. Sigüenza is careful to point out that the erection of triumphal arches is an American as well as a European tradition. The Viceroy is welcomed to a hybrid state where the Spanish rulers have replaced the Aztec sovereigns but, crucially, no attempt has been made to efface the latter's memory.[58] The baldaquin held over the head of the Viceroy, the Marqués de la Laguna, is not only alluding to his status as representative of the King of Spain but also to the shadow of Aztec royalty: the baldaquin of Moctezuma as depicted in the early eighteenth-century painting by Juan Correa of *The meeting of Cortes and Montezuma.*[59]

Sor Juana and Sigüenza are aiming to instruct and inform their honorand. This festival aims to articulate the entrance to the city as a transformative progress. The Marqués de la Laguna may arrive simply as the representative of the King, but, by the time that he has contemplated and passed through the arches which have been erected to greet him, he can be left in no doubt of the antiquity and distinctive identity of his new territory. He is the successor of the Aztec kings as were the preceding viceroys.

Questions of centrality and marginality have been readdressed, so that at once the dignity of the Americas is asserted and Spain and New Spain take on an equality, both ancient Christian territories, monarchies sharing the plural antiquities of the baroque world.

This mythologising of origins is a contentious and fantastical aspect of Sigüenza y Góngora's text, especially his derivation of a Mediterranean, Old World origin for the Aztecs: his argument is a virtuoso piece of baroque elision of boundaries to combine the Israelite Old Testament Misraim with the Neptune of the Gentiles and to suggest that this composite figure was a ruler in Africa and possibly the progenitor of the Aztecs.[60] Athanasius Kircher's observations of comparative religion and of writing systems are adduced as proof of the connection.[61]

Further, the Aztec king Huitzilopochtli is placed in direct parallel with Aeneas, the ancestor of the Romans.[62] The *impresa* or device which is offered for the king Chimalpopocatzin is the pelican, sometimes used as a type of Christ in the Eucharist, the bird which traditionally feeds its young with the blood from its own breast and is thus the visual signifier for a king whose people are dearer to him than himself.[63] This is all potentially problematic, in that it denies a degree of autonomy and validity to an American origin, by suggesting a remote 'old' world origin for the Aztecs. This preoccupation with Mediterranean roots is observable in many European myths of origin, the most remarkable being the derivation of the origin of the Scots from Scota, the daughter of Pharaoh, and 'Scot' from late Greek *skotos* meaning 'darkness'.

Jesuit painting in the Far East

There is a continuous process of accommodation of a 'high' culture with a 'native' culture visible throughout recorded cultural history. Such phenomena as Chinoiserie and Turquerie are anomalies and to be set aside here, in that they are not the product of dialogue. Oddly, it is the Chinese pavilion of the European garden which is an uncomprehending copy of a drawing or engraving. Of necessity the European buildings in Peking or Agra were the products of dialogue and an attempt at cultural understanding, although it is to be suspected that the western elements were considered by the Manchu or Mughal emperors as little more than curiosities.

But there is a real sense in which 'high' culture in Europe has been in dialogue with, and assimilating elements from, autochthonous popular culture for millennia. Such phenomena as carnival and the absorption of local pagan cults into some of the stranger observances of the Christian churches are testimony to this. What is also consistent is that the high or classical culture always convinces itself that it is proceeding with reference only to antiquity and tradition and that it is making no accommodations with, and drawing no strength from, the popular beliefs of its day, manifested in phenomena such as Christmas and carnival.

From discussion of the cultural bilinguality of the baroque mode, of its ability to function simultaneously within a local and an international discourse, I would move to the discussion of the same phenomenon in the visual arts internationally, particularly in the Far East, where the cultural translations attempted by Europeans were not equally successful in all spheres.

The activities of the Jesuits in the Far East test the inclusiveness of the Baroque to its limits. The artwork from the Jesuit missions expresses a willingness to engage very fully with alien cultures, and to seek and exploit moments of cultural convergence which, if effectively exploited, might permit cultural translation.

One interesting instance of aesthetic and cultural convergence in the Christian art of Japan is the damaged painting known as *The madonna of the snows*, now in the Museum of the Martyrs in Nagasaki. This painting is probably based on an oil sketch by a European, Giovanni Niccolò, and is in any case referential to a European tradition of oil painting

on canvas or panel. But it is a watercolour on Japanese paper: as Gauvin
Bailey observes,

> the artist transforms every element of his image into equivalent Japanese
> style and technique. The brilliant colours on a gold background reflect
> current trends in mainstream Momoyama painting, as do the high,
> arched eyebrows, the narrow eyes, the double chin, and the 'bee stung'
> lips . . . The Virgin demonstrates Japanese concepts of beauty; as in typ-
> ical Japanese portrayals of women of the period, her head is accented by
> sensuous wisps of hair, and her cheeks and forehead shine with an ivory-
> like brilliance.

At the same time, the shadow beneath her jaw, modelling the round-
edness of the neck, is entirely European.[64]

The Counter-Reformation Catholic conceptualisation of the Virgin
Mary requires that she must, above all, be both lovable and familiar,
so she is invariably represented as a beautiful woman. In this Japanese
image, therefore, she is portrayed in a mode which expresses local, not
European, concepts of attractiveness. But another very interesting
aspect of Japanese Christian art is that, not only is the Virgin assimilated to a lively native tradition of representing beauties, but Christ is
assimilated to an existing tradition of representing foreign religious leaders
which goes in a somewhat different direction from Jesuit models.

Buddhism originates in India, and, with an admirable historical
sense not found in European images of Christ (whose Semitic origins
are seldom, if ever, represented), Japanese *zenga* (a tradition of Japanese
Zen ink painting) portray Buddhist hermits, particularly the Indian
missionary Bodidharma, locally called Daruma, as gnarled, elderly
men with the large nose and big eyes of a Caucasian. *Zenga* paintings
not infrequently portray head and shoulders only, permitting convergence with incoming European models. This convergence goes in two
directions. On the one hand, from the first half of the seventeenth
century onwards, a series of coloured pictures of Daruma and Zen
hermits and eccentrics was painted using European techniques of
shading taken from Jesuit art. On the other, the artist of a painting of
Christ as *Salvator mundi*, painted in the European mode in oil on a
copper panel, roughens and exaggerates the features of his model.
This is not because he was unable to copy the fine, youthful features
of Christ in the engraving he used, but because his culture offers him
an iconography for 'a foreign holy man', to which the *Salvator mundi*
is assimilated.[65] Jesuit iconography of Christ represent him as not
only European, but young and handsome: the Japanese tendency to

represent him as an older, rougher and more formidable figure indicates direct crossover from the representation of Daruma.

The tendency of Japanese Christians to appropriate the images they were shown and to make them their own is also evidenced by a fine painting of St Michael slaying the dragon (oil on panel) in the Seminario de São José in Macao, which makes an interesting parallel to Mexican treatment of the same theme.[66] Inspired by a Dutch print, Jerome Wierix's *Quis sicut Deus?*, this image of the archangel exchanges the lance he traditionally carries for a samurai sword, gives him a helmet and sleeves adorned with variations of the Chinese-inspired *lingzhi* fungus pattern, and outlines the borders of his costume in bright gold. His stance is also warrior-like in a Japanese as opposed to a European way. The archangel stands with his legs turned out like a dancer, a pose frequently found in Japanese representations of samurai, which presumably reflects the particular training underlying effective use of a samurai sword, though by a European eye it is not perceived as martial. The image of Michael, so often seen as a protector, here converges with the iconography of traditional images of Buddhist guardian kings.

The Jesuit missions also gave rise to 'Occidentalist' artworks in both Japan and China, suggesting considerable mutual curiosity. Japanese *Namban byōbu* ('southern barbarian screens') portray figures in European dress against a golden background or in a rich verdant landscape. Like European chinoiserie, the images on the screens have a strong tendency to be miscellaneously rather than specifically exotic.[67] Technically also, they tend to be composite. Some use oil paints for the figures and Japanese colours for the background; while others are painted in indigenous water-soluble pigments, but these are thickened with a white body and glue binder to simulate the opacity of oils.

One of the most curious by-products of the Jesuit missions is a scroll-painting of the Yongzheng Emperor wearing the heavy, curled wig, brocade coat and waistcoat of the European elite, created entirely within the techniques and representational system of Chinese portraiture. This is an experiment with representing oneself as high status within an alien set of conventions, comparable to Van Dyck's portrait of Sir Robert Shirley in Persian dress, or the various paintings of Jesuits in mandarin robes.[68]

In China, as in Japan, the Jesuit missionaries found that their Christian art was interpreted with reference to alien cultural patterns, but within a more complex structure. Buddhism aside, Japan had a native animist religion (Shinto), which was, from a Jesuit point of view, mere superstition and could be dealt with as such. The Jesuits were able to

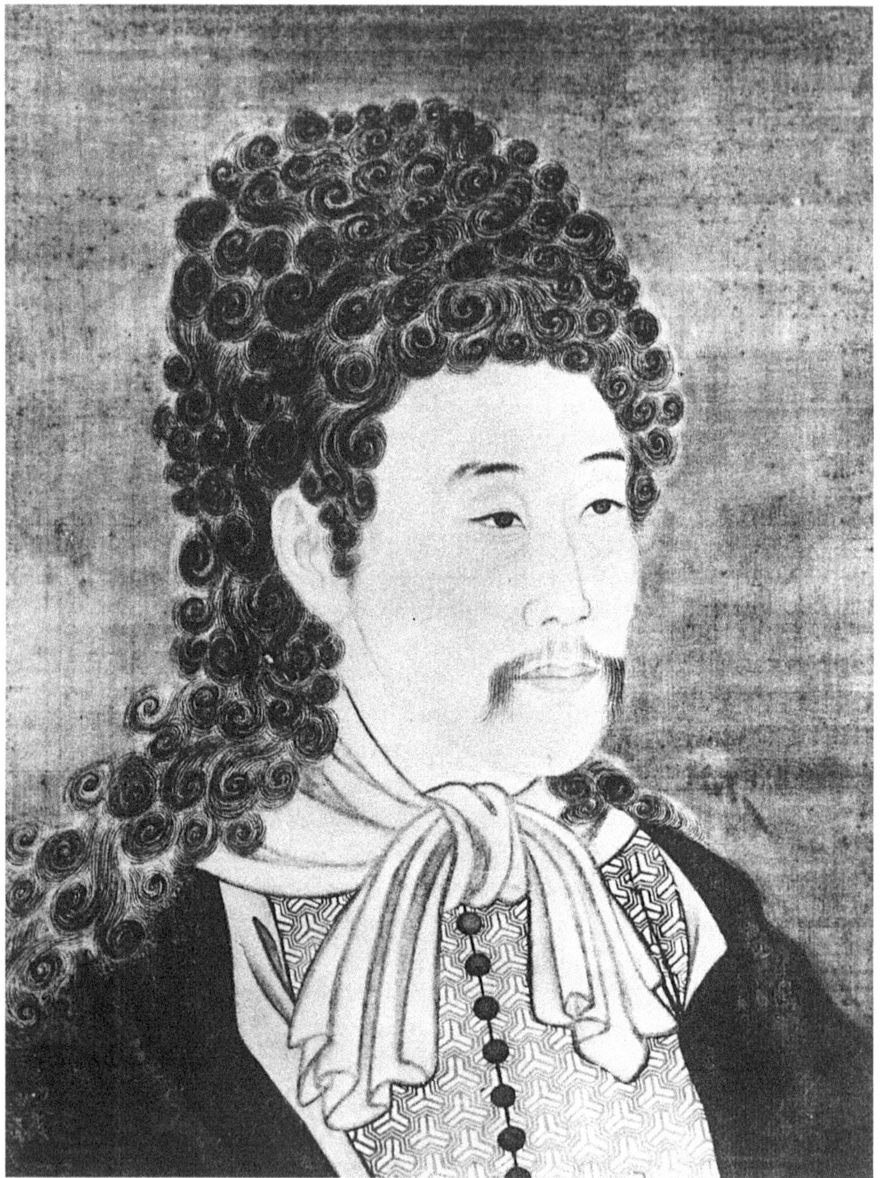

5 The Emperor Yongzheng in European dress, eighteenth century.

establish a group of believers sufficiently firm in their faith to survive dire persecution and maintain themselves to the present day. In the case of China, the situation was fundamentally different. While, similarly, there were Buddhism, Daoism and a host of native deities to take into account, there was also Confucianism. Confucianism, while not quite a religion, was an all-embracing cultural phenomenon which represented what is *zheng* (orthodox) in a religious, ritual, social and political sense. In order not to be branded as *xie* (heterodox) and treated as a subversive sect, a marginal religion had to demonstrate that it was on the side of *zheng*.[69]

As in Japan, the Jesuits in China discovered that, whereas the representation of the crucified Christ caused endless problems, images of the Virgin were potentially attractive, since there was a genuine convergence of associations between the Madonna, the Buddhist Bodhisattva of Mercy, Guanyin and the Chinese goddess protector of sailors, A-Ma. Bodhisattvas play a similar intercessory role in Buddhism to that played by saints in Catholicism, and the Virgin Mary as *Stella Maris* also had a specific role as a protector of sailors. Furthermore, China was a culture which exalted male babies, and among the most popular images made for Buddhist devotion in the home in sixteenth- and seventeenth-century China was *songzi Guanyin*, 'Guanyin the sender of sons', in which the deity assumes a female form and is shown holding a young male child. This image was also popular in Japan, and thus the Hidden Christians worshipped household statues of Kannon/Guanyin, holding a baby boy in her arms – this figure was known as Maria-Kannon.[70]

One image which illustrates this crossover very clearly is the Madonna of St Luke, taken from one of the many altarpieces on the subject in Ricci's mission, a large silk scroll painted entirely in a flowing, calligraphic Chinese style in indigenous watercolours. The original image, head and shoulders, depending ultimately on a Byzantine model, has been extended by the Chinese artist into a full-length figure, slender, willowy and wearing a flowing gown in a way that brings the Virgin very close to Guanyin, her slim body leaning to one side to offset the weight of a robust infant, with a Chinese boy's shaved head and topknot.[71] Another strikingly syncretic image, from Vietnam, is a hanging scroll representing the Last Judgment, painted in the second half of the eighteenth century, and heavily dependent on Buddhist representations of hell. 'Chinese pagodas and dragons, Buddhist demons and *apsaras*, make this one of the most strikingly syncretic religious images to come out of the Asian missions.'[72] Hell-mouth (bottom right) is a Chinese dragon. The kneeling ranks of angels/*apsaras* suggest the court of the heavenly Jade Emperor rather than the Trinity, which is actually depicted centre top.

Jesuit relations with the other religions of China were complex. From a Confucian perspective, Buddhism and Christianity were very similar. Both were institutional religions with a system of theology, rituals and an organisation which was independent of secular institutions. They shared a belief in the afterlife, the idea of heaven and hell and the practice of celibacy. To some extent, this created an area of convergence which the Jesuits could exploit. Unfortunately, Buddhist monks had a very low status within Chinese culture. Thus the Jesuits, after an initial false start, preferred to assume the dress of, and to associate with, the Confucian literati.[73] Chinese Christian art, while making use of Buddhist motifs and useful convergences such as Guanyin/Mary, therefore, simultaneously deploys a register of imagery which seeks to represent the Virgin and Christ as high-status within the conventions of *wenren hua*, 'paintings of literati'.

Chinese Jesuit woodblock prints show a deliberate use of double messages. In an *Annunciation*, the Virgin sits in a Chinese timber cantilevered pavilion, her prie-dieu converted to a black lacquer table of the kind commonly found in the homes of Ming literati. Clouds surround the shaft of light and the angel, boldly Chinese, with lobed heads and tails of flame, drawn in the traditional form used in China as vehicles for Daoist immortals or Buddhist Bodhisattvas, where they enclose or support holy figures. In the *Annunciation*, they clearly denote the status of the Holy Ghost and the angel, who himself resembles a Bodhisattva – a remarkable example of convergence in action, since the artist has capitalised on a motif which serves a very similar role for both cultures. In this, and in a comparable *Agony in the garden*, an anonymous artist presents Christian stories in a way which plays into traditional Buddhist imagery but also conjures up the world of the cultured literati, presenting the Virgin and Christ as high-status figures in the same way that Italian renaissance Annunciations give the Virgin a cultivated princess's bedroom (in which she is often, as here, interrupted while reading). These prints represent a calculated attempt to give Christian imagery an appeal to educated Chinese.

A significant part of the Jesuits' failure in China was due to a fundamental error. Jesuit painters, above all Guiseppe Castiglione, may have achieved an effective synthesis of European and Chinese painting, but painting was not a high-status art. The key fact which the Jesuits never grasped was the aesthetic dimensions and cultural importance of calligraphy, the art, par excellence, of the literati. Unable to write with elegance – in most cases, unable to write at all – they could not expect to be taken seriously. They were victims of their own cultural prejudices, in that they did not grasp that the hierarchy of art forms might be totally different in another culture; but they were also brought up sharply against the essential fact that, while baroque Christianity could assume a Chinese modality as well as it could assume any other, Chinese high culture was absolutely unwilling to engage seriously with alien ideas other than on an entirely superficial level.

In contact with uneducated Chinese, the Jesuit approach was, once more, to offer a parallel and alternative religious experience – or, to put it another way, to compete directly with Daoist masters, sorcerers and faith healers. Using Catholic practices such as exorcism and apotropaic prayer, the Jesuits offered themselves to simple souls as alternative shamans, and from the perspective of the Chinese authorities, fell under the same suspicion of *xie* (heterodoxy) as Daoist magicians. The Jesuits engaged in what Standaert calls the pastoral of fear: telling gruesome stories of hell, which, since Daoist and Buddhist popular traditions offered similar narratives (as the Vietnamese Last Judgment scroll indicates), were far more comprehensible than the Creed.[74] On this level, they achieved some modest success, but at the risk of alienating such literate support as they had. It was a paradox which could not be resolved.

Visual arts in Ibero-America: arquebusier angels

The visual arts were considerably more successful in the Iberian territories in the Americas, not only in terms of creating a culturally hybrid school of painting, but also in accommodating elements of indigenous culture into what became, in effect, a completely new school of painting which persists in its influence to this day.

This enterprise was sustained by the dividedness and permeability of the Spanish colonial project. It created many gaps and *lacunae* where areas of cultural fusion and literal intermarriage could take place. Sabine MacCormack makes it clear in her comprehensive *Religion in the Andes: Vision and Imagination in Early Colonial Peru* that the conquest of Peru was hostile to and destructive of a complex elegiac native religion based on presence of the honoured dead as sacred mummies, and on colloquies with blessed ghosts, often ghosts of those who had been willingly sacrificed.[75] Her equally incisive later piece about the Jesuit mission in Peru sees the Jesuit epoch as a very different thing, the creation of a culture of accommodation on the ruins created by earlier intransigence.[76]

There are clearly different degrees of religious accommodation in Mexico and Peru. Mexico has a considerable amount of simple overlay. Sor Juana de la Cruz's syncretic prologue to her play *The Divine Narcissus* records the sanguinary religion of the old 'god of seeds' and the spontaneous conversion of America thereafter to the 'new god of seeds' who is Christ in the Eucharist. The conversion and transformation is instantaneous, with the inevitability of a masque or a dream. The same dance refrain serves both divinities.[77]

In the popular art of Mexico a similar syncretism caused the Jesuits in particular to allow the people to recollect the old observances of

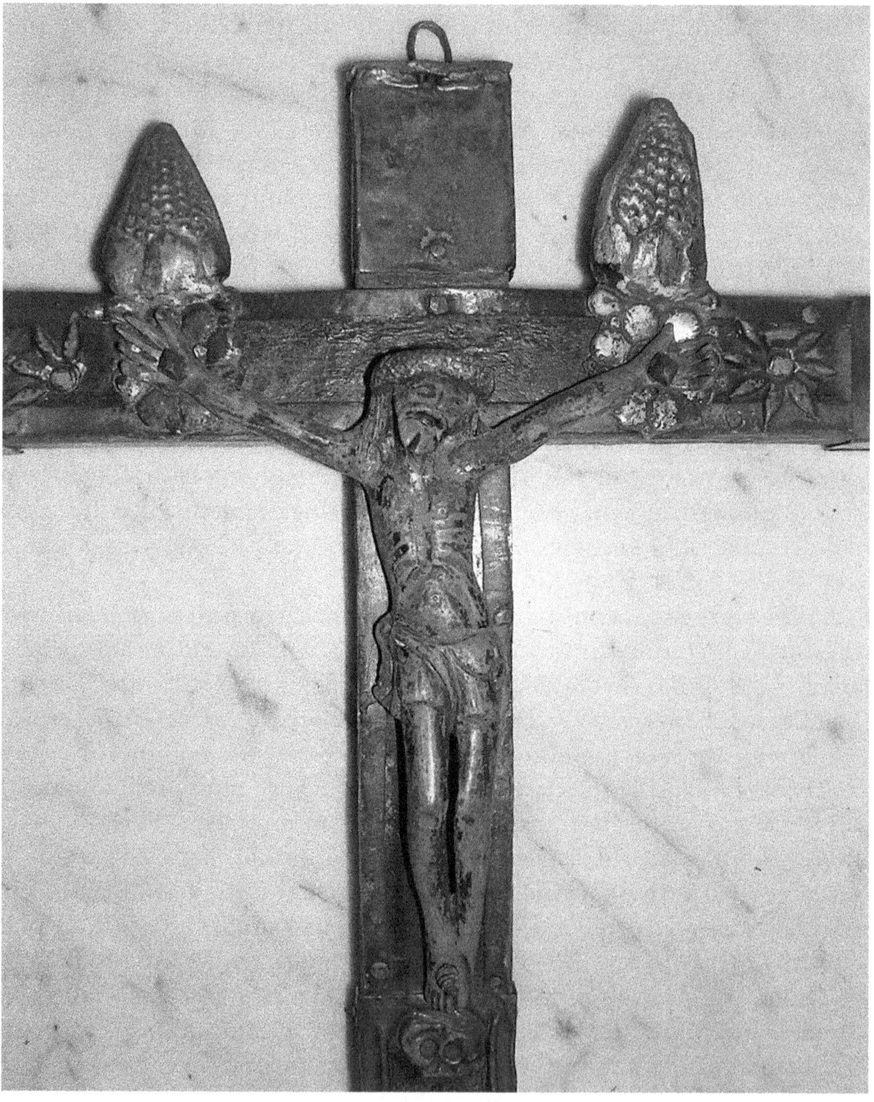

6 Metal crucifix with maize-cobs, Mexican (?eighteenth century).

the 'god of seeds' in contemplating the crucifix, by making crucifixes of the formerly sacred corn pith.[78] A Mexican metal crucifix now at Stonyhurst, a late manifestation of this cult, has ears of corn instead of blood emerging from Christ's wounded hands and feet.[79]

*

The religious position in Peru was considerably more complicated. An initial period of confrontation with little accommodation eventually gave way to a complex process of syncretism, essentially the work of the Jesuits. Although certain Christian devotions were grafted early onto the stock of indigenous religion, the assimilation of a complete system long remained problematic. In the end, it produced a school of painting which went further than any other in making works which fuse the international and the indigenous to produce objects which can be decoded simultaneously by local and international systems.

Indeed the arts of the indigenous Americans of what are now Argentina, Bolivia and Peru consistently demonstrate this phenomenon of double signification. In the visual arts it is those territories which now compose Peru and Bolivia which give us the most compelling schools of hybrid art in Ibero-America. They have a large repertory of sophisticated images, almost all of which carry multiple significations. Culturally, Peru represents the fusion of two sophisticated peoples both of whom, Inca and Spaniard, were conquerors with a highly evolved culture. Santo Domingo Cuzco is built on the foundations of the temple of the sun and the merging of the two traditions was manifested in elite intermarriage.

The Jesuit church in Cuzco preserves a stylistically hybrid painting of a significant dynastic marriage: that of the nephew of St Ignatius Loyola to Doña Beatriz Clara Coya (sometimes called Beatriz Ñusta), the niece of Tupac Amaru. Their daughter went on to marry the son of the widower-Jesuit St Francisco Borja. Both families are represented according to the pictorial conventions of their own traditions. This double marriage formed a significant part of the way that the Jesuits presented themselves in Peru. As part of their affirmation of the ties of blood between the Society and the Incas, the pupils of the Jesuit College at Cuzco re-enacted this auspicious marriage annually.

The intensity of hybridity in the arts in Peru can be seen most clearly in the Andean images of the Virgin: an image of the draped statues of the Iberian tradition can move into the image of (literally and metaphorically) the Virgin of the Andes, as in the astonishing picture called the Virgin of Potosí. This is a genuinely multivalent image of the Iberian Madonna draped in a mantle which is itself the treasury of the Andes, the metalliferous mountain of Potosí.

But we can go further: the Clement Mother vested in the hill, in the earth itself, is the old Virgin of the Andes, Pachamama, Mother of the Earth, the breath of life itself to all created things.[80] This is not any simplistic manifestation of compromised cultural translation. It is rather the manifestation of a cross-cultural act of baroque poetic imagination.

The Latin hymn to the Virgin 'Salve Regina' resonates with the Inca recognition of the mountain as queen, manifestation of the universal mother of living things; the Christian devotion gathers the indigenous belief unto itself, and vice versa. The symbolic or poetic languages of the universal Baroque have functioned as a bridge between the indigenous worship of the hill as the Mother, and European worship involving Marian statues which are, in visual form, parallel to the form of the sacred mountain. The Augustinians of the *altiplano* in the first years of the seventeenth century explain the identification by way of the baroque language of the *impresa*, the 'hieroglyphic', the *jeroglífico*.

Mary is the mountain from which was quarried the stone without hands or feet, Christ, (i.e. Christ the patient sacrificial victim, incapable of self-defence). The Church as Bride, as earthly manifestation of the heavenly Jerusalem, often identified imaginatively with the Virgin, is an edifice of precious stones of which the most precious is the diamond of the purest water, Christ, the true refractor of the glory of the Father, of the light of the Sun.[81]

The Trinity crown Mary in her manifestation as the Holy Mountain of Potosí. The Pope and the Emperor in the foreground worship a truth represented in the fusion and hybridity of visual imagery. And the Inca is present on the hill.

The earliest version of this image from the year 1520 (this version is now in the Museo de la Moneda, Potosí) shows Charles V and Pope Paul III, flanking a globe in the foreground. This image is replicated as time goes on, with substitutions to keep the pontiff and monarch up to date, with a final version (now in a private collection in Potosí) dating from 1720, without the globe and with the figure of Philip V.

The operation of lines of power and status in this image are far from simple. How does the terrestrial globe relate to the Virgin/Mountain? Are pope and monarch in the positions of donors alongside the indigenous donors? Or are they suppliants or pilgrims to the Virgin of the Andes? Is the globe between them their province, or does it indicate a further extension of the domain of the Pachamama/Virgin as universal Mother? Within the universalism of the Baroque it is rarely a simple matter to decipher in which direction the lines of power and creativity are running.

*

The other remarkable visual manifestation of the Baroque of the high Andes comes in the figures who attend the Virgin in the remote churches of the native American villages, of the remote Jesuit stations. These figures represent an imaginative fusion of the idea of the indigenous deities of the stars – merciful, handsome young warriors – with the European merciful warriors of heaven, the angels and archangels.

What is compelling and moving about these images (they are being painted in Cuzco to this day) is that they represent the heavenly warriors as the armies of the baroque centuries: Flemish engravings illustrative of musket drill are transformed in the Americas into the angel

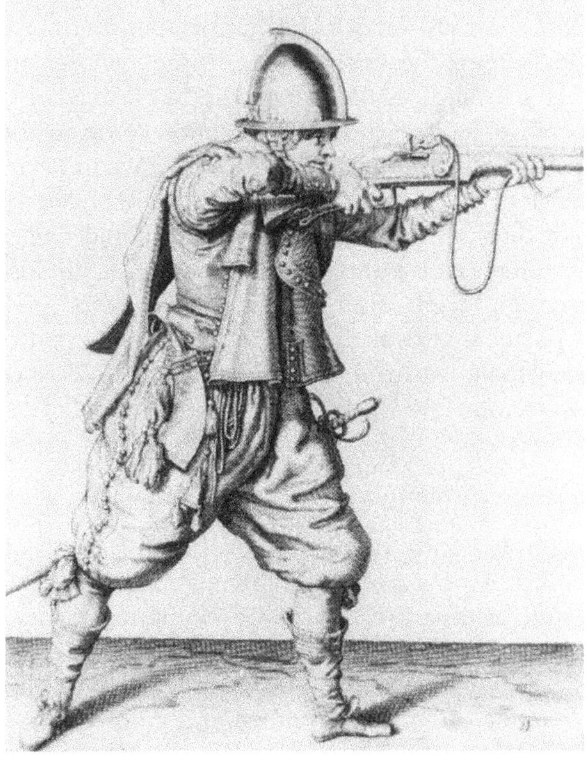

7 Engraving of musket drill from Jacob de Gheyn, *Waffen handlung von den roren, musquetten undt spiessen* (The Hague, 1608), plate 2.

arquebusiers who attend the Virgin of the Andes.[82] Plumes, which are an indigenous signifier of sacred and royal status, adorn European hats, part of the brocaded uniforms of baroque officers, in these works of fusion and complex signification. Each posture of the musket drill comes to identify a particular angel, with a name and a particular function.

The angel who levels his gun at the horizon is, in one of the most extraordinary and compelling paintings of the Master of Calamarca, the angel called Aziel who is the Fear of God, *Aziel timor Dei*.[83] Gisbert associates these Andean angel-paintings with confraternities of indigenous peoples fostered by the Jesuits under the patronage of St Michael.

The meeting of cultures in the Altiplano gives the names of the angels from the apocryphal book of Enoch to these postures taken from the engravings of musket-drill published for the armies of those endless wars in Flanders which consumed most of the riches of the mountains of Potosí. Sometimes the attribute of one of these angels is a translation of his Hebrew name; more often they have taken on an attribute of the merciful heavenly warriors of the Inca pantheon. Salamiel is the Peace of God, Aziel is the Fear of God; Aspiel, whose gun is reversed as for a prince's funeral, is *apetus Dei*, the Marksman of God.[84] These paintings are an object of endless fascination, even in the apotropaic functions which their replicas are believed to have in Peru to this day.[85]

One sequence of musketeer angels even returned from the New World to Spain, providing an extra layer of international complexity: these are in the hermitage of Ezcaray in the Rioja. Their shields are charged with aspects of the Virgin from the Litany of Loreto. As in the Andes, they are the palace guard of the Virgin, but their accoutrements have been, as is inevitable with the baroque arts, localised to conform with Spanish expectations.[86]

Sculptures of the Guarani

One final example of the hybrid arts is, like the Jesuit arts in China, partly the record of a defeat for the international system. The Guarani people adopted international baroque elements very cautiously and retained an overiding indigenous visual language of abstract patterning. (This is a highly instructive instance of the usually sensitive Jesuit missionaries *misapprehending* the nature of a culture.)

The figures produced by the indigenous sculptors in the Jesuit mission stations among the Guarani people of what is now Argentina are conceived in a significant local idiom drawing on, but not dominated

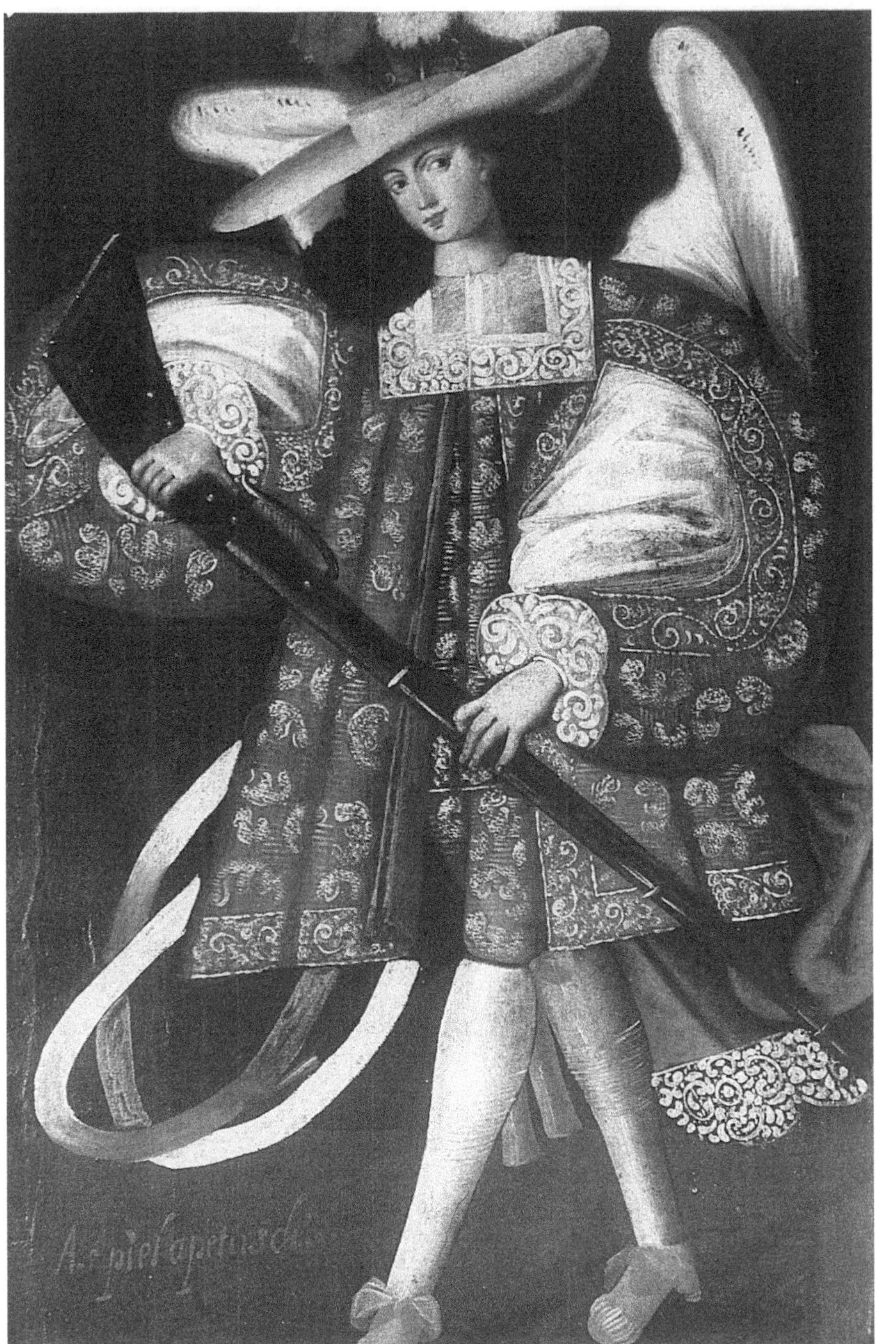

8 Follower of the 'Master of Calamarca', *Aspiel apetus Dei, arcángel arcabucero,* oil on canvas, late seventeenth century.

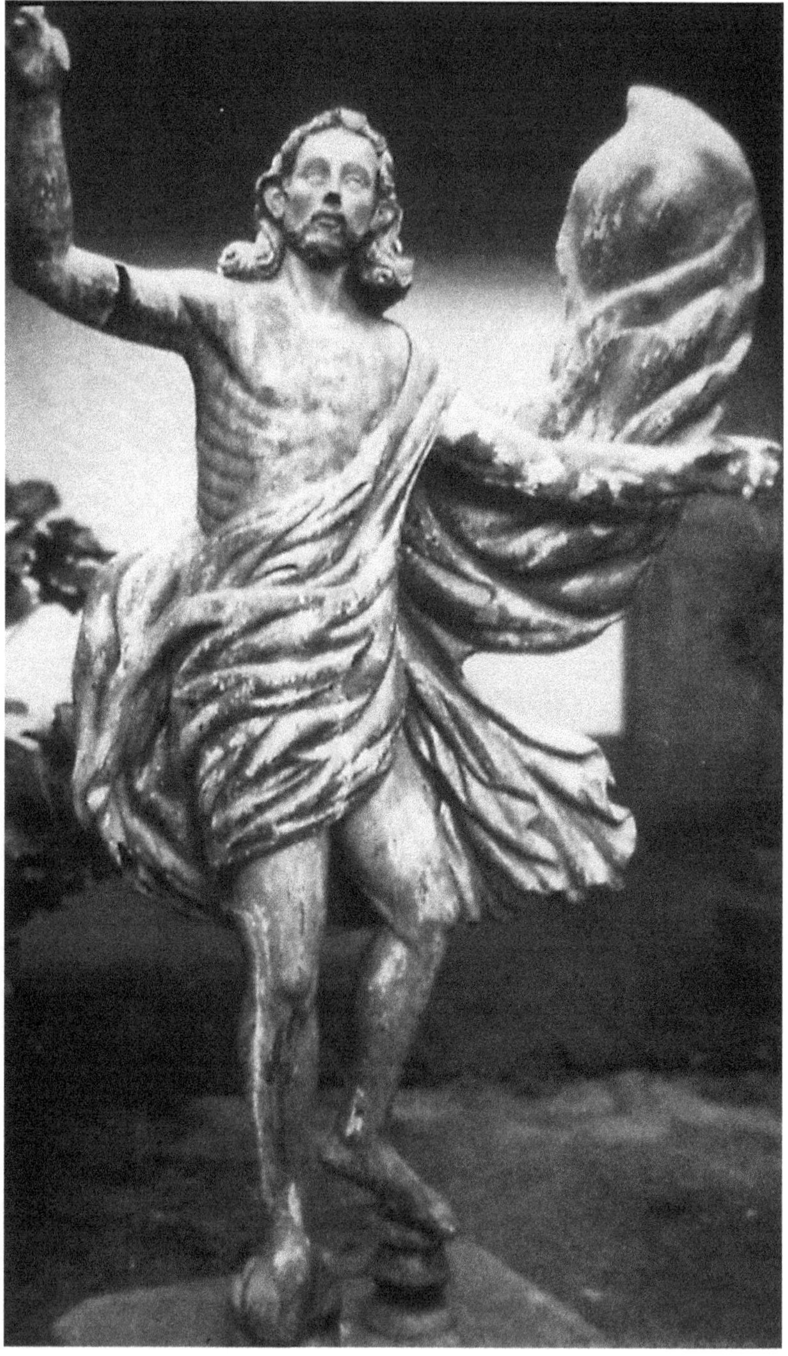

9 Guarani sculptor, Paraguay, *Risen Christ*, second quarter of eighteenth century. Santiago Museum, Paraguay.

by, the international Baroque. Gauvin Bailey makes the point that this artistic adoption only of certain aspects of Christian art is of a piece with the Guarani selectivity with regard to those aspects of Christianity itself which they adopted. He notes also the serene monumentality of their Christian figures, in sharp contrast to the affective and tortured images of Hispanic derivation, and again attributes this to the calmly visionary aspects of Christianity which the Guarani people chose to adopt. Many aspects of the Guarani figures correspond to the conventions of baroque Europe, but the handling of the drapery is almost defiantly non-naturalistic.[87] Bailey's description of the handling of the drapery on a statue of *Santa María de la Cabeza* now in the Santiago Museum, Paraguay, is worth quoting in full:

> But the static nature of this figure is completely counteracted by her garments. Her dress churns with concentric energy, drawn into a whirlpool that is driven by powerful, wavelike folds, yet nevertheless remains perfectly contained and tightly controlled.[88]

And his thoughts on the sculptures of the Guarani people extend in their importance far beyond his immediate subject:

> Such questions again force us to go beyond concepts such as 'folk' or 'primitive' art and examine how these works might represent a distinctive dialect of the common Late Renaissance and Baroque language that is equally indigenous and part of that global phenomenon.[89]

Hybrid arts of New France; obsidian nativity; Christmas at Macao

It is worth meditating on this formulation, 'the common Late Renaissance and Baroque language that is equally indigenous and part of that global phenomenon', as we consider one last work of hybrid art from the Americas, this time from Canada: the wooden altar frontal in the church of Notre-Dame de Lorette, Wendake, from the beginning of the eighteenth century, with its literal overlay of an international shallow-relief carving of the Virgin and Child, foliage and cherubs over a wholly indigenous scratch-carved background with a depiction of a mission with a church, a Huron woman worshipping and two bark wigwams.[90]

*

Christmas is a locus of cultural hybridity in the Old World as the whole unstoppable tradition of the Neapolitan *praesepio* demonstrates[91] – even Corelli's Christmas Concerto, with its reminiscences of the shepherd

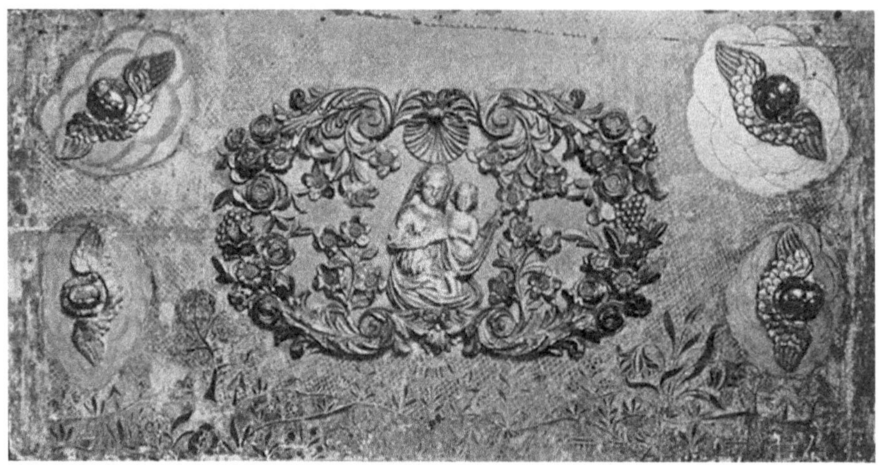

10 Carved wooden altar frontal, Notre-Dame-de-Lorette,
Wendake, Canada, early eighteenth century.

musicians in the streets of Rome, is an action of *mestissage* between
European popular and elite traditions. A remarkable example of the
layering of the arts of Europe and the Americas is a group of three
religious paintings by Bartolomé Esteban Murillo (*c.* 1618–82) – a *Nativity*
in Houston, Texas,[92] and an *Agony in the garden* and a *Penitent St Peter
kneeling before Christ at the column*[93], both in the Louvre. They are
painted not on canvas, but on Mexican obsidian mirrors, the sacred
'smoking mirrors' of the Aztec god Tezcatlipoca.[94] These are haunting
objects, raising many questions, not all of them easily answered.

The deep black of the obsidian is used to represent night in these
paintings, a darkness which dominates all three compositions. The *Agony*
represents the night vigil before Christ's Passion; the *Christ at the column is* not a representation of a moment in scriptural narrative, but a
meditation-picture in which St Peter, as paradigmatic repentant sinner,
kneels before the bleeding Christ.[95]

It is difficult to apprehend the precise intention of this group of paintings. On the one hand, they are very much a part of the baroque
aesthetic of the marvellous, of found landscapes and prodigious representations in split stones, as described in great detail by the Jesuit
savant Athanasius Kircher in his *Mundus Subterraneus.*[96] On the other,
the pagan and sacred origin of the obsidian is very much present underlying the Christian artefacts. These 'smoking mirrors' had 'long been
an instrument of divination and sorcery in central America' but, as

Meslay's comprehensive article also points out, by the time that Murillo superimposed his Christian images on the obsidian, 'a vision of a confrontation between Spanish and Pre-Columbian cultures is probably an anachronistically romantic one . . . The colonisation of Mexico and its forced Christianisation were old history by this date.'[97] An interim placing of these objects might relate them to those Mexican festivals and writings which represented the Aztec past as a formative, if transformed, part of the Mexican Christian present: the world of Sigüenza y Góngora and Ixtlilxóchitl.

Murillo's use of figurations in the stone is a recognition of a curiosity, a ready-made element of representation which he renders specific as the depiction of light. In the Louvre *Agony* he has composed his image so that some flecks of whiteness in the stone are positioned so as to suggest the first light of dawn in an otherwise profound darkness.

Even more, in the Houston *Nativity*, baroque ingenuity in the use of materials and baroque permeability between different media of representation unite the craft of the mirror-polisher in central Mexico with that of the painter in Seville. The Holy Family occupy the foreground, attended by the shadowy depictions of the ox and ass. The black gleam of the volcanic glass suggests the darkness of the stable and the surrounding night. But there are vertical inclusions in the obsidian, streaks of paler lustre running from top to bottom which are made to appear as rays of light descending from a group of cherubs who tumble through a bright cloud high in the picture space. In contrast to the sombre overlay of dark reflection with agony and penitence in the two Louvre pictures, this Christmas picture is playing with the marvellous. In the same spirit of sacred play, marble panels in the Jesuit church of St Charles Borromeo in Antwerp, their swirling patterns already suggesting mountain landscapes, are fixed as representations by the addition of painted figures of saints and hermits. The altar rails of that church are ornamented with emphatic carvings of the grain-plants of Africa and the Americas, expressing the universality of the Eucharist, the universal possibilities of the signs presented by art and nature. Thus too Murillo's paint overlays the sacred obsidian artefact by transforming it into the deep night of Christ's passion or the bright night of his nativity. The Christmas *villancicos* of the Americas are even more permeable than other festivals to popular and indigenous elements. There could be no more conclusive testimony to baroque internationalism than the three continents which come together in the lines of the Chinese Jesuit poet Wu Li as he describes, in Classical Chinese, Africans dancing their own dances before the Christmas crib in the Jesuit church in Macao:[98]

> A thousand lanterns glitter from a cliff of tiny trees:
> brocades forming cloudy peaks, candles forming flowers.
> They decorate these winter mountains and all come to enjoy:
> Black men's dancing feet keep time to the guitar.

Notes

1 Cf. Eugenio Lo Sardo (ed.), *Athanasius Kircher, il museo del mondo* (Rome: de Luca, 2001), pp. 250–3; Daniel Stolzenberg (ed.), *The Great Art of Knowing: The Baroque Encyclopaedia of Athanasius Kircher* (Stanford: Stanford University Libraries, 2001).

2 Cf. also Patrick Mauriès, *Cabinets of Curiosities* (London: Thames and Hudson, 2002).

3 Sor Juana Inés de la Cruz, *Obras completas,* ed. Francisco Monterde (Mexico City: Porrua, 1989), p. 200.

4 Jonathan Chaves, *Singing of the Source Nature and God in the Poetry of the Chinese Painter Wu Li* (Honolulu: Hawaii University Press, 1993), p. 134.

5 Information from Prof. James Knowles. His source is East Sussex Record Office, Glyne MS 314.

6 Detlef Heikamp, *Mexico and the Medici* (Florence: Edam, 1972), p. 34, quoting the 1539 Medici inventory. There was also feather-work in Habsburg collections in Vienna and Innsbruck, cf. Alfred Auer, *Ambras Castle* (Milan: Electa/Vienna Kunsthistorisches Museum, 2000).

7 His statement, in its original Spanish, is the epigraph to this book.

8 French text and translation in Introduction p. 9; Spanish text quoted as epigraph.

9 *Epistolae* 2.1, 156–7.

10 Bailey, *Between Renaissance and Baroque*; Bailey, *Art on the Jesuit Missions*; O'Malley and Bailey (eds), *The Jesuits and the Arts*. A case-study of Jesuit cultural translation is found in Bailey *The Jesuits and the Grand Mogul: Renaissance Art at the Imperial Court of India* (Washington: Smithsonian Institution, 1992). Bailey has discussed the hybrid art of the Mogul seventeenth century so fully that I omit any further reference here to its felicitous hybridities: illusionistic baroque miniatures surrounded by the patterned and calligraphic page-borders of the Indo-Islamic tradition.

11 Croce, *Storia dell'etá barocca in Italia,* p. 4; illuminating discussion of the idea of Jesuit baroque in Bailey, *Between Renaissance and Baroque*, pp. 6, 30.

12 This openness to others is very much part of that cultural system which gave the early modern Society its identity: contemporary references identify this attitude simply as part of 'how we do things', *modus noster procedendi.*

13 John Prest, *The Garden of Eden* (New Haven and London: Yale University Press, 1981), pp. 7–9.

14 Stonyhurst College, MS A.v.4. Davidson and Sweeney (eds), *The Collected Poems of St Robert Southwell*, p. 88.

15 Louis Richeome SJ, *Les Oevres du R. père Louis Richeome . . . revues par l'autheur avant sa mort* (Paris: Sebastien Cramoisy, 1628), p. 461.

16 See my article 'The Jesuit Garden', in O'Malley SJ and others (eds), *The Jesuits II: Cultures, Sciences and the Arts* (Toronto: Toronto University Press, 2006), pp. 86–107.

17 Richeome, *Oevres*, p. 463.

18 *Ibid.*, p. 463.

19 *Ibid.*, p. 480.

20 *Ibid.*, p. 480.

21 *Ibid.*, p. 480.

22 Johannis Eusebius Nieremberg, *Historia Naturae* (Antwerp: Plantijn-Moretus, 1635), pp. 299–300.

23 Thomas Downing Kendrick, *Mary of Ágreda, the Life and Legend of a Spanish Nun* (London: Routledge, 1967), pp. 46–56. There are about 5,000 folios relating to Maria as a candidate for canonisation in the archives of the Congregation of Rites in the Archivio Segreto Vaticano – an unrivalled source for the hopes and beliefs of early modern Spain. The document which first made the whole narrative public, Alonso de Benavides, *Memorial of 1630*, has been published (Washington DC: Academy of American Franciscan History, 1954).

24 *Ibid.*, p. 302.

25 *Ashrea: or, the Grove of Beatitudes, represented in Emblemes: and, by the Art of Memory, to be read on our Blessed Saviour Crucifi'd: with Considerations and meditations suitable to every Beatitude, and to the holy time of Lent* (London: 'W.P.', 1665).

26 *Ibid.*, sig. A2v.

27 The cornel tree; the Indian fig tree; the myrrh tree; clove tree; banana (called 'Adam's apple'); the fig; the honeysuckle; the vine: mapped on to His nakedness; His bowed head; His eyes; His mouth; His wounded side; His wounded heart; His hands; His feet.

28 *Ashrea*, p. 17.

29 See Ijsewijn, *Companion to Neo-Latin Studies*, p. 298. Abad ended his life as an exile in Italy after the suppression of the Society of Jesus in 1773, as did another great Jesuit poet of the Americas, Rafael Landivar from Guatemala, who wrote the peerless Georgics of the Americas in his *Rusticatio Mexicana* (1781–82).

30 Marc Lescarbot, *Les Muses de la Nouvelle France*, ed. Bernard Emont (Paris: Harmattan, 2004), p. 134.

31 *Ibid.*, pp. 141–3.

32 'This town lieth upon a great river, wherunto belong many boats and canoes, wherin those Indians have been taught to act sea fights with great dexterity, and to represent the nymphs of Parnassus, Neptune, Aeolus and the rest of the heathenish gods and goddesses, so that they are a wonder of their whole nation.' Also they act in sham fights over canvas castles, which Gage thinks is giving them military skills which they could use against 'the Spaniards and the Friars'. Thomas Gage, *The English-American* (London: Routledge, 1828 [1648]), p. 165.

33 Cf. Dietrich Briesemeister, 'Inszenierungen des Fremden in Frankreich und Portugal (1550/1619)', in *Die ganze Welt ist Bühne, Festscrift für Klaus Pörti* (Frankfurt: Peter Lang, 2003), pp. 51–69. I must acknowledge here the generosity and good advice of Professor Briesemeister, his gift of several works about the literature of the baroque Americas, and his kind encouragment of my work.

34 António de Sousa SJ, *Relación de la real Tragicomedia* (Lisbon: Jorge Rodriguez, 1620), p. 59. A Portuguese translation is printed alongside the Tupí original. The admixture of Latin, vernaculars and various creoles in this play is a true representation of baroque universality.

35 Alexander Pope, 'Windsor Forest', in *The Works of Mr Alexander Pope* (London: Lintot, 1717), pp. 70–1.

36 Sor Juana Inés de la Cruz, *Obras completas*, p. 235.

37 Fernando de Alva Ixtlilxóchitl, *Obras historicas*, ed. Alfredo Chavero (Mexico City: Editora Nacional, 1952), pp. 235–6.

38 Alfonso Méndez Plancarte, *Poetas Novohispanos, primer siglo (1521–1621)* (Mexico City: University of Mexico, 1964), pp. 171–2. The textual history of these verses would appear to be very complex, and this text contains a good number of the editor's emendations.

39 *Ibid.*, pp. 175–7, 'Romance del Rey Don Sancho'.

40 The contrast with the experience of Anglophone America is considerable: the translations involved in that very different negotiation did not produce a hybrid third term readily, if at all.

41 Carlos de Sigüenza y Góngora, *Glorias de Querétaro en la Nueva Congregación Eclesiástica de María Santissima de Guadelupe* (Mexico City, 1680), pp. 47–51.

42 Careri, *Baroques*, p. 24.

43 The passage is translated in full in Irving A. Leonard, *Baroque Times in Old Mexico* (Ann Arbor: University of Michigan Press, 1966), pp. 128–9.

44 See Chapter 3, pp. 166–80 below for an extended discussion of the baroque motif of the heart.

45 David Brading, *The First America* (Cambridge: Cambridge University Press, 1991), p. 342.

46 There is also a little-known sequence of twelve paintings of this kind, of the Inca rulers of Peru ending with Pizarro, dated to the seventeenth century, as well as a stupendous eighteenth-century Cuzco painting of the Virgin with saints, in the collections of Stonyhurst College.

47　*Ibid.*, p. 403.

48　For this whole tradition see the excellent discussion in Teresa Gisbert, *Iconografiá y mitos indigenas en el arte* (La Paz: Linea Editorial, Fundación BHN, Editorial Gisbert y Cia, 1994), pp. 128–40 and her plate facing p. 128 and illustration no. 130.

49　Andrés Pérez de Ribas SJ, *History of the Triumphs of our Holy Faith*, trans. Daniel T. Reff, Moureen Ahearn and Richard K. Danford (Tucson: University of Arizona Press, 1999), pp. 714–15.

50　*Ibid.*, p. 715.

52　Bernardo Illari, *Fiesta Criolla*, CD and booklet issued by *Chemins du Baroque* (K617139).

53　Sor Juana, *Obras*, p. 231. 'Allá va, cuerpo de Cristo,/de esgrima el mayor maestro'.

54　Much information on this 1680 festival, and a full text and translation of the second part of it, which was written by Sor Juana de la Cruz will be found in (eds), Watanabe-O'Kelly, Helen Mulryne, J.R. Margant Shewring, *Europa Triumphans: Court and Civic Festivals in Early Modern Europe* (Aldershot: MHRA and Ashgate, 2004) vol. 2, pp. 345–434.

55　Peter Davidson, 'The Theatrum for Claudia de'Medici, Urbino 1621', in *Festivals of the Renaissance and After*, ed. Elizabeth Goldring and J.R. Mulryne (Aldershot: Ashgate, 2002), pp. 311–34. 'The Entry of Mary Stewart into Edinburgh, 1581, and Other Ambiguities', in *Renaissance Studies*, 9:4 (December 1995), pp. 416–29.

56　*Ibid.*, p. 365.

57　*Ibid.*, p. 371.

58　Carlos de Sigüenza y Góngora, *Teatro de virtudes politicas*, in *Seis obras*, ed. I.A. Leonard and William G. Bryant (Caracas: Biblioteca Ayacucho, 1984), p. 172.

59　*Ibid.*, p. 17; *Los siglos de oro in los virrenatos de América*, pp. 181–3.

60　Sigüenza y Góngora, *Teatro de virtudes políticas*, pp. 179–82.

61　*Ibid.*, p. 181.

62　*Ibid.*, p. 197.

63　*Ibid.*, pp. 210–11.

64　Bailey, *Art on the Jesuit Missions*, pp. 75–6.

65　*Ibid.*, p. 76.

66　*Ibid.*, p. 77.

67　*Ibid.*, pp. 79–80.

68　Midil Beurdeley, *Peintres Jésuites en chine* (Arceuil: Anthèse, 1997), p. 31.

69　Nicolas Standaert, 'Jesuit Corporate Culture as Shaped by the Chinese' in O'Malley, *et al.*, *The Jesuits*, p. 356.

70　Bailey, *Art on the Jesuit Missions*, p. 89.

71　*Ibid.*, p. 97.

72　Gauvin Alexander Bailey, 'Jesuit Art and Architecture in Asia', in O'Malley and Bailey (eds), *The Jesuits and the Arts*, p. 312.

73 Standaert, 'Jesuit Corporate Culture', p. 356.

74 Standaert, 'Jesuit Corporate Culture', p. 359.

75 Sabine MacCormack, *Religion in the Andes: Vision and Imagination in Early Colonial Peru* (Princeton: Princeton University Press, 1991).

76 Sabine MacCormack, 'Grammar and Virtue: The Formation of a Cultural and Missionary Program by the Jesuits in early Colonial Peru', in *The Jesuits II*, ed. O'Malley, Bailey, Harris and Kennedy (Toronto: Toronto University Press, 2006), pp. 576–601.

77 Sor Juana Inés de la Cruz, *Obras completas* pp. 383 *et seq.*

78 Bailey, *Art of Colonial Latin America*, pp. 101–2.

79 There are many indigenous elements surviving into the twentieth century in the *penitente* rituals of New Mexico and in the representations of saints by New Mexican *santeros*, the *crucifixus* sometimes has a heart visible through the ribcage, which can be moved. Cf. Thomas J. Steele SJ, *Santos and Saints, the Religious Folk Art of New Mexico* (Santa Fé: Ancient City Press, 1982).

80 Cf Bailey, *Art on the Jesuit Missions*, pp. 96–7.

81 This whole question is splendidly documented in Gisbert, *Iconografiá y mitos indigenas*, pp. 17–22.

82 European engravings of musket-drill would seem to constitute one source for these hybrid images. A specific example which seems likely to have played a part in so doing is Jacob de Gheyn, *Waffen handlung von den roren, musquetten undt spiessen* (The Hague, 1608).

83 Museo Nacional de Arte, La Paz, Bolivia. See the excellent discussion by Luisa Elena Alcalá in *Los Siglos de Oro*, pp. 351–4. See also Gisbert, *Iconografiá y mitos indigenas*, pp. 86–8.

84 The definitive work on the angels of the Andes is Ángel Kalenbery *et al. El retorno de los angeles* (exhibition catalogue, Montevideo: Museo National de Artes Visuales, 2000). The essay in it 'Angeles y arcángeles' by Teresa Gisbert and José de Mesa (pp. 25–31) is the classic summary of the subject.

85 The dealer in Lima from whom I bought a contemporary representation of the angel Laeiel priming his musket, described him as a demonifuge, but his older function would seem to be as protector in the hours of the night.

86 Bérchez (ed.), *Los siglos de oro*, pp. 365 *et seq.*

87 *Ibid.*, pp. 164–9. I have, clearly, nothing to add to Bailey's comprehensive account, but the conclusion which he draws from his description of the art of the Guarani people is a keystone of the argument which this book seeks to construct.

88 *Ibid.*, pp. 166–7.

89 *Ibid.*, p. 165.

90 O'Malley and Bailey (eds), *The Jesuits and the Arts*, pp. 370–1.

91 Nina Gockerell, *Nacimentos* (Munich: Bavarian National Museum/Taschen, 1998); Roberto De Simone, *Il presepe popolare napoletano* (Turin: Einaudi, 1998).

92 Inventory number is 94.1143; the work is dated *c.* 1665–70.

93 Inventory numbers 931 and 932 respectively. There is a comprehensive doscussion of the two paintings in the Louvre: Olivier Meslay, 'Murillo and "Smoking Mirrors"', *The Burlington Magazine*, 143: 1175 (February, 2001), pp. 73–9. The Louvre paintings are also discussed in the context of the European reception of Mexican obsidian mirrors, and of the black mirror as a magical object, in Arnaud Maillet, *Le miroir noir* (Paris: Kargo/L'Éclat, 2005), pp. 24–8, 39–46. Perhaps the most celebrated of these obsidian mirrors in a European collection is the 'Devil's Looking-Glass' in the British Museum, which is believed to have been used as a scrying-glass by the English *magus* John Dee.

94 Analysis of the obsidian supports of Murillo's pictures confirms that they are from Ucareo or Zinapécuaro, that is, from the same central-Mexican sources as the 'smoking mirrors' in many collections worldwide. Cf. Thomas Calligaro *et al.*, 'PIXE Reveals that Two Murillo Masterpieces Were Painted on Mexican Obsidian Slabs', *Nuclear Instruments in Physics Research*, 240: 1–2 (2005), pp. 576–82.

95 The repentance of St Peter is the subject of a long, widely read meditation by the English Jesuit martyr St Robert Southwell. Cf., *Collected Poems of St Robert Southwell*, ed. Davidson and Sweeney.

96 Athanasius Kircher, *Mundus Subterraneus* (Amsterdam, 1665), vol. 2, pp. 30–48. Cf. especially p. 47 for Kircher's description of a 'miraculous' naturally formed image of the Virgin and Child discovered in a cave in Chile.

97 Meslay, 'Murillo and "Smoking Mirrors"', pp. 73 and 79.

98 Chaves, *Singing of the Source*, p. 153. Wu Li adds the note: 'When the blacks sing, they move their feet in a dance which keeps time with the sounds of the guitar. This all takes place around the time of Jesus's birth.'

III

The shape of the baroque world: learning the Baroque

Having argued for the essential hybridity of the baroque world, and having offered examples mostly from places which would be thought conventionally 'remote' from cultural centres, I would like to develop the argument that, because of its flexibility and adaptibility, the Baroque lends itself particularly to what one might call *cultural devolution*.

The shape of the baroque cultural world is not by any means the shape of the cultural world after the emergence of the nation states, with their emphasis on the metropolis as the location of artistic training and achievement. Indeed, the cultural centres of the Baroque can be places conventionally (or retrospectively) identified as very remote indeed, and yet function wholly successfully within the baroque system of the arts. The two examples which I would advance here, two out of potential thousands, are both concerned with the production of distinctive baroque music which, like the Andean paintings considered above (pp. 127–31), fuse the international manner with a local vernacular. My examples are the 'reduction' music of the Jesuit settlements in the jungles of South America and the chamber music of eighteenth-century Scotland.

I move from these to the consideration of two bodies of baroque architectural drawing, both accomplished and stupendous combinations of local and international elements, and both likewise chosen out of thousands of potential examples for their (again by conventional mappings) remote points of origin. These are the imaginary projects for the renovation of his own lands (and indeed of the imagined London of the restored King James VIII and III) made in his migratory continental exile by the Jacobite Earl of Mar; and a not-dissimilar body of work, drawings of the greatest fantasy and invention for numerous estate buildings and for the building of a complete baroque town, all proceeding from a small country-house circle centred on Birr Castle in County Offaly in Ireland. The inventive Baroque of both of these sequences of drawings (and indeed their use of local and vernacular elements) relate them back to a work of canonical English architecture actually realised – John Wood's Circus in Bath – which draws on a wholly baroque tradition of 'hieroglyphics' (pictograms which are not, in fact, Egyptian hieroglyphs) to convey its intended meaning.

The proposed model of the baroque world is not of a hierarchy or chain of command originating from the European capitals, but rather of a network embracing infinite and distinctive local centres of production. This model works even within Italy itself, with its multiple centres of cultural production, each town and city with an *accademia* or cathedral or university which was itself a nexus of the baroque arts. Similarly, every town worldwide which had a Jesuit college would of necessity, by the customs of the Society, have functioned as a centre for oratory, exhibitions of emblem material and drama. Architecture is inevitably the most devolved of the arts, but what is not completely appreciated is the degree to which, in the great age of the magisterial pattern-books (Pozzo, Gibbs, Palladio), the local interpretation of these models was in fact idiosyncratic, aware and consciously localising.

In this context, it is worth remembering the degree to which dramatic regional variations occur within the territories which are now Italy and Spain. Lecce especially, capital of the Salentine peninsula of Puglia, springs to mind as a centre which not only produced a highly distinctive local baroque architecture, spreading a damask of fine detail across the breadth of the façades of its major buildings, comparable to (and yet radically different from) the façade decorations of the mestizo-Baroque of the Americas, but also trained Antonio Verrio, paradoxically one of the leading wall-painters to the elite of Georgian London.[1]

It is crucial to the apprehension of this argument to realise that the baroque arts can be practised, devised and taught within a relatively small compass, on a relatively small scale. This is unsurprising in a world of regional cultural centres of modest size, at least by the standards of the metropolis of the nineteenth century. From this perspective, the Baroque of Potosí or Montréal is not to be interpreted as a provincial dilution of the Baroque of Madrid or Paris, but rather as an autonomous idiom, drawing on local as well as metropolitan traditions. There is an anachronistic danger in superimposing the idea of the metropolis on a world of regional cultural centres. The idea that all regional versions of the baroque style must be imitative dilutions is again a product of the retrospective distortions of thinking about the early modern world from the perspective of the nineteenth century nation state, which by its nature strives to produce a clear primary loyalty in its citizens superseding the ambiguous, multidirectional loyalties of individual localities.

The idea enshrined in the nineteenth-century *Bildungsroman* of the need for artists to leave the provinces and make their way to the capital city, is not relevant to the early modern world. In a *Bildungsroman* of the eighteenth century, on the other hand, a talented individual might choose to make her or his way, for example, to a dukedom where there was a celebrated theatre company. Baroque culture was infinitely more culturally devolved in a geographical sense than we can comprehend. The plurality of dukedoms and republics which were merged in the nation states of the nineteenth century had all functioned, at least to some degree, as autonomous cultural centres. Universities, colleges, painters' studios and musical societies of considerable cultural significance flourished at some geographical distance from centres of political power. An excellent example of this is the exiled English Catholic colleges at St Omer and Douai on the frontiers of France and the Spanish Netherlands. Both were centres of literary and controversial writing from the exiled Catholic community, and they also functioned as centres of the production of recusant Latin drama. There are documented instances of this drama being appreciatively revived in Rome after an initial performance in Flanders – in a city which is one of *the* paradigmatic cultural centres of the European imagination.

Before the expansions of road and railway in the nineteenth century, the geography defined by the slowness of land travel and the uncertainty of sea travel reinforced an infinitely greater concentration of cultural production in regional centres. But these geographical factors also worked for the preservation of the local tradition within which the architectural pattern-books and the new musical scores could feed into the baroque culture of that particular place. Above all, this redrawing of the map of cultural centres radically refocuses the precedence of Old World and New World: much of the real energy and achievement in all the baroque arts was centred in 'colonial' territories' and the more the Baroque is studied the more the truth of this becomes evident. The Anglophone empires neither set nor followed a universal pattern.

In the baroque world each of these cultural centres had its dignity, and each could appeal equally to the dignity conferred by the antiquities which lay at the root of the cultures of the baroque world. It is wholly serious to call the Aberdonian pupil of van Dyck '*Apelles noster*'[2] or to dignify the Mexican historian Ixtlilxóchitl as 'the Livy of Anahuac' or to identify Sarbievius as 'the Sarmantian Horace' or, indeed, to compliment Gironda Cerrini of Perugia as '*Sappho nostra*'. Only in retrospect, and in local self-deprecation, can the provincial self-hatred, the inevitable by-product of the rise of the metropolis as an exclusive cultural centre, make such designations grow even potentially facetious or risible.

Music is potentially the most devolved of the performing arts: works of the first quality do not necessarily demand more than a few performers; many are for one performer alone. Music can function *pars pro toto* as a way of exploring the idea of the devolved cultural centre, of the devolved culture. At the same time, music is the art in which the mingling of the indigenous with the international to produce a style distinctive to one centre is perhaps most apprehensible. If we explore this idea without anachronistic prejudice, a considerable quantity of musical activity of the early modern period comes into parallel with the biculturalities we have already observed in the verbal and visual arts.

The problem created by cultural history based on the nation state has left a corpus of music of the seventeenth and eighteenth centuries stranded between categories and therefore difficult to discuss and difficult to place. On the one hand, this repertory is perceived as a simplified or dilute version of the most complex works of the chief European musical centres (works written for exceptional groups of elite performers). On the other hand, from the perspective of the musical ethnologist of the twentieth century, music which combines elements of international with vernacular can be seen as simply 'tainted' or 'contaminated'. I would propose rather that, within the model of universal Baroque which this book advances, musical works exhibiting in varying degrees combinations of local and international styles should be seen as an expected or normal musical expression in the numerous *devolved* centres of cultural production which circled the baroque world.

Music in New France and New Spain

This approach is relevant to the music of the Jesuit missions in Canada, the operas and instrumental music of the 'reductions' (Jesuit towns) of the Amazonian forests, and the rich musical tradition poised between the vernacular and the international in the Celtic countries.

As is being increasingly demonstrated, in its sheer extent and richness, the musical life of colonial Ibero-America is directly comparable with that of many European countries (pp. 191–2). In the discussion of the festivals at Sucre in 1712, the degree to which the musical and cultural language of the Americas were becoming hybrid followed, in that urban setting, those elements of hybridity which had already entered festal and liturgical observance throughout the Hispanic world.

There is some seventeenth-century witness to a parallel musical development beginning in *la Nouvelle France*, the French settlements in what is now Canada: a musical manuscript from Québec contains not only sophisticated organ and choral music from the contemporary French repertory, but also locally composed works combining indigenous with international traditions.[3] The combination is almost like that of the altar-frontal discussed in Chapter II (see pp. 131–2): the Latin words are mostly set in a simple international style like the bas-relief carvings of the Virgin and angels, but two pieces from the *Office du Salut du Très Saint Sacrement chez les Indiens Abénakis*, like the scratch-carved background of the frontal, have a responsory form and richly lingering melodic movement which owes a great deal to indigenous musical modes. This music from New France shows a tradition in some ways halted before it reached its fullest development, and, like the visual arts from the same regions before they were cut off, already remarkable in its fusion of the indigenous with the international.

To see the development of a fully hybrid musical tradition, it is necessary to turn to the 'reduction' settlements of South America, especially in those territories once identified as the Jesuit 'republic' of Paraguay. These were towns into which the Jesuits gathered the indigenous peoples to protect them from the depredations of the 'San Paulistas', the slave-traders who infested the coasts and the river estuaries. The intensity of musical life in the reduction towns and the degree to which the indigenous people were instructed in and enabled to practise music, were remarkable.[4]

> From 1607 . . . until the expulsion of the Jesuits from the Spanish lands in 1767 . . . in what has been referred to as the Jesuit republic of Paraguay . . . virtually every town of about two thousand members boasted its own orchestra, and several of the larger towns were set up as conservatories or as factory towns for making musical intruments. As a result, the Jesuits were constantly asking their European colleagues to send the most recently composed music to the the townships.

Music in the Amerindian towns was encouraged to take root locally, in terms of performance, instrument-making and even composition. A repertory of liturgical and festal music grew up in the Jesuit territories, reflecting the very considerable activity in polyphonic as well as popular religious music throughout Ibero-America.

Among the most extraordinary discoveries is the survival of plentiful evidence of operatic activity in the 'reductions', with records of many operatic and festal performances, as well as fragmentary scores of two chamber operas and one complete chamber opera from the Jesuit settlements in what is now lowland Bolivia. Both the fragmentary operas – the very damaged *El Justo y el Pastor* and the recoverable *San Francisco Xavier* – have libretti partly in the indigenous language of the people for whom they were composed.

The most complete of these 'mission operas', which has been given the title *San Ignacio de Loyola*, has a Spanish text, although there are clear local elements in the imagery and dramaturgy. There is also very clear evidence of a long performance tradition in different centres of population, since there are variant scores surviving from different mission communities among the Chiquitano peoples: one from the community of Santa Ana y San Rafael,[5] and one from the town of San Ignacio in the territory of the Moxos people. The scores from the Chiquitano sources are deposited in the Archivo Musical de Chiquitos at Concepción.[6] This textual information is not merely of technical interest, but also a testimony to the extraordinary career of this chamber opera, composed initially by Europeans but explicitly for an Amerindian audience, an artistic offering to the indigenous people in what was esteemed in Europe the most prestigious art form at court or university.

The opera was preserved by a series of indigenous copyists. The decision to preserve it and keep a performance tradition alive was therefore made by indigenous Americans, after the suppression of the Jesuits. The earliest elements in the text are by the esteemed Italian composer Domenico Zipoli SJ, presumably dated by the final period of his life which was spent in the Americas, 1717–26; then there is a period of contribution from the Swiss Martin Schmid SJ, which can be dated between 1733–60. What is remarkable is that all subsequent copying, including quite possibly the addition of numbers to the second part of the opera, must have been carried out by indigenous musicians.

After the suppression of the Jesuits in 1773, the Chiquitano people were infinitely more open to exploitation and enslavement than they had been in the days of the reductions. Yet, in these times of adversity, the opera of *San Ignacio* was preserved, revised, and kept in repertory exclusively through the work of Chiquitano copyists and performers. The existence of multiple versions confirms that there were multiple places of performance. The copies made in the 1830s and again in the early twentieth century demonstrate the length of time for which the opera was preserved and performed, as Bernardo Illari argues, as an essential part of the Chiquitano cultural patrimony.

This is a bewildering (but magnificent) reverse of what might be expected from a musical transaction at a colonial frontier between peoples. Primarily, the indigenous peoples are offered the skills and training to mount a performance in what was the defining elite form of Europe (recent research would also suggest that in so far as the 'reduction' operas were educational or school pieces, they were in accord with the kind of school opera being offered at the elite Jesuit college in Vienna).[7] Given the demands of the last aria, in particular, with its highly ornamented vocal line and trumpet *obbligato*, it is clear that the level of musical education offered was of considerable sophistication.[8]

The action is brief, didactic and allegorical. In the first part, St Ignatius is depicted resisting the rather languid worldly temptations offered by a demon, whose apocryphal name of 'Luzbel' echoes the invented or apocryphal names of the angels of contemporary Andean painting, a theatrical type not unfamiliar to the Americas with their apotropaic *diablerias*. This dramatises Ignatius's choice to renounce his life as an aristocratic soldier and to become the founder of the Society of Jesus. In the second part he sends his companion St Francis Xavier on his mission to the Far East, a mission which becomes representative of the global scope of the Jesuits. Their parting is conveyed in a duet which uses many of the conventions of the operatic love-duet of the early eighteenth century, but shifts adroitly into the central section. The voices move towards unison and resolution as soon as the words '*Jesús amoroso*' (loving Jesus) are sung. The opera's action ends on their resolved duet as they sing of their confidence that Christ can transform all sorrow into the greatest happiness: '*convertirá el dolor/en gran contento*'. The commentator's virtuoso aria with trumpets follows, about the glorious banners of the Regiment of Jesus and the power of Ignatius and his successors to work for the salvation of the people.

There is one more unmistakably local reference in the text of the opera: European Christian imagery has the devil as a 'lion', the 'devil like a lion seeking for prey' is part of the text of the canonical hour of Compline which closes the day. Adapting this image to the pumas of the American rainforests, evil becomes, in the local word 'un tigre'. The text of the fourth aria of the first part of the opera begins:

Contra este tigre rampante
con mi Dios corre a pugnar,

y con mi escuadrón volante
te quiero guerra presentar.

[Against this rampant tiger, I run with my God to the fight; and with my
flying squadron I want to join battle.]

The process which begins in the opera of *San Ignacio de Loyola* reaches
a further degree of cultural development in the set of catechetical arias
and linking text called *San Francisco Xavier,* which is in the Chiquitana
language, and sung by two people representing St Ignatius and St Francis
Xavier. It is not clear whether the linking text was designed to be
spoken or whether recitative settings have been lost: certainly there is
considerable damage to the surviving score.[9]

Despite the sophistication and the markedly hybrid feeling of its music,
this piece is dramatically very much more static and catechetic than is
the opera of *San Ignacio.* St Francis Xavier, the great Jesuit missionary
to the Far East, who died on his mission, arrives in heaven where he
meets St Ignatius, the founder of the order. From there onwards
their colloquy, their arias and duets are all catechetic: explanations
of Christian belief, elaborations on the felicity of the blessed. These
descriptions of the felicity of the blessed continue until the last duet
of the two saints, in 6/8 time, close in its idioms to music for the dance:

Irikibo ñana Iyai
Yiroti ichimo aesai
Irikibo ñana Ichupa
Yirotanu aesa ape.[10]

[You are called eternal father. I will come to join myself to you. Your
name 'my God' forever. I will come to you in heaven.]

The last fragmentary piece of spoken dialogue identifies the mission
of St Francis Xavier to the East as the forerunner of the Jesuit mission
to the Chiquito people.

A heavenly messenger, like those who appeared to Ignatius in the
opera of *San Ignacio,* addresses the two saints in turn, telling Ignatius
that he has been given literally 'five ears of [American] maize' and has
returned a rich harvest. To the travelling Francis Xavier the angel says
that the feet of the bringer of the gospel are blessed (from Isaiah 52:7),
and then, universalising his missions, he says, 'Aiñataityo au nimi
unama chikito, kaima ariakupo auna Yesañi'[11] ('You have visited the kingdom of the Chiquitos, now enter my heavenly kingdom').

One of the chief local markers of the score of *San Francisco Xavier*
is the composer's delight in repetitions of two-bar phrases, with

ornamentation of the repeated element, very extensively deployed throughout the opera. These short units of repetition are consistently used within the overall conventional *da capo* structure of the baroque aria. The vocal lines particularly tend to consist of two or four bar units, inevitably followed by a *ritornello* of equal length on the same harmonic progression, but offering a variant of the same melodic shape or simply melismatic ornament on the phrase which has just been sung. To some extent this musical procedure is well within the scope of the metropolitan Baroque: echo effects and, indeed, echo choruses are part of the international repertory. But the degree to which voices or voice and ritornello occur throughout this score in succint echo-units of imitation clearly also displays elements of musical aesthetic and practice indigenous to the Chiquitanos themselves.

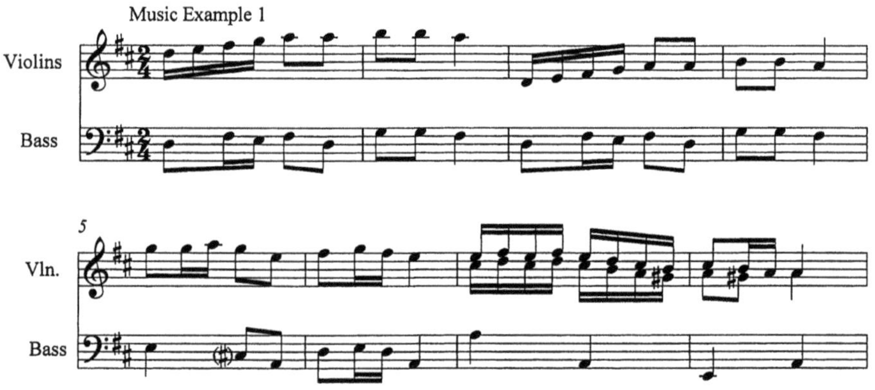

Music example 1: Nawrot, p. 31.

The degree to which music and musical performance defined the culture of these remote 'reductions' – whose sheer level of cultural achievement is, in itself, a powerful argument for the possibility of the baroque arts proceeding from cultural centres geographically far remote from any metropolis – can be seen in the description of the celebrations for the coronation of Charles IV of Spain, held in the reduction town of San Borja, in what is now Uruguay, in November 1760. Members of the colonial army acted in three comedies; there were bullfights and sung church services; and the indigenous peoples of four reduction towns performed operas.[12] Interestingly, the anonymous officer who recorded the festival in verse said that the church music of the combined musicians of the reductions was the equal to any celebrated music of Europe: '. . . en todas circunstancias igualaba,/A Musica de Europa mas famosa'. The banquets were accompanied by 'celestial' music. Fireworks closed each day. As in the description of an improvised triumphal arch quoted in Chapter II (see p. 14 above) the plaza in front of the church was ornamented with arches of green branches lit with little lamps when night fell – 'arcos esmaltados con Laureles'. The Guarani sang their four operas 'with skill and art to move admiration'. The subjects of the operas are recorded, although no scores have hitherto come to light: *The King of Egypt, King Philip V,* and two *Nativities.*

The character of the festival was culturally yet more hybrid than it first appears, in that all the time not occupied by services, operas, bullfights and comedies was spent in the performance of indigenous dances in honour of the coronation of the distant King and Queen.

Even after the 1773 expulsion of the Jesuits and the destruction of many of the 'reductions', the musical traditions they had fostered amongst the Canichana and Moxo peoples found expression in musical composition. Three sets of songs and cantatas are recorded from the winter of 1790,[13] all from the former Jesuit territories among the Guarani and Moxo. All are on the occasion of the coronation of the King. The district officer's report accompanying the music sent on from the Moxos (this music is now in the General Archive of the Indies in Seville) mentions 'more than thirty-five flutes and violins which compose the orchestra of this town . . . of La Trinidad, playing in alternation with a warlike consort of native instruments'.[14] A fair copy of music from this town was sent to Spain, signed by the composers Francisco Semo, Marcelino Icho and Juan Josef Nosa. Their songs for the name-day of the Queen contain graceful assertions that the festival may be celebrated more magnificently in Spain, but nowhere can it be celebrated with more sincerity than among the people of La Trinidad and San Xavier. Four arias for solo voice and two obbligato violins with continuo lead to a final chorus for three two-part choirs with violin and continuo.[15]

There are also songs in praise of Charles IV and Queen Maria Luisa from the Canichana people of Pueblo San Pedro. Throughout the texts are in the indigenous languages and the music is in a manner unique to the region, being a local development and variation of over a century of musical contact with the international manner, a contact which may have been greatly reduced in the 1770s with the suppression of the Jesuits.

These praises of a European monarch in a tongue far removed from the language of their court and in a literary style essentially derived from local traditions of praise-poetry is not a phenomenon confined to Ibero-America, any more than is musical hybridity of style. Many cultures can coexist within a state or an empire. Profession of loyalty to a ruler can work with diverse cultural forms and artistic traditions.

Scotland: praise-poetry and hybrid music

In early modern Scotland, there can be found equivalents of the Moxos and Canichana praises of the Queen of Spain, in those Gaelic praise-poems where the formal apparatus of the Celtic bardic tradition is brought into play for the laudation of the house of Stuart. A fine example comes from the poem of Iain Lom (John Macdonald) on the coronation of Charles II:

> Thug Dia dhuinn furtachd
> As na cliabhan druidte
> 'N uair dh'iarr sin iuchair a ghàrraidh
>
> 'S a Theàrlach ig Stiùbhairt,
> Ma chuaidh an crùn ort,
> Dia 'na fhear-stiùrdigh air t'àrdraich.[16]

> [God has delivered us from the closed beast-pens, when we asked of Him the key of His garden. And young Charles Stuart, if you have been crowned, may God be the steersman of your ship.]

This is no naive utterance, any more than are the birthday cantatas of Pueblo San Pedro: Iain Lom is thought to have studied the baroque literary and philosophical curriculum which acted as as the preliminary to study for the priesthood in the universities of Spain. As with Pierce Ferriter in Galway, he has access to Latin and to the diverse voices open to a Celtic poet of the Baroque. It is only a matter of circumstance that Iain Lom expressed himself in bardic Gaelic: the Biblioteca Apostolica in Rome preserves a number of pamphlets, all Latin poems of praise for the house of Stuart, written by another Catholic exile, James Alban Gibbs (1611–77), who had stayed on in Rome.[17]

The consideration of the plural possibilities open to a poet in the Celtic countries leads us inevitably to the hybridity manifested in the music of those countries, particularly in the eighteenth century. Much of this activity has simply fallen below the radar of cultural historians. If we consider that hybrid of vernacular and international which is my particular interest here, one falls foul of orthodoxies on two different sides. On the one hand, the composers who have succeded to some degree in the international style are thought to be losing caste by admitting an element of the traditional or vernacular. On the other hand, nationalist historians of the last century and ethno-musicologists of the same epoch were rendered deeply unhappy by 'contamination' from the international manner.[18] The fact remains that much of the musical activity of the Celtic countries was indeed hybrid, that many composers remembered for their dance music in the vernacular style also wrote minuets and trio-sonatas in styles derived from the universally admired Corelli. This is as true of Turlough O'Carolan in Ireland as it is of William MacGibbon or Robert Mackintosh in Scotland. The composers who mastered the international style – such as John Clerk of Penicuik, the musician Earl of Kellie – manifested, however occasionally, their familiarity with the vernacular tradition of music-making. There were also composers of some achievement, Alexander Munro most notable amongst them, who chose to work exclusively in a hybrid style which sets and develops traditional melodic material in the 'international' forms of variations or suites of dances.

Space here precludes discussion of the seventeenth-century Netherlandic publication of song-tunes from many European countries in collections for wind instruments, or of early evidence for song-tunes which can be transformed into dance-tunes in a way that implies potential variation sets.[19] Evidence for a consolidating hybrid musical tradition comes in the work of a Scot already mentioned, who had studied law in Leiden and music in Rome (exceptionally, he was for a short time a pupil of Arcangelo Corelli), John Clerk of Penicuik.[20] His G-major sonata for violin and continuo was written about 1705, not long after his return from the continent.[21] The last movement is a G-major *giga*, three repeated strains of eight bars, generally Corellian at a first hearing, indeed not at all unlike the *giga* finale of Corelli's F-major violin sonata, Opus V, no. 4. In the fourth bar of the movement, a C in the violin is supported by A in the bass, both resolving to a D. But in the manuscript the C is a natural, and thus for a second the international texture is shot through with an implication of something altogether more specific to the origins of the composer. Similarly, the triplet figures which dominate from bar nine have a poised quality: if the repeated top notes define the melodic line, then all is unexceptionally international again, but if the pattern sketched by the lowest note of each triplet is taken in concert with the movement of the bass, something again much more of the character of a Scottish jig emerges. This is emphasised by the octave fall in the violin part in bar sixteen.

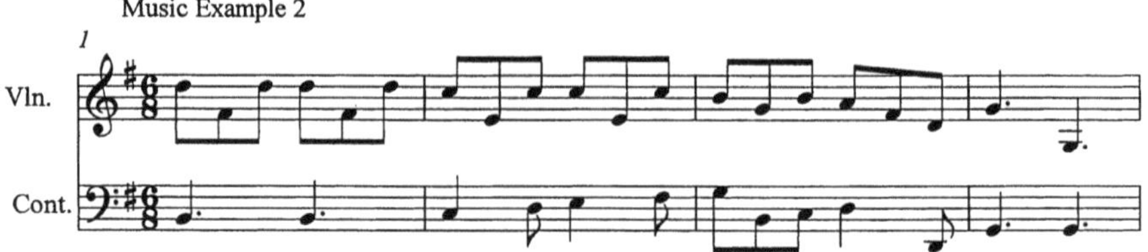

Music example 2: Clerk giga bars 13–16.

What is beguiling here is that the same piece in the same performance can appear to be in a different idiom depending on which way a hearer wants to hear it on a given occasion, indeed dependent on whether a hearer's experience includes the Scottish jig as well as the Italian *giga*.

What we have in the Clerk sonata is a matter of a brief movement of delightful stylistic ambiguity. Like Arthur Johnston's poems on Frendraught it is *both* international and intensely local, and perceptions of the balance of those elements will depend on listening or reading individuals. Both are present simultaneously.

On a rather larger scale, a more developed hybridity, the product of a comparable cultural background, is expressed in the series of violin pieces published at Paris in 1732, *A Collection of Scots Tunes*. The name of their composer is Alexander Munro. It is far from certain that he was identical with the distinguished Edinburgh professor of anatomy, Alexander Munro *primus* (1697–1767), although the increasing number of Scottish medical graduates from Leiden who are known to have been musicians and composers, including some of Munro's most distinguished pupils, suggests that the identification is not unlikely.

Munro picked up the Scottish form of the air and jig (with the two pieces sharing the same musical material). 'Munro's idea of crossing the Scottish air-jig with the Italian *sonata da camera* form was simple but daring . . . The most famous *da camera* sonatas of the time were Corelli's Op. V, nos. 7–10.'[22] These typically have a prelude followed by four or five dance movements. This was the pattern which Munro followed in his variation sonatas, so that, for example, his finest sonata, on the air *Bonny Jean of Aberdeen*, sets the air at length, then begins his transformations of it with a *sarabanda*, a *corrente*, a *gavotta* and a *giga*. This is a work of real interest because it is so poised between idioms, so much at home in both musical styles, that it is difficult for a listener to anticipate by which idiom the piece will proceed from bar to bar. The transformations of the initial air are adroitly handled, the final *giga* constituting an almost complete Italianisation of the original material, without destroying its vernacular identity entirely.

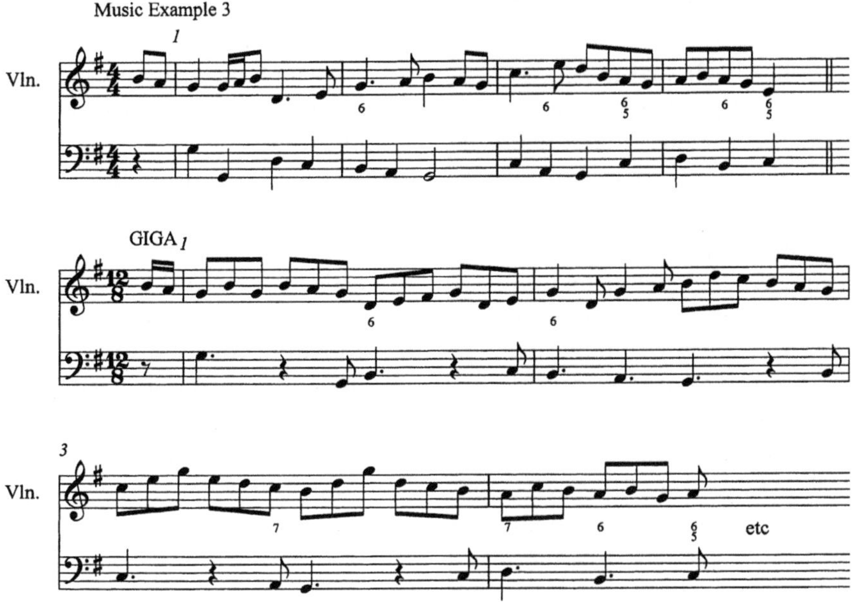

Music example 3. Bonny Jean first strain, melody and bass; giga bars 1–4 dittto.

At one point in his *gavotta*,[23] Munro achives a momentary overlay of two musical systems, where a falling pentatonic scale is syncopated over an Italianate bass line.

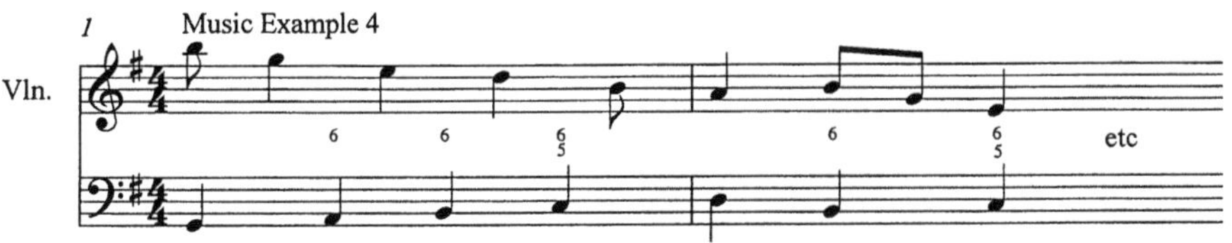

Music example 4. Gavotta bars 11–12.

From that point, the variation sonata was established as a meeting ground for the international and the local in the music of the Celtic countries. There are numerous Scottish examples, collected and discussed by David Johnson. Many numbers from the fine collection of harp pieces assembled by Edward Jones in his *Musical and Poetical Works of the Welsh Bards* are also furnished with sets of variations,[24] which combine in themselves varying styles, reflecting Jones's own indication that these pieces would be playable on a variety of instruments. The majority of his variations are developments of the material within the idiom of international keyboard music, but many of the sets have at least one variation which indicates, usually by alternating-hands figurations, that it is conceived securely within the harp tradition.

One final Scottish example shows the development of the process of musical hybridisation. Thomas, sixth Earl of Kellie (1731–81), son of another Jacobite branch of the Erskine family, was trained in traditional violin playing near his family's castle in Fife and subsequently, pursuing an extraordinary devotion to (and gift for) music, trained in the most advanced manner of his day, studying the violin with Stamitz at Mannheim in the early 1750s. There are numerous compositions of his in the international manner, symphonies, sontatas and quartets, which have led him to be considered Scotland's leading composer in the *galant* style. At least one Strathspey and reel, in the vernacular tradition of his youth (although with an unusually sophisticated leaping syncopation in the second strain) are consistently attributed to him also.

But there is one work, his best, certainly his strangest, which juxaposes and combines the two manners. This is his 'Largo in B flat' for violin/flute and continuo, which survives in manuscript, possibly autograph and certainly signed, in the National Library of Scotland.[25] It is of fifty bars, with the conventional *da capo* repeat of the first eighteen. It works throughout around a traditional song-tune, a particularly sad one, but the way in which it surrounds and punctuates this vernacular material with what one is tempted to call reflections and reconsiderations in the *galant* manner is extraordinary. The traditional song is called 'The Lowlands of Holland' and is a woman's avowal of fidelity to a man carried away by circumstances to 'the Lowlands of Holland'. The words are expressive of enforced parting and it is tempting to associate them with the Scottish diaspora which followed the Jacobite risings.

> The love who I have chosen, I'll therewith be content,
> The salt sea will be frozen before that I repent . . .
> But the Lowlands of Holland have twined [parted] my love and me.

Kellie sets the first eight bars with absolute simplicity, adding only appoggiaturas at the cadences, but then bars nine to twelve are a reflection upon them in the full *galant* manner: melancholy, distant, regretful. Twice he resolves 6/4 to 5/3 with an implied pedal B-flat.

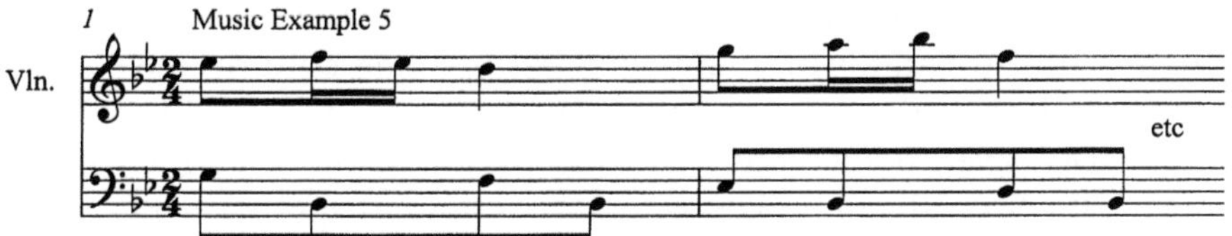

Music example 5: bars 9–12 melody and bass.

Then there is a unison, major key statement of a version of the eighth bar of the song, a suspension for a bar on the seventh and then an ornamented statement of the last two bars of the traditional tune. The trio repeats essentially the same harmonic shape, although with considerably more elaboration over the 6/4, 5/3 resolutions, before moving out into triplet ornamentation and, finally, in the last few notes, an echo and transformation of the last notes of the traditional tune. The degree of fusion of manners (or the complexity of the music for which a traditional tune provides the point of departure) is astonishing, an anticipation in some respects of musical developments of the following century. On the one hand, it is the highest development of the 'folk-song setting'; on the other, it is a reflection upon and summary of a whole century of hybrid music. One might even go so far as to say that it uses the most advanced language of the international musical manner to develop and comment upon a traditional song, unusually accomplished and expressive in itself, and, of course, to reflect also upon the centuries of revolutions, partings and disasters which lie behind the song.

It is worth reflecting that this is the tradition which is inherited by Burns and Scott. Robert Burns's lyrics, revising and contrafacting to airs in the vernacular song tradition, were originally published with harpsichord accompaniment in the late eighteenth-century *Scottish Musical Museum*. The *Scottische Volkslieder* of Beethoven and Haydn are not anticipations of the Scott-inspired craze for romantic and primitive Scotland which was soon to sweep the opera-houses of Europe, they are rather commissioned *from* Scotland as the last examples of the hybrid musical traditions which had been sustained throughout the long eighteenth century.[26]

And what more of Scotland can we extrapolate from this music, from the condition of hybridity inherited by Burns and Scott?[27] The first chapter argued that Arthur Johnston's poems on the Fire of Fendraught inhabited at once the international world of the Ovidian elegy and the local world of the Gaelic lament for the dead. Even more than that of Ireland, where the contrasts between cultures have always been as clear as their confluences, the culture of Scotland was and is a *métissage*. Even before the enriching complication of Gaelic is introduced, the Scottish cultural experience was *mestizo* experience: the blending of metropolitan and vernacular informing art, architecture and painting as well as music, literature and (always) the spoken language. To a considerable extent, this holds true of Scotland to this day.

Irish music

When we come to consider the music of the most celebrated of the Celtic harp composers, the Irishman Turlough O'Carolan (1670–1738) we find again in his music a hybridity between vernacular and international styles. Paradoxically, O'Carolan, working at a time when the Treaty of Limerick had effectively marginalised the Irish-speaking aristocracy who were his natural patrons and thereby limited his opportunities for wider study, is among the most consistently internationalist in his own style.[28] His response to the music of Vivaldi, Geminiani and, especially, Corelli is vividly present in the greater part of his output. Like the Scottish composers, he makes considerable use of the proto-variation-sonata implied in the air with a related jig derived from the same musical material. He also, indicating a chain of unexpected influence, wrote an accomplished sets of variations on a Scottish traditional tune.[29]

The textual history of O'Carolan's work is a melancholy one, emblematic of the subsequent history of his music, as of so much of early modern Irish high culture. Fragments of a unique printed copy of his work survive from 1748, lacking title page but presumably printed at Dublin, possibly by O'Carolan's son in collaboration with the liberal protestant clergyman Patrick Delaney. The music is presented with a bass line and implied harmonisation: its appearance bears out Gráinne Yeats's assertion that,

> The strongest influence was that of the music of contemporary Italian composers. According to his friend and patron Charles O'Conor 'Vivaldi charmed him and with Corelli he was enraptured'. He greatly admired Geminiani whom he almost certainly met towards the end of his life . . . Many of his tunes attempt Italian forms with sequences and imitations.[30]

In 1780, O'Carolan's music was published at Dublin in John Lee's compilation *A Favourite Collection of the so much admired old Irish Tunes*. Like Edward Jones's Welsh collection, this is advertised as suitable for harpsichord and flute and violin. Again the tunes are harmonised, and particularly in 'Mrs Poer' (also known as 'Carolan's Concerto') connection to the international style is clear. The alternative title is a serious indication of how O'Carolan's music may have sounded to those last Irish aristocracy with connections in Salamanca and Rome, and among the officers in the *brigades irlandaises*. Later editions of O'Carolan tend more and more to give a melody line alone and to assimilate his work more and more to the vernacular tradition. The sequences and echo effects of the baroque international mode are lost in moments of what can seem vagueness, melodic indirection.

There is every indication that harp music elsewhere in eighteenth-century Ireland went far beyond the composition of short dance-tunes and airs: one Kerry harper is indicated as composing funeral music as well as what are referred to as 'Elevations', possibly instrumental music for liturgical use:[31]

> ... the chiefest Master of that Instrument in the Kingdom in his time. Mr. Nic: Pierce of Clenmaurice ... for his singular capacity of compos-ing Lamentations funerals addition and Elevations etc.

Architectural projects: the Chearnley circle and the Earl of Mar

We will move shortly to the consideration of an extraordinary Scottish repertory of imaginary or projected architecture by the Earl of Kellie's Jacobite kinsman, the Earl of Mar, imagined and drawn in various places of continental exile after the failure of the 1715 Jacobite rebellion. But first there is a remarkable set of Irish architectural projects to consider, again demonstrating the degree to which the baroque arts can flourish at an extraordinarily sophisticated level in a remote cultural centre, here at Birr in County Offaly. The circle out of which these projects came was a small one of minor aristocracy, gentry and clergy, elite protestants of English descent living in the midlands of Ireland in the decade after the death of O'Carolan and the eclipse of the indigenous Irish arist-ocracy who had formed the majority of his patrons.[32]

These drawings were made, at Birr, by Samuel Chearnley (*c.*1717–46) in collaboration with, and under the patronage of, his cousin Sir Laurence Parsons, Bart (1708–56). Stylistically these drawings are wide-ranging, fantastical and brilliant: as William Laffan says in his intro-duction to the recently published album,[33]

> Chearnley's designs are multi-sourced and sometimes wilfully eccentric in their combination of different architectural modes, demonstrating,

in addition to the prevailing Palladian idiom, the clear influence of the European Baroque, even at times that of sixteenth-century Italian Mannerism.

Samuel Chearnley and the Earl of Mar (both architects of stupendous imaginary buildings) were designing in a climate of forlorn hope: there was little more chance that Mar would live to be the architect of the restored, baroque London of James VIII and III than that the Parsons family would ever have the money to realise the Chinese obelisks and casinos of Chearnley's fantasy in the demesne of Birr Castle, or that they would have been able completely to rebuild Birr after the Parsons/ Chearnley designs, however much the fortunes of the Ascendancy might have improved with the Jacobite threat finally banished. If only they had built their Irish Borrominian-Palladian town, with a row of grand palazzi in the Mall, terminating in a great court house with arcades, statues and belvederes, approached through triumphal arches and the skyline of Birr bristling with trophies of arms and statues on Salomonic columns, this would be by now one of the wonders of Europe in its 'fantastical grandiosity', words which Toby Barnard used in describing these designs.[34] There is indeed a hint that these designs were meant for more than fantasies to pass a politically anxious winter for a remote elite circle – one or two of the drawings are annotated to show how they could be accomplished with brick and stucco without going to the expense of cut stone, with capitals of columns counterfeited with slates or flag-stones set on edge.

The collection is baroque in every sense: in its magnificence but also in its hybridity, and its incorporation of indigenous elements. Its editor observes the connection with Irish tradition:[35]

> The *groteschi* which feature so strongly at the beginning of the sequence of drawings are cognate with the lengthy Irish tradition of masks and skulls, extending from the Celtic 'cult of heads' as found at nearby Clonmacnoise and Clonfert, to the faces which decorate the corners and aprons of Irish Georgian furniture . . . more conjecturally, the central grotto of Plate 7 seems to be modelled on an Irish *clochán* or beehive hut . . .

It is also baroque in its sheer scope and ambition: the curious echoes of the monster-garden of Bomarzo (see p. 19) in the deliberately disproportionate 'surprises' of plates 11 and 12; the gothic window-tracery formed by jets of falling water, a remarkable example of baroque games and paradoxes with materials. The designs for columns, partic-ularly plates 31 and 32, use the full baroque repertory of trophies of arms and Salomonic twisting and vine-wreathing.

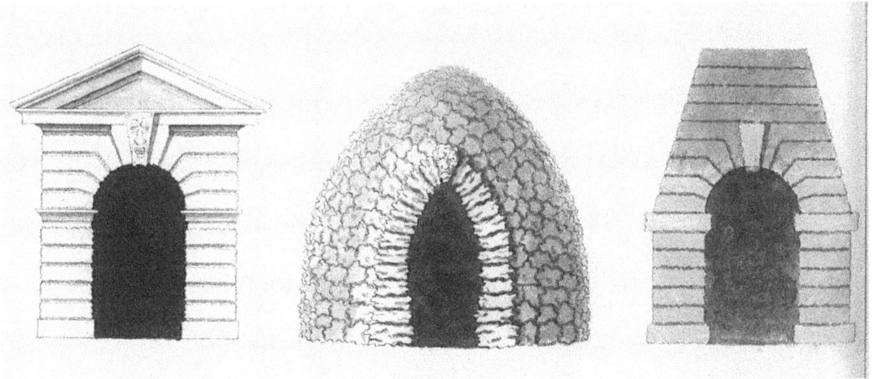

11 Samuel Chearnley, grotto in the shape of an Irish beehive hut with other designs for grottoes, from the manuscript 'Miscellanea Structura Curiosa' (1745–46).

The styles of most of the farmhouses and town houses are Palladian with Vanbruggian overtones, but the court house and house in the 'theatrical taste' go beyond the invention of Puglia or the 'earthquake Baroque' of Sicily towards the fictitious magnificences of opera-settings by the Bibiena. This ebullient magnificence raises interesting questions about the provenance of the architectural ideas which the sequence of drawings incorporates and develops. While the chief influence is Palladian, there are distinct elements of the most developed French as well as Roman Baroque, and elements of fantasy beyond that.

Chearnley's buildings date from the winter of 1745–46, anxious times for the protestant Ascendancy in Ireland, as Prince Charles Edward Stuart's advance on England got as far as Derby in the month of December. It is interesting that in a year of potential disasters for his community, Chearnley's dated series seems to begin with a sequence of six designs for ruins, the first, oddly, appearing to be at the head of a long drive from a country-house gate, thus in the place of the house itself, perhaps a sophisticated rueful joke about the contemporary political situation.

Chearnley's calligraphic title-page, promising (the list in itself is an Irish baroque poem) 'Ruins, Grottoes, Surprizes, Cascades, Fountains, Bridges, Obelisks and Pyramids, Columns, Terminations for Vistows, Temples, Triumphal Arches, Monuments...' is dated 24 October 1745; the last dated design is from May 1746, when the sequence was interrupted by Chearnley's final illness. There is a number of designs for triumphal arches towards the end of the album, and it is tempting

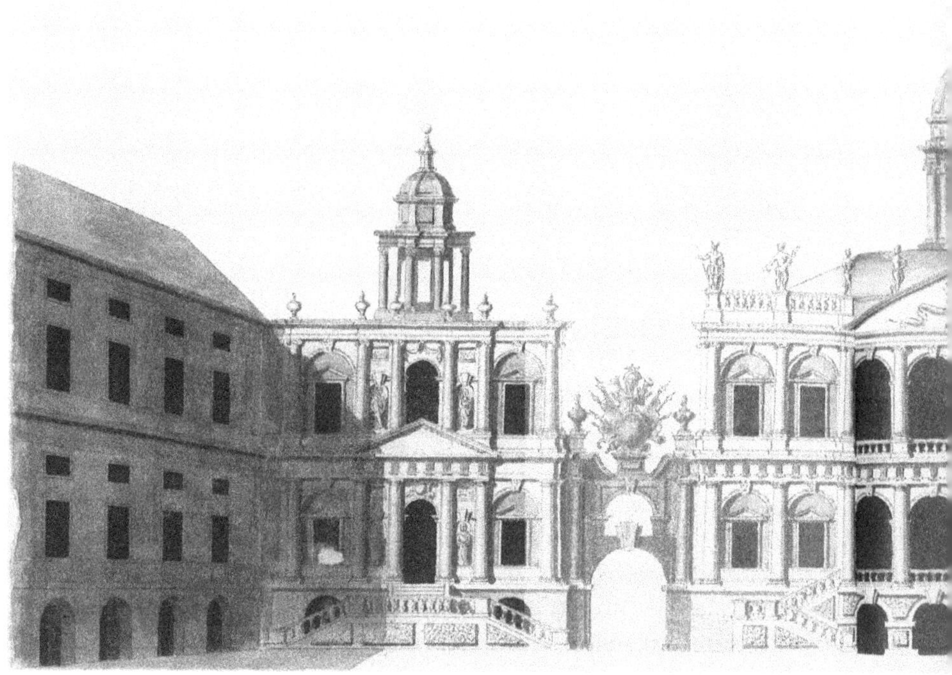

12 Samuel Chearnley, *Design for a court house,* from 'Miscellanea Structura Curiosa' (1745–46).

to wonder whether they reflect the arrival of the news of Jacobite reverses and imminent Hanoverian victory.

The iconography of the triumphal arches in plates 47 and 48 would certainly seem to set forth reminiscences of past Jacobite defeats with a mounted figure of Cumberland surmounting all. Despite his many projects, only one structure by Chearnley is known to have been built. This is the column in the Mall at Birr, erected originally to commemorate the Hanoverian victory at Culloden (and thus the securing of the position of the Protestant ascendancy) with a lead (apposite material) statue of Cumberland.[36] By the time that Chearnley's one posthumous work was built, the Jacobite Earl of Mar had been dead for over a decade and had been in continental exile for seventeen years before that.

It would be of real interest to follow the developing political theories of the Earl of Mar in his exile from 1715–32, especially his

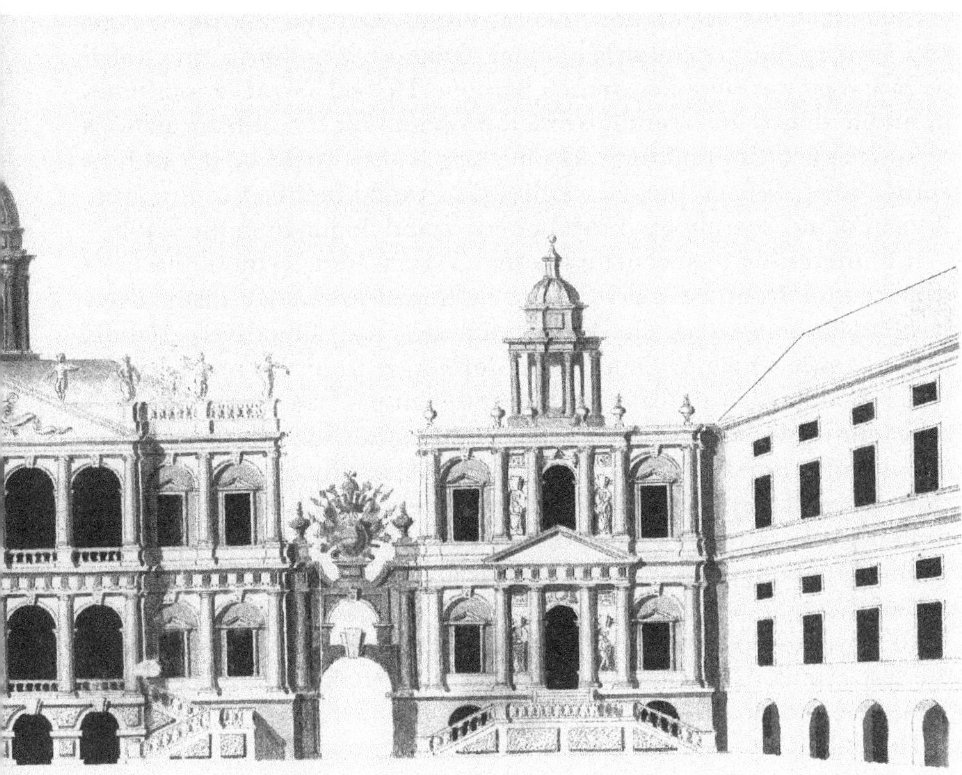

repudiation of the 1707 Union of Scotland with England; his whole-hearted, and personally catastrophic, adoption of the Jacobite cause; and his belief that Scotland had taken a disastrous (Presbyterian, Whig, Unionist) wrong turn from which it needed to withdraw in the direction of Episcopacy and a settlement which would incorporate close links with the ancient ally, France, and the respecting of highland as well as lowland traditions.

Many of these ideas are reflected in Mar's architecture, especially in the house he would have built for himself at Alloa, one which would, in its expressive hybrid-baroque style, lying (like Birr in Ireland) in the centre of lowland Scotland, have become itself a kind of epitome of the Scotland of his retrospective aspirations.[37]

The subject has been discussed fully and painstakingly elsewhere, so I will not write about Mar's detailed plans for the rebuilding of the palace quarter of London as he would have liked to have seen it done for the imagined, unimaginable day when the capital would welcome James Francis Edward Stuart as James VIII and III.[38] Made in his restless continental exile at Avignon, Lucca, Pistoia, Geneva, Bourbon, Paris and Antwerp, the general style of the vertiginously grand structures which he proposed was emphatic French Baroque. He had also at various times in his life drawn up carefully worked proposals for the transformations of ancient Scottish buildings: Drumlanrig House would be left with its corner towers intact, but the central void would be filled with a great Roman dome, soaring up into a belvedere and dominating the whole.[39]

It is interesting to speculate whether Mar evolved, in these places of exile remote from the places where he hoped to build, a distinctively Jacobite Baroque to parallel (even contradict) the calmer Netherlandic baroque style which William Adam developed from the precedent of Dutch buildings of the later seventeenth century.[40] Margaret Stewart's excellent dissertation on Mar's plans emphasises that Mar was a conscious and learned architect, but one capable of bringing his own early experience of vernacular castle architecture back into his most sophisticated plans as one element blended into a stylistic range of international Baroques.[41] Mar also had ideas to express about Scotland, and one of these, as later manifested in his 'B' design for his own house at Alloa, devised and drawn in 1730, was a belief that the highlanders were the last remnants of the Old Scots and that their culture should be respected and protected.[42]

The Alloa 'B' scheme is also remarkable for a fantastical use of hydraulics; water is drawn up through the body of the house to fountains and lead tanks on the roofs. Stewart connects this back to the tower of Kildrummy Castle in Strathdon which had been Mar's childhood home, the Snow Tower, which had oculi at the centres of the floors for water to be drawn up. But what a transformation of childhood and mature experience can be seen by the time that Mar made his plans for his own house at Alloa–plans never carried out, for a house he would never see again. The treatment of roof level in Alloa 'B' is remarkable, a real baroque development of the marvellous, of the ambition to astonish, with considerable fluidity about the materials used to achieve the effect. Mar's roofs were to be of lead, with fountains and trees in tubs, but the flat leadwork was itself to be painted with green and sand-colour in imitation of the parterres visible to the south below.

The Alloa 'B' design is Mar's most accomplished baroque work, and also his strangest. It is a rectangular structure, with a portico in the centre of each nine-bay façade, and porticoes also in the seven-bay shorter sides. The two longer fronts, facing east and west, have the two centre bays recessed. There is an attic storey in the French style and above this a flat roof with roof garden with trees and fountains surrounding a central belvedere, a square rising into an octagon with another tree surmounting the whole composition.

The positioning of the imaginary house is significant: Alloa is at the centre of the Lowlands, east to west, and also situated on a fertile plain, but in view of both the sharp rising of Ben Cleugh to the north and the associational and monumental block of Stirling Castle on its rock to the west. (Indeed among Mar's fantastical drawings are a project for a baroque recasting of Stirling Castle with vast, extraordinary thistle finials punctuating the roofline.) Mar perhaps intended his imaginary palace to be a microcosm of the state of his nation as well as a built autobiography.

On elevation 'D' there is a fictive drapery of stone over the recessed portico: it is held up by the beasts of the Erskine arms – eagle, lion, griffin – and the drapery bears a laurel wreath descending on the master of the house in a fantastical vindication of the rightness of his disastrous political career. The other long side, elevation 'C' is martial and Roman, with weapons of war between the metopes of the frieze and figures of Mars and Justice above. The south façade (elevation 'F') facing down across the gardens and parterres towards the fertile river-plain of the Forth, is Corinthian with female figures presumably meant for Ceres (perhaps Astraea, perhaps Persephone), flanking an attic-level terrace with a fountain on it. The last elevation (marked 'E') is the sternest: the massive columns have banded rustication. This façade faces north towards Ben Cleugh and into the hills. At the cornice level are two giant statues of highlanders.

> They commemorate the debt Mar acknowledged to them for their generosity to him during the '15 uprising, and his description of their future role in Scotlnd's history as being to assist in 'relieving our country' from the Union . . . Mar seems to draw an analogy between the most robust and 'primitive' of all the orders, the rusticated blocked Tuscan Doric, and the nature of Highland life.[43]

Mar's designs for his lost estates at Alloa include a complete recasting of the church there, with grand lofts like opera boxes for his own family and for that of his local Erskine kinsfolk. The most spectacular element of the recasting of the church was to be the formation of a great top-lit void within the walls of the old church building where, behind Mar's loft and the burial-place below it, was to stand a black marble obelisk monument to the families of Mar and Erskine. The arms of the branches of the Erskine family are round the base; gilded reliefs on the obelisks combine the international and the local: Roman

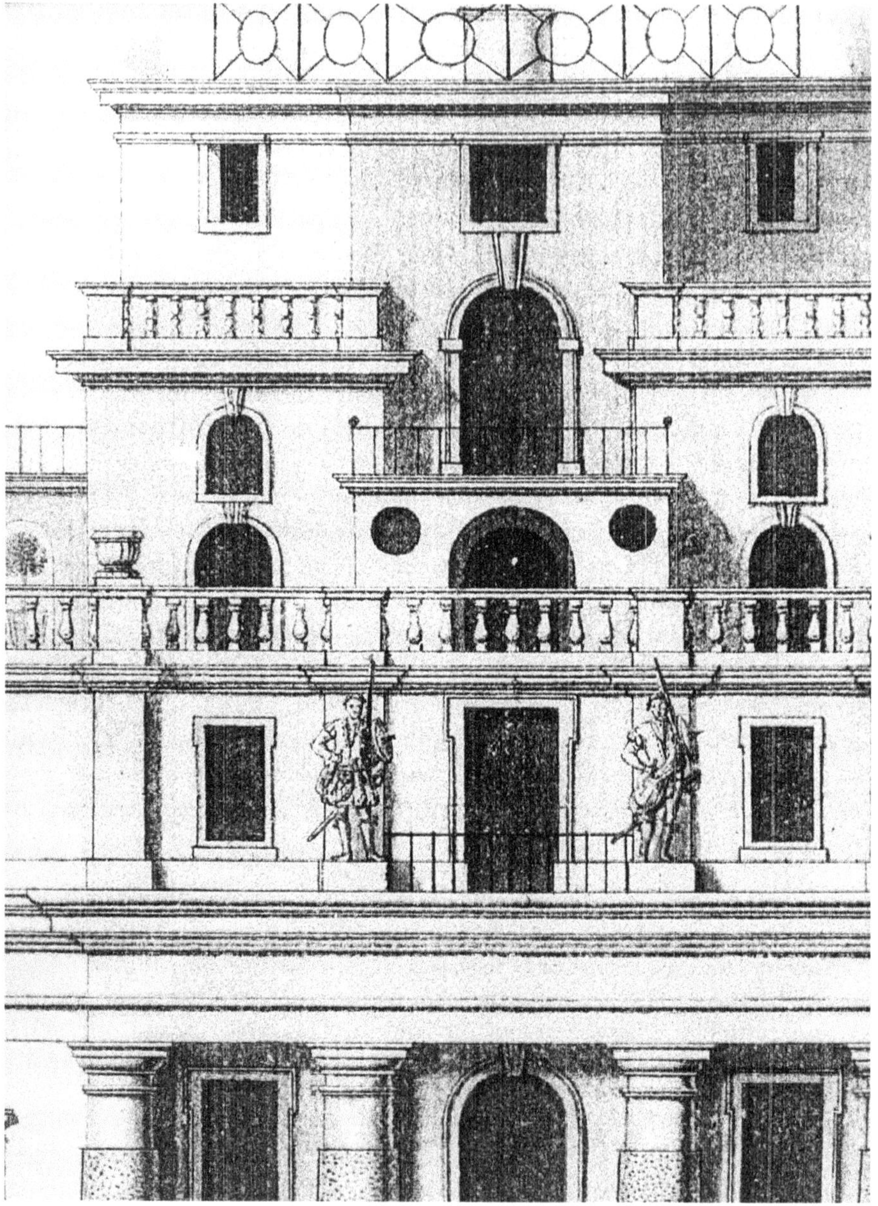

13 John, Earl of Mar, detail of the north façade from a proposed design for Alloa Tower, with giant statues of highland warriors.

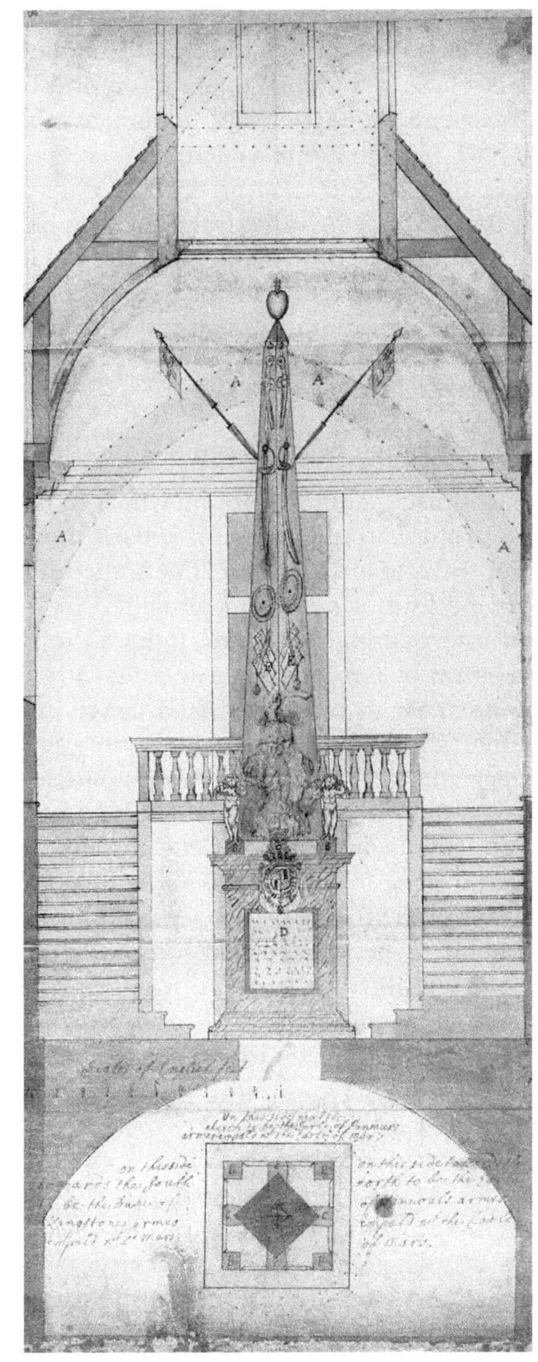

14 John, Earl of Mar, proposed obelisk monument to the Mar and Erskine families to be erected in Alloa Church.

trophies of armour and the claymores of the highlanders. Crowning the obelisk is, in Mar's own annotation, '[a] heart on the top of it is to be of white marble with a flame comeing out of it of guilt brass'. It is possible that the overall design of Mar's monument relates to an obelisk with emblems and illuminations which was erected in the Scots College at Paris in 1688 to celebrate the birth of Mar's monarch, James Francis Edward Stuart. In that context, the flaming heart represented the ardour and devotion of the followers of the Stuarts,[44] just as the preparation of an emblematic display for a festal day is a good example of how colleges and institutes worldwide educated the people in the symbolic languages of the Baroque.

The flaming heart: baroque education

The flaming heart is itself a good point on which to conclude this survey of the shape of the baroque world: it is itself the baroque symbol *par excellence*, expressive of ardours and affects, the interpenetration of temporal and divine love, a metaphor visualised so habitually that it becomes part of international language. Indeed the flaming heart as a symbol is so central to baroque discourse that it changes, expands and deepens its meaning as it spreads as an image universally.

If the continuities which I have argued for in the baroque world internationally are real, then it is necessary to demonstrate, albeit briefly, that these international discourses of emblem and symbol were inculcated through education, as well as by the dissemination of printed exempla, and that instruction in symbol and emblem was an essential component of education (in the widest sense) internationally.

Everything argued so far depends to some degree on this matter of dissemination. How did the baroque mode spread and how was such an international system inculcated? The distribution of pattern-books and emblem-books has been touched on at various points in this book, (see pp. 36–41 and pp. 96–8) but the fact remains that the underpinning of such a universal system is necessarily educational.

There is abundant evidence from which to argue for the world-wide networks of the Jesuits (see Introduction' pp. 8–11) from Cuzco to Kilkenny, and we may assume that wherever there was a Jesuit college there was also a standardised element of instruction in images and 'figures', rhetorical and symbolic. We may also assume easy access to the writings of other Jesuit colleges and houses as well as the circulation of records of the emblem exhibitions, pinned-up verses, plays and orations which accompanied special festival days.[45]

The early modern world also, regardless of religious confession, absorbed a good deal of instruction by means of the sermon, whether as part of a religious liturgy or as an independent event. The other occasions on which the public would be required at some serious level to engage with symbolic languages would be the frequent festal occasions which provided the public manifestations of the movements of political life in the early modern world, indeed made political events public in a visually legible form.[46] The 1688 illuminations for the birth of James Francis Edward discussed above are one educational establishment's modest participation in such an event.

These events, at a college or university level, could take place on a very much larger scale: the English Catholic college in Valladolid, for example, received the Queen of Spain in September 1600 as guest of honour at a ceremony in which a statue of the Virgin, vandalised in the course of the Earl of Essex's raid on Cadiz, was ceremonially installed in the college chapel to serve both as its patroness and as a perpetual reminder of the wounded and diminished state of heretical England and its apostate queen. Symbolic pictures were exhibited to interpret and convey this message: the Virgin figured as the Rose which nourishes the fruitful honeybees and kills the sterile 'dores' like Elizabeth, the Keeper of the Vineyard, the Beacon to guide home the ship of faith to England.[47]

These emblematic exhibitions were carried on regularly and on a larger scale at the town colleges throught the Catholic world. But at the same time, the dissemination of emblem books and the use of emblems as material for vernacular painted decoration was universal in the Protestant countries, and there is plentiful evidence that Protestant school and university education included the devising of emblems as part of the curriculum, part of social life.[48]

From the necessity for even quite small cities to produce festivals from time to time, and therefore the further requirement that citizens must have some sense of the use of symbolic languages, arose what might be identified as evening classes for ambitious or talented artisans. These gatherings, under the auspices of the Jesuits, were a complementary activity to those of the Jesuit confraternities which led their members through a programme of meditations (very often making the most extensive use of emblems and symbolic pictures in the process) with more exclusively spiritual ends.[49] Inevitably, during the process, the confraternity member would learn a great deal about how to read (or devise) an emblem, and how, for example to 'read' the iconography of an elite place like the imaginary Marian garden in the text for Hawkins's confraternity's meditations, which is itself very like some of the larger baroque gardens with a detailed scheme of symbolism and meaning, such as the prodigious garden of Valsanzibio in the Veneto.[50]

The Jesuits also ran congregations attached to their town colleges which were devoted to the social and cultural eduction of their members. Those run by the young Jesuit Claude-François Menestrier have been especially studied: they are well documented and their curriculum is particularly interesting, focused as it is on *honnêté*, that constellation of qualities which would make a member an admired participant in social gatherings.

The summary of the progress of such studies is so germane to this phenomenon of 'learning the Baroque' that I quote at some length from a descripion of the course.[51]

> The first part having been devoted largely to instructing the student in how to become an *honnête homme*, the second part consists of a series of treatises intended to help him to operate as such, so that he can participate intelligently in the creation of festivals and related decorations for his city. This series of treatises led the congregationalist through the building blocks from which festivals were made: inscriptions, symbolic imagery (here called 'la peinture sçavante', erudite painting: heraldry, devices and emblems) all culminating in festivals (*pompes sçavantes*), and a genre of related performance, ballet. All these subjects were considered essential, since they were deemed to be instruments of rhetoric, broadly understood by Menestrier as 'persuading through images'.

Education in the confraternity or congregation taught images and symbols, beyond doubt. Essentially, for our purposes, education in the material and imagery of the arts occurred in the academies, the *accademie* which flourished throughout Italy and France, sometimes in comparatively small centres of population. As well as these there are the 'rhetorical societies', the *redderikerskamers*, who devised and staged pageants for town festivals in the baroque Netherlands. In all of these institutions the apprehension of the symbolic languages of the Baroque is to a greater or lesser extent at the centre of educative and cultural activity.[52]

What baroque education taught, apart from reverence for (plural) antiquities and their languages, was how to read imagery and to use symbols. Christian education has for its end instruction in how to live and how to die, the literal schooling of the heart. But this, and here we return to the heart in flames, is also achieved through symbols and emblems, and, as most famously in the *Spiritual Exercises* of St Ignatius, through acts of visualisation, sensual imagination. The most famous and widespread of the heart-books is the *Pia Desideria* of Herman Hugo, with its imagery of hearts as agents, representing the affect, the moved and schooled emotions and desires which can be turned to God and to virtue.

There is space to offer only one instance of the dissemination of a speaking picture. We find numerous devotional books of the type of 'the school of the heart', all in one sense or another imitating Herman Hugo's seminal *Schola Cordis* (Antwerp, 1619). In Christopher Harvey's imitation, *The School of the Heart* (London, 1647), we find endless instances of the central image, widely distributed.[53] These derivatives of the *Schola Cordis* were translated into almost every language of the western world, including, significantly, those of central and eastern Europe.

For the moment, let us return to the maligned and exiled English poet Richard Crashaw (see pp. 52–5) and read his lines on St Teresa and her mystical experience of her heart being pierced by an angel with the arrow of divine love

> His be the bravery of all those Bright things.
> The glowing cheekes, the glistering wings;
> The Rosy hand, the radiant Dart;
> Leave Her alone *The Flaming Heart.*
> Leave her that; and thou shalt leave her
> Not one loose shaft but love's whole quiver.
> For in love's feild was never found
> A nobler weapon then a Wound.
> Love's passives are his activ'st part.
> The wounded is the wounding heart.[54]

These are elegant lines of sacred gallantry which express the ardent, wounded heart, wholly receptive to God as more powerful than the divine arrow, active in its sheer capacity to receive love. The burning heart taking fire is the opposite affect to the other great baroque outpouring of love: the dissolution in tears so lauded by the Jesuit theologian St Robert Bellarmine,[55] whose special praise of the tears of St Mary Magdalene relates closely to Crashaw's generous, maligned poem 'The Weeper'.

The flaming heart appears in another form in the vastly influential *Iconologia* of Cesare Ripa, where the heart is less inflamed than illumined, and sheds light as from a taper. As such, it is carried in the hand of Ripa's personification of *Catholic faith.*[56] An anonymous seventeenth-century Andean *Guardian angel* leads a child by one hand and in the other hand holds aloft a flaming heart as symbol of love for God and for his charge.[57]

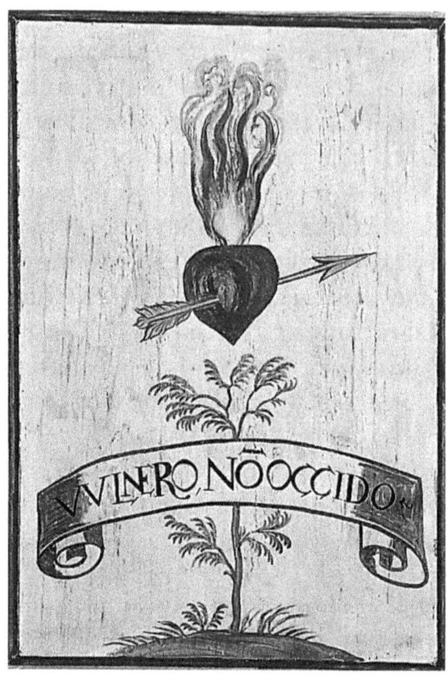

15 Heart emblem on painted ceiling, parish church,
Hergiswald, Lucerne, Switzerland, 1654.

On the extraordinary emblem-ceiling of the parish church of
Hergiswald, in the Canton of Lucerne, the heart emblems are all
expressive of aspects of the Virgin. The heart flowering into a lily is
borne up the sky by the hand of God, with the inscription *Virginale
Praeconium*; the heart with the Christ-child within it and a dove
perched upon it is again borne up the sky by God's hand with the motto
In pace locus eius, 'his place is in peace'. We have the flaming heart pierced
by an arrow, with the motto *Vulnero non occidio*, 'I wound but I do not
kill', with its source in the vastly popular *Schola Cordis* of 1629 by
Benedictus van Haeften (especially plates 436 and 350, which show
God's cherub wounding the devout heart).[58] Finally, there is the heart
wounded by the eye (depicted with heart and eye being held by hands
issuing from clouds, with the motto *Uno oculorum tuorum*, 'with one of
your eyes', a signal instance of sacred Baroque adopting the language of
profane). The flaming heart in a silver field, with the tetragrammaton
above, is the emblem of the Academy of the Ierofili of Livorno.[59] At
the Jesuit College in Québec, a tempera-painted emblem was made in

the eighteenth century showing a heart on an anvil being formed with a hammer. The anvil is placed between a tree and a building like a mission church with a prominent cross on its roof. The motto is 'Sauvage', signifying either the cultivation of the wilderness, or the instruction of the native American.[60]

In Rome, flaming hearts attend the shrines of one major saint and one beata of the Counter-Reformation. Throughout the Oratorian house attached to St Maria in Vallicella, but most specifically in those rooms in which St Philip Neri lived and died, the lock-plates on all the doors are silver flaming hearts, commemorations of the ardour of the saint. In Bernini's chapel of the Blessed Lodovica Albertoni in the church of San Francesco a Ripa in Rome (containing the statue of a mystic dissolving in ecstasy, a work very closely parallel to his celebrated St Teresa) the grille which pierces Albertoni's sarcophagus-altar is another heart with flames streaming away below it (there are also flaming hearts in the decoration of the two side-windows of the chapel).[61] As Giovanni Careri observes, this has an effect of generalising the state of transport in which Bernini's statue depicts her, indeed of generalising her experience until it connects with such feelings of religious ardour as are comprehensible to the spectators.

A further example comes from the sequence of emblem exhibitions which were held in the Jesuit college in Brussels. In the year 1650, the theme of the *affixiones* was the charity of St Ignatius and the steadfastness of St Francis Xavier. All the emblems devised on the theme of Ignatius's love and charity are framed in the winged and flaming heart. The fire is a pun on the *ignis* hidden in the name 'Ignatius', also a reflection of the Ignatian motto 'Go and set fire to the world'. This tremendous example of an explosion (complete with astonished spectators) contained within the flaming heart is expanded in the motto *S. Ignatii Charitati mundus angustus* – 'for the love of St Ignatius, the world is too small'.[62]

Orthodox Baroque: Kiev and Karlovci

The emblem of the ardent heart presides over the early stages of fusion between the literary and artistic traditions of Orthodox eastern Europe and those of the international baroque.[63] On Easter Sunday 1632, the pupils of the Spiritual Academy of Kiev in the Ukraine presented a panegyric of their patron and founder, Archimandrite Peter Mohyla. The imagery of this poetic composition, heraldic, historical and allegorical, declares the extent to which this new Academy represented an opening-up of a formalised post-Byzantine cultural tradition to the Latin learning of the west. The liberal arts are given voices to announce the arrival of the Muses in Kiev and the poem concludes on the heart emblem, with a prayer that a flame may be kindled in the Archimandrite's heart to give warmth to the flowers growing on the new Helicon of Kiev.[64]

The central and eastern European culture which developed from contact between an ancient post-Byzantine tradition and new baroque literary and artistic influences is worth exploring as a distinctive example of the phenomena which have been considered elsewhere in this book: contact with the baroque arts of western Europe and a subsequent period of hybridisation until a distinctive local manner emerges. From such points of initial contact as the Orthodox academies and the influence of the Jesuit missions to (or, more precisely, *against*) those Orthodox communities within the Empire, a 'transitional period' developed which saw the composition of specifically Orthodox emblem and heraldic books, as well as the emergence of a dramatic and festal tradition combining indigenous with international elements. Then an assimilated 'Orthodox Baroque' emerged, a hybrid interpolation of many stylistic elements of western European Baroque into the Orthodox world, but still interpreted wholly in terms of Orthodox tradition.[65]

Inevitably, emblems and historical and allegorical drama play their part in the transitional period of cultural negotiation. There were western emblem-books in the library of Peter Mohyla himself and in that of the Kiev dramatist Teofan Prokopovich. In 1712, a Russian-language emblem-book illustrated with sixty-seven engraved plates was published at Kiev. This *Itika Ieropolitika* was a crucial document in the development of Orthodox Baroque, serving as a pattern-book for ecclesiastical painting, as on the baroque *iconostasis* at Kikinda. There were numerous editions, including one published at Vienna in 1774. By means of such works, a baroque style was established during the eighteenth century in central and eastern Europe which appeared to conform to international models while retaining intact a complex and specific repertory of Orthodox meanings.[66]

As the influence of western and Orthodox emblem-books grew in the Ukraine, the flaming heart was used to decorate the apex of the arch on the ceremonial entrance into the church complex of St Sophia – the seat of the Archbishop of Kiev, rebuilt in the 1750s.

The theatre of the academy of Kiev derived in part from indigenous marionette and street plays called *vetrep*, popular with the students at the chief festivals of the Christian year.[67] But the need to rival the

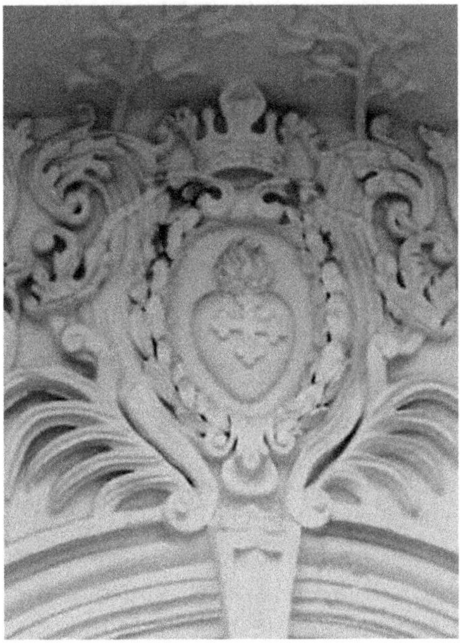

16 Stucco flaming heart, Triumphal Metropolitan Gate on the St Sophia complex, Kiev, Ukraine, 1730–54.

seductive political and historical allegories set forth in the dramas of the Jesuit colleges led to the emergence of a distinctive Orthodox baroque drama: texts filled with complex readings of histories and origins, set forth with illusionistic scenery and theatrical machines. In this enterprise of using history to illumine and comment upon the present, these Orthodox dramas are a part of an international phenomenon including such examples as the *Mercia* performed at St Omer and the *Titus* performed at Kilkenny (see p. 51 and pp. 68–9 above). In Kiev, this appeal to historical precedent was most notably expressed in the works of Teofan Prokopovich, especially in his *Vladimir*, which offered the glories of the arrival of Christianity in Russia as an analogue to the glories of the reign of Peter the Great.[68]

*

The cultural life of the Orthodox Serbians within the Habsburg Empire constitutes an Orthodox Baroque negotiated at the literal frontier of western Europe. They appropriated the baroque style fairly late, by the end of the seventeenth century. This cultural and stylistic change had been mainly conditioned by the 'great exodus' of Serbs from the Ottoman Balkans to the safer territory of the Habsburg Empire in 1690. The Habsburg Emperor Leopold I had offered them freedom of Orthodox worship and freedom to elect their own archbishops as both spiritual and temporal leaders. In return, he expected them to form a military bulwark reinforcing the borders of the Empire against the Ottomans.

Serbian existence in the Empire was marked thereafter by perpetual political struggles to preserve faith and autonomy, as Habsburg officials whittled away the Serbs' privileges and indemnities, rendering the entire eighteenth century in the archbishopric of Karlovci, their semi-independent province within the Habsburg lands, a constant cultural and diplomatic battle.

To survive, the archbishops of Karlovci initiated political and cultural reforms which inevitably entailed a cultural negotiation with the Baroque of the Empire. This involved the visual arts, the printed image and festal spectacles of state. In all these aspects, the first 'transitional' or hybrid works appeared as early as the late 1690s and the process of hybridisation reached its culmination from the middle of the eighteenth century.

Although slower to change, the religious art of the Orthodox assimilated new influences to its established Byzantine and Athonite traditions, in order to maintain a dialogue with the late baroque style in the Empire. By the 1780s, the archbishopric of Karlovci had fully appropriated the current artistic idiom of the Baroque. Through the transitional phase from 1690 to the mid-eighteenth century, Serbian Baroque remained suspended between the two visual idioms, two modes of expression and two worlds – a post-Byzantine and a baroque one. But the sources for its Baroque were themselves complex: the baroque art of the Habsburg Empire combining with the already hybrid Baroque of Kiev.

For that very reason both Ukrainian scholars and artists were invited to Karlovci from 1720s onwards, while Kievan books had been a source of guidance and inspiration there from the beginning. German printed Bibles and emblem-books also entered the archiepiscopal libraries. On the formal level, the adoption of the new visual idiom meant that the elaborate baroque imagery legitimately shared pictorial space with the remnants of the post-Byzantine style. The eastern tradition remained dominant in the treatment of faces and in the disposition of space within the painting.

In 1741, an archiepiscopal commission to the painter Hristofor Žefanović and the poet Pavel Nandović produced a revision of a heraldic handbook, the *Stemmatographia*, which includes an image of the historical Serbian Emperor Dušan, to all appearances drawn by western baroque conventions, shown in a medallion supported by Minerva and the personification of Time.[69] What is important here is that the adoption of an international style is used to convey a specifically local message: time preserves and sustains the image of the exemplary medieval Emperor, himself the embodiment of the independent identity of the archbishopric within the Empire.

A similar assertion is made by the baroque drama composed by the Kievan scholar Manuil Kosachinskii, who arrived in Karlovci in 1733 to take up the post of rector of the Latin school there. The play, and the school itself, were a response to the initiatives, dramatic and educational, of the Jesuits, who had established a college in Belgrade as early as the 1650s. Kosachinskii's *Traedokomedija*, which probably dates from the year 1736, uses the full baroque machinery of scenery and allegories to assert historical continuity between the medieval Serbian emperors and the archbishops of Karlovci.[70] After an allegorical prologue, the first part of the play concerns itself with the last medieval ruler of the Serbians, the fourteenth-century Emperor Dušan. After the interventions of the figures of Serbia, the Virtues and the Liberal Arts as well as sibyls and angels, the second part of the play, masque-like, emphasises that the archbishops are the true inheritors of the emperors, culminating in the glorification of the contemporary archbishop.

One of the most complex works of Serbian baroque art is also the festal apotheosis of a clerical dignitary, in this case the Bishop of Bačka, Mojsej Putnik. Zaharija Orfelin's work takes the form of a complex illustrated festival-book 'The Festive Greeting to Mojsej Putnik in 1757', partly a pangyric, partly a record of the Orthodox rite of episcopal investiture, partly a 'paper-triumph' setting forth the splendours which the Orthodox community were prevented from enacting in public.[71]

One of the most conspicuous images from the international Baroque in this festal synopsis is the flaming heart, repeated in several of the illustrations and calligraphic ornaments of the manuscript. It first appears in the scenes of Mojsej's enthronement and it figures most importantly on the concluding page as the centre of an elaborate word-labyrinth. (One of the pairs of angels who hold up the feigned drapery on which Orfelin's word-labyrinth is inscribed, also sustains a flaming heart.) The flaming heart, in this context, comes to the archbishopric through the Russian emblem book *Itika Jeropolitika*, in which the emblem of the flaming heart symbolises the endurance of faith – the very quality that the ideal prelate set forth in Orfelin's panegyric should possess,

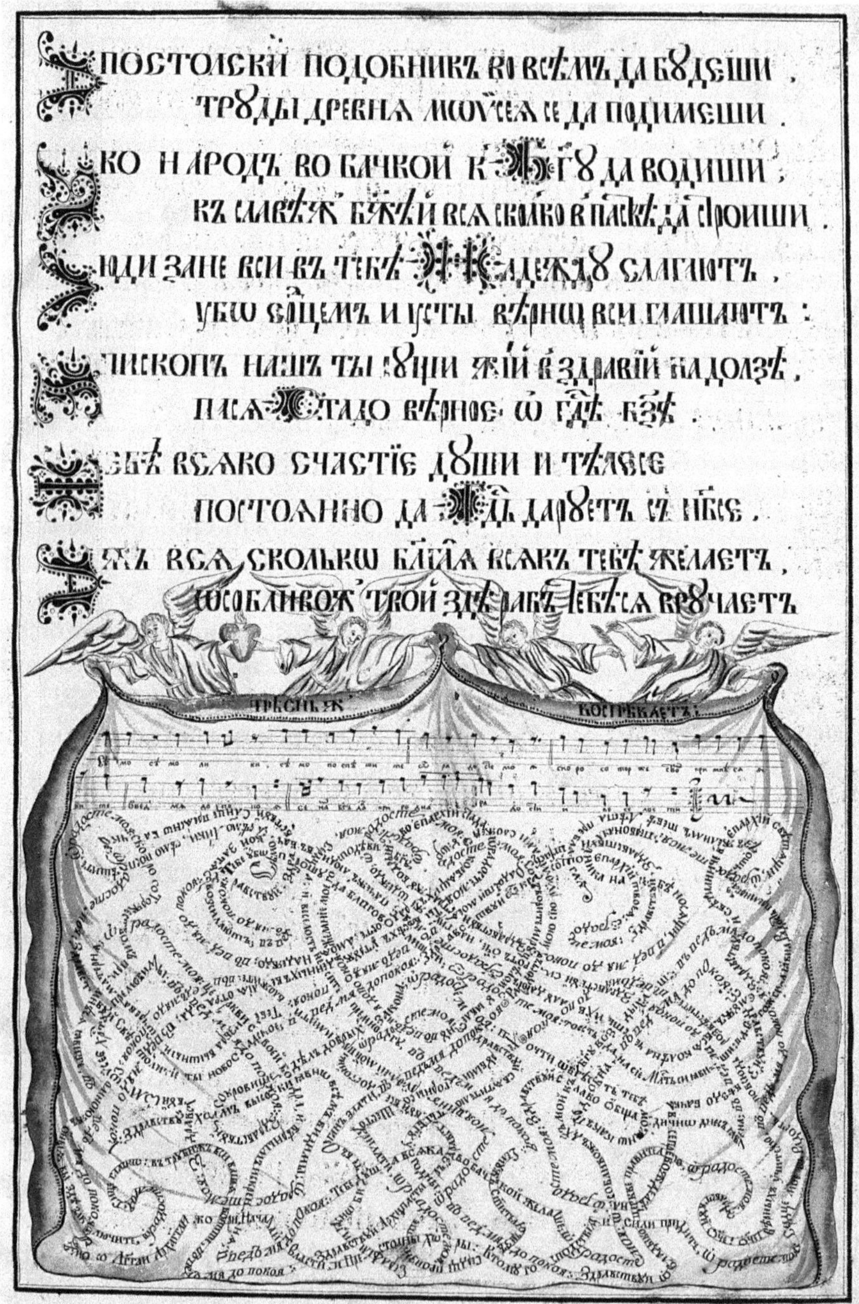

17 Zaharija Orfelin, *The festive greeting to Mosei Putnik*, Karlovci, 1757.
Final page of the calligraphic manuscript, with a pattern
poem forming a flaming heart.

especially in the besieged circumstances of the Orthodox community within the Empire.

The flaming heart, created as *carmina figurata* at the end of Orfelin's manuscript and also presented as angelic attribute, carries a double weight of meaning, Orthodox and international:[72] its Orthodox significations include the endurance of faith and the divine love which draws the soul upwards; but it also carries the overtones of the ubiquitous international emblem-books which use the winged or flaming heart to represent the affects of the Christian soul in relation to God, the *Schola Cordis* of Benedictus van Haeften and the *Cardiomorphoseos* of Francesco Pona.[73]

The flaming heart: the hearts of the saints

In the writings of St Carlo Borromeo, and in the writings and images marking his funeral and the translation of his own heart to its final resting place in the church of San Carlo al Corso in Rome, the flaming heart becomes the symbol of the ideal cleric, epitomising his love for his congregation and his devotion to his pastoral duties. We have become familiar with the emblematic use of the flaming heart, with its fires aspiring upwards to divine life. But in the ceremonies which accompanied the translation of the heart of St Carlo on 22 June 1614, the physical heart, taken from the body of the saint, itself took on the status of an emblem as well as of a relic.

For the procession on that day, the relic was adorned by a silver and rock-crystal reliquary, which still exists, with its gilded rays shimmering about the mummified heart. Along canopied streets, under great arches of green branches and garlands at the corners of the squares, the heart was carried to an altar prepared to receive it in the church of St Carlo. Here, it entered into its aspect as an emblem, the disembodied devout heart floating in radiance in the heavens: it took its place upon '. . . *una nuvola fatta artificiosamente . . . ornata da molti raggi*'[74] (a cunningly made cloud, adorned with many rays).

In the pamphlet issued to commemorate the festival of the heart, Jacopo Lauri published a print, *Cardiogramma*, that represents the heart overlaid with a *carmen figuratum* composed of a reticulation of sentences rehearsing the virtues of the sanctified bishop, with the word COR at the knots of the net.[75]

Another riddling flaming heart, also a heart of flesh, is ciphered in one of the most compressed and elliptical poems of St Robert Southwell. This poem, 'Christs Bloody Sweate', is encoded even beyond the usual allusive discretion which marks the recusant poems of this Jesuit mission-priest and martyr, circulated in full texts only in manuscript copies.[76] The poem begins with a *carmen figuratum*, a 'magic square' readable horizontally, vertically and diagonally, to describe Christ's sweat in the garden of Gethsemane as an anticipation of the effusion and the effects of the blood and water of the Passion.

Fatt soyle,	full springe,	sweete olive,	grape of blisse
That yeldes,	that streames,	that powres,	that dost distil
Untild,	undrawne,	unstampde,	untouchd of presse
Deare fruit,	cleare brooks,	fayre oyle,	sweete wine at will

The second stanza speaks of burning love, of the one who will imitate the emblematic fates of the pelican, lacerating its own breast to feed its young with blood, and the phoenix, casting itself into the flames to be reborn from them. The one who undergoes the fates of phoenix and pelican, 'Whome flames consume whom streames enforce to die', is possibly Christ himself; but the more one reflects on the stanza, the more it seems possible that the emphasis on the burning fate of the phoenix is the covert indicator that the following line is the explicit description of a death on an English scaffold: 'How burneth bloud howe bleedeth burning love/Can one in flame and streame both bathe and frye'. The Jesuit martyr, like St Edmund Campion, cut down from the gallows alive, eviscerated, and hacked to pieces, his entrails thrown into the executioner's brazier, his heart elevated in the executioner's hands, is a literal answer to Southwell's dark riddle: 'How coulde he joyne a Phenix fyerye paynes/In faynting pelicans still bleeding vaynes'.

The flaming and bleeding heart is a heart of English flesh as well as the emblematic heart, the phoenix-heart of Christ. The conclusion of Southwell's poem appears to support such a reading. It is partly the kind of *imitatio Christi* to be expected in the work of a priest-poet, asking metaphorically to be destroyed and revived like the phoenix, 'O sacred Fire come shewe thy force on me/That sacrifice to Christe I maye retorne' but also, in Southwell's condition as a fugitive in England it is an acceptance and anticipation of his own death.

yf fleshe and blood will burne
I withered am and stonye to all good.
A sacke of dust a masse of fleshe and bloode

But it is also a quintessential baroque victory, the symbolic transformation of the excecutioner's fire which will in time consume Southwell's own heart, into an emblematic fire of supernal love.[77]

The flaming heart: revolutionaries and antiquarians

So widespread was the image of the flaming heart that it was used to express Calvinist and revolutionary fervour for the bringing about of Sion on earth on the Civil War banner of the Parliamentary Captain John Blackwell. This shows a troop of silver flaming hearts with the motto *Accendia cura Sionis* (aflame with love of Sion) below a turreted city representing London transformed into the new Jerusalem on earth.[78]

The flaming heart has an afterlife even amidst the Classicism of the French Revolution: a fragmentary coloured print in the Musée Historique d'Orleans shows a female personification of Liberty with banners and Phrygian cap. Above her head are crossed palm branches (presumably emblematic of victory after oppression), and, at their junction, is a flaming heart, ornamented by a cap of liberty and an inscription to the local revolutionary brigades: *Aux Sans Culotes D'Orleans.*[79]

*

The flaming heart is found too even in that citadel of English reasonableness (which is also a place for the expression of perplexities about the complication of the Romano-British past), the spa-town of Bath. The Circus in Bath has a metope frieze with symbolic and hieroglyphic elements between the triglyphs, the ardent and wounded heart among them, as a late reflection of the baroque feeling of the evocation of a plural antiquity, both archaeologically Roman in the allusion to the Colisseum but also romantically British in its evocation of King Bladud of Bath and in its implicit reference to Inigo Jones's very baroque treatise on Stonehenge, which reads that monument as a circular Roman temple to Coelus the god of the heavens. And amongst the many associational 'hieroglyphics' which adorn the Circus – anchor, spear and banner, bow and quiver, serpent and spear, palm and sheaf of corn, trumpet and palm, oak leaves – is a flaming heart pierced with a spear. The current symbol of the sorrow and ardour of the baroque epoch, here perhaps with the application of the sorrows and ardours of the hybrid history of England and of this particular place.[80] Bath is so axiomatically claimed as a classical or Augustan site that it is salutary to recall the backward-looking symbolism of the Circus, recalling a tradition which stretches back in English architecture to the recusant 'hieroglyphics' in the frieze of Sir Thomas Tresham's Lyveden New Bield in Northamptonshire'[81] and untimately to the invention of 'hieroglyphics' in the renaissance dream-narrative the *Hypnerotomachia Poliphili.* The buildings of John Wood at Bath are often thought of (as is the semi-formal garden of the poet Alexander Pope at Twickenham) as the beginning of an autonomous English style – the Georgian city, the landscape garden. But it is intensely salutary to consider that both artefacts also stand at the end of centuries of a developing baroque tradition of symbolic ornament and symbolic articulation of place and history. Viewed from an international perspective, they are late-baroque artefacts, speaking in the international language of that mode, but with local elements poised to develop into an indigenous style.

A Jacobite memorial object

I would like to end with an example of the internationalism of the Baroque considered in every way: symbolic language, Latin, internationalism of materials, manufacture and intention. An object which combines all these things, as well as taking us full circle to the heart as image of Jacobite loyalty, as on the obelisk planned by the Earl of Mar, is the whole blend of cultures and exiles embodied in an ostrich egg carved in memory of James Francis Stuart, 'The Old Pretender' – or James VIII and III, depending on the beliefs and allegiances of his contemporaries.

I have chosen deliberately to end on an object which brings once more before the reader the inconvenience and sheer oddness of Baroque as well as its magnificence and internationalism. The ostrich is baroque in its plumes (adornment for the corners of beds of state, for the headdresses of the riders in the carousel which welcomed the convert Queen Christina of Sweden to Rome, for the helmet of the cult statue of San Crecentino in the church of San Francesco at Urbino). The ostrich attends the personification of *DIGESTION* in Cesare Ripa's universally useful and universally used directory of anthropomorhic personifications, the *Iconologia*.[82] Ostrich eggs themselves were formed into cups and set in precious metals, in which form they ornamented many cabinets of curiosities in the baroque world.

This carved ostrich egg, made in the year of the death of James Francis Edward Stuart, is one of the strangest artefacts in the Marischal Museum of the University of Aberdeen. The eldest son of James VII and II, James Francis Edward was both in St James's Palace, Westminster, on 10 June 1688; fled with his mother on 9 December that year; and thence entered a lifelong exile. He died in Rome on 1 January 1766. The provenance of this object is uncertain, indeed its design is interestingly hybrid. The lettering of the inscription is recognisably Scottish, as is the drawing of the symbols ('hieroglyphics', in the terms of the eighteenth century), but the other work, especially the

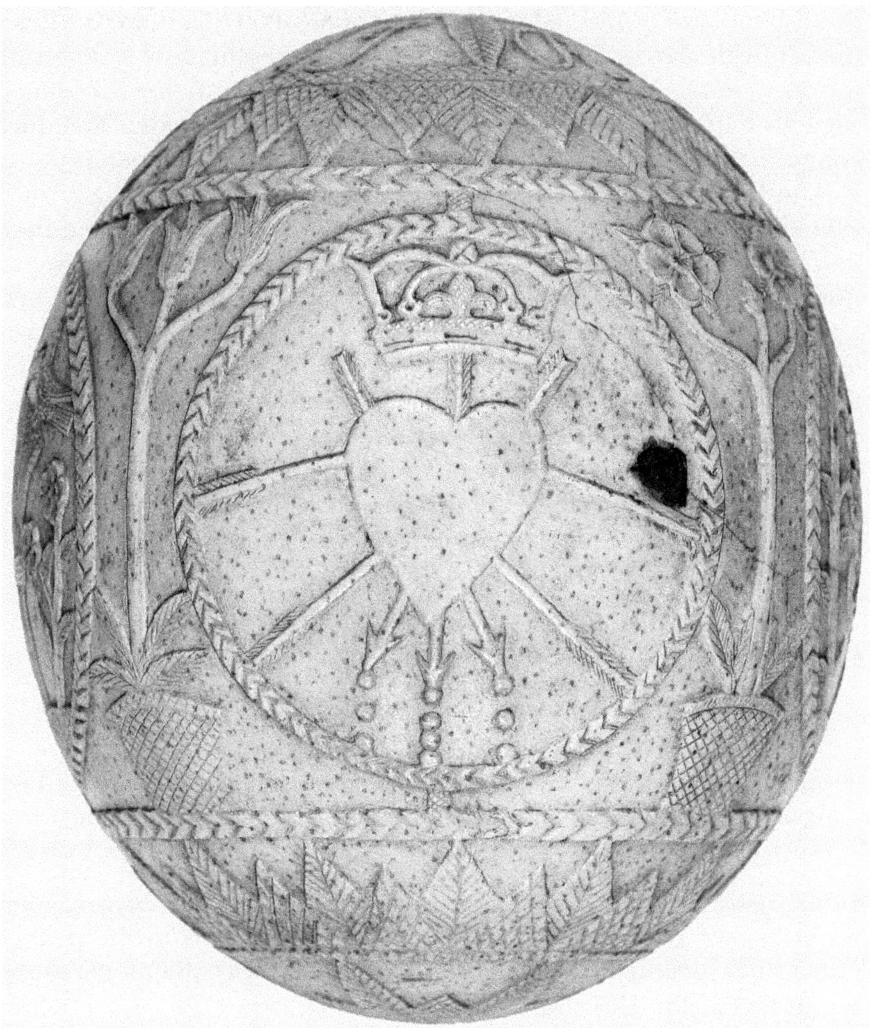

18 Ostrich egg carved in low relief with emblems in memory of James Francis Edward Stuart, 1766. Possibly West African, for a Scottish patron.

conventionalised tulip trees which divide the four compartments in which the three symbols and one monogram are carved, would seem to belong to a West African decorative tradition. The inscription reads J[ACOBUS] R[EX] 1766: the monogram is also of the initials 'J.R.'. The first symbol is of a crowned thistle: this has a long history in Scotland (even as a printer's ornament) and essentially conveys the idea of the

Scottish monarchy invested in the house of Stuart. Then there is a heart pierced with arrows: this is a conventional representation of suffering within Catholic iconography, here the fact that the heart is crowned suggests that it represents the sufferings of the king in exile. The third symbol is the most enigmatic: a sheaf of corn with birds perching on it. The birds themselves may indicate no more than that the corn is ripe and the grain is ready to be eaten. The symbol of the sheaf itself may go back to the French emblematist Claude Paradin's representation of a mature prince by the maturing of the corn, harvested and bound into sheaves. Paradin's motto for his *impresa* is 'They grow yellow', originally the device of Orazio Farnese; the image was taken up and adapted for Mary Queen of Scots with the added anagram MARIA STUARTA: MATURA ARISTA (Mary Stuart: the corn is ripe). This very conceit, this anagram, was a mainspring of the Dutch poet Joost van der Vondel's martyrological conceit when writing about Mary.[83]

INCOMPARABILIS HEROINA ANAGRAMMA.

MARIA STUART ERAT MATURA ARISTA

EPITAPHIUM

VIVICANTE FIDE MATURA RESURGET ARISTA, SECTA ODIO, JESU LECTA, STUARTA, MANU[84]

[An epigram on the matchless heroine: Mary Stuart was the ripe ear of corn (or 'harvest'). Epitaph. Brought to ripeness by living faith the ear of corn grew up, cut by hatred, O Stuart, gathered by the hand of Jesus.]

So this ostrich egg, made in Africa for a Scottish Jacobite patron, sums up in its own bizarrerie, its modest claim to be a part of the marvellous, its international languages, the complex of ideas which I have tried to put forward in this short book.

*

Conclusion: a map of the baroque world

The apophthegm of Eugenio D'Ors (itself, of course, a restatement of Horace, in true baroque style) will bear repetition: *le colonisateur est en quelque sorte colonisé, le vainqueur vaincu.*[85] The coloniser is some degree colonised, the victor vanquished. In conclusion, I would suggest that we have to replace the old, conventional map of the cultural shape of the early modern world, which consisted of radial lines, looking rather like the maps of the world's airline routes. In those maps, lines of power and energy stretched out into what were then the 'new worlds' from their centres in the European capitals, representing one-way lines of influence. The diagram with which I would seek to replace this old chart, however tentatively, would look much more like a net.

Each nodal point of that net could be held to represent a centre of cultural or artistic production, be it a fortress on the coast of New France, the academies of Leiden or Kiev or Mexico City, a country house in the midlands of Ireland or a Jesuit 'reduction' town in the Bolivian lowlands. Every knot is ultimately connected to all the other knots by a shorter or longer route. And the medium, the stuff of the net itself, would have to be the international languages: Latin and the shared visual systems of iconography and emblem ultimately derived from a *plurality* of antiquities. Quetzalcoatl inhabits the classic past alongside the gods of the winds and the stars who manifest themselves as the angels of the Andes, and these co-exist with Osiris and with the winter Persephone.

But the image will only work if we can visualise each of these knots in the universal net being of composite materials: the golden thread of that which is supranational interwoven with that which is truly local to Kilkenny or Wolfenbüttel or Lecce or Nun Appleton. Each knot in its composition represents the degree to which the baroque culture of each place is a fusion of the international, universal Baroque with that which is truly local. The world of the seventeenth century was composed of a series of hybrid cultures, each blending to a different degree the vernacular with the international.

St Augustine hazarded a metaphor for God as 'A circle whose centre is everywhere and whose periphery is nowhere', and we might hazard a counter-metaphor for the international, universal Baroque as 'A circle whose circumference is everywhere but whose centre is nowhere'.

Notes

1　See, for example, the glorious inventions, including what might be identified as the 'siren-order' and the 'phoenix-corbel' of Salentine architecture and decoration in Mario Manieri-Elia, *Barocco leccese* (Milan: Electa, 1989).

2　George Jamieson (1589/90–1644) is so identified on the frame of the self portrait now at Fyvie Castle, Aberdeenshire (National Trust for Scotland); Prescott so names Ixtlilxóchitl in his *Conquest of Mexico* (London: Richard Bentley, 1854); Sarmantian in this case identifies Sarbievius as Polish/Lithuanian. Cerrini is so called in *In Funere Iosephi A Giaceto Castelvillani Comitis &c. Oratio Felicis Verduccioli* (Perugia: Typographia Episcopali, 1643).

3　These are found on the K617 'Chemins du Baroque' CD, *Le chant de la Jérusalem des terres froides*, with the Studio de Musique Ancienne de Montréal directed by Christopher Jackson. This is CD 3 of a 4-CD set of 'Musiques Sacrées Missionaires'.

4   T. Frank Kennedy SJ, 'Jesuits and Music', in O'Malley and Bailey (eds), *The Jesuits and the Arts*, p. 424.

5   This information is from Bernardo Illari's 1996 essay 'La ópera y el Otro: *San Ignacio de Loyola* en las reducciones jesuíticas', which he communicated to me directly. I would like to acknowledge his generosity in making available so many of the fruits of his researches.

6   There is a preliminary catalogue by Waldemar A. Roldán, 'Catálogo de manuscritos de música colonial de los archivos de San Ignacio y Concepción (Moxos y Chiquitos), de Bolivia', *Revista del Instituto de Investigación Musicológica 'Carlos Vega'*, 11 (1990), pp. 225–478.

7   See T. Frank Kennedy, SJ on the musical life of the Vienna college in 'Jesuits and Music', in O'Malley and Bailey (eds), *The Jesuits and the Arts*, especially pp. 421–2.

8   Prof. Bernardo Illari kindly communicated to me his (as yet) unpublished score of *San Ignacio de Loyola*: the work is recorded from his edition in the *Chemins du Baroque* series on the K617 label directed by Gabriel Garrido, and by Abendmusik, directed by James Christie, on the Dorian Label, *The Jesuit Operas*.

9   Anonymous Paraguayan master (*c.*1740), *San Francisco Xavier*, ed. Piotr Nawrot SVD (Cochabamba, Bolivia: Editorial Verbo Divino, 2000). The difficulties with the text are outlined on pp. viii–ix. This opera is also recorded, directed by Gabriel Garrido, in the *Chemins du Baroque* series on K617.

10 Anoymous Paraguayan master (*c.*1740), *San Francisco Xavier*, ed. Piotr Nawrot SVD (Cochabamba, Bolivia: Editorial Verbo Divino, 2000), p. 124.

11 Nawrot (ed.) *San Francisco Xavier*, p. 141.

12 Nawrot, (ed.) *San Francisco Xavier*, pp. v–vii, quoting a manuscript original in the Institute for Brazilian Studies at the University of São Paolo, Cod.68.8.A8.

13 These are edited by Piotr Nawrot SVD, in *Cantos Guaranies y Moxeños* (Cochabamba, Bolivia: Editorial Verbo Divino, 2000).

14 *Ibid.*, p. 61.

15 *Ibid.*, pp. 96–130.

16 *Orain Iain Luim*, ed. Annie M. Mackenzie (Edinburgh: Scottish Gaelic Texts Society, 1964), pp. 76–7.

17 Gibb was a prolific and accomplished Latin poet in Rome. The Biblioteca Apostolica, Vatican City, holds multiple copies of his *Carminium Jacobi Albani Ghibbesii* (Rome, 1668). The number of copies in BAV and their provenance from the libraries of the Barberini and Chigi families, amongst others, would suggest that Gibb enjoyed a fair degree of success.

18 This problem of the degree to which Scottish 'traditional' music was formed by awareness of international 'composed' music is responsible for the

curiously primitivist performance traditions which have grown up (for example) for songs to words by Robert Burns. Few orthodoxies, however, are proof against a good tune: among the material collected in the mid-twentieth century by the poet and musicologist Hamish Henderson from seasonal workers in Blairgowrie is a quadrille by the Viennese composer Johann Christof Schetky, none the worse for a couple of centuries of oral transmission.

19 There is a useful discussion of this background in David Johnson's *Scottish Fiddle Music in the Eighteenth Century* (Edinburgh: John Donald, 1984) especially pp. 161–9, including a very detailed analysis of Munro's sonata discussed here.

20 For brief discussion of Clerk as a representative figure for the transmission of continental culture to Scotland, particularly in the field of architectural style, see pp. 76–7 above.

21 The manuscript of the sonata is in the National Archives of Scotland, Edinburgh (Clerk Papers, GD 18/4538/5); an edition by Dr David Johnson was published at Edinburgh in 1990.

22 See Johnson, *Fiddle Music,* pp. 160–4.

23 Johnson points this sequence out on p. 164; the observation is his.

24 (London, 1784). Note that Jones also offers two of his other compositions for sale: a book of Italian songs and a book of sonatas – another Celtic composer clearly moving with ease between the vernacular of his native Wales and the international musical style.

25 Edinburgh, National Library of Scotland, MS 1782. David Johnson, who has transcribed and edited this piece, dates it to around 1770.

26 Discussion of the romantic musical apprehension of Scotland, and of George Thomson's commissions for arrangements, is found in Roger Fiske's classic *Scotland in Music* (Cambridge: Cambridge University Press, 1983); discussion of the career of the Earl of Kellie and of the rise and fall of 'international' music in eighteenth-century Scotland is in David Johnson, *Music and Society in Lowland Scotland in the Eighteenth Century* (London: Oxford University Press, 1972).

27 Which condition of linguistic and cultural hybridity, Scott's son-in-law Lockhart is at great pains to deny in his life of his father-in-law.

28 A comprehensive edition of O'Carolan's works (with a concise and useful account of their textual tradition) is Graínne Yeats (ed.), *The Complete Works of O'Carolan* (Cork: Ossian Publications, 1984), which reproduces in facsimile pages from the earliest states of the text.

29 *Ibid.,* pp. 138–9.

30 *Ibid.,* p. 4. Some pieces of O'Carolan's, one attributed (perhaps facetiously, perhaps not) to 'Sig. Carrollini', were published at Dublin in 1724 in *A Collection of the Most Celebrated Irish Tunes.*

31 Alan J. Porter, *Drama and the Performing Arts in Pre-Cromwellian Ireland* (Woodbridge: D.S. Brewer, 2001), p. 489, quoting eighteenth-century MS *History of Kerry* (Royal Irish Academy, MS 24 K 43).

32 This wonderful album of drawings is published with excellent essays by Toby Barnard, Christine Casey and Peter Harbison, as well as an introduction by the editor: Samuel Chearnley, *Miscelanea Structura Curiosa*, ed. William Laffan (Tralee: Churchill House Press, 2005).

33 *Ibid.*, p. 16. Laffan also advances the fascinating idea of 'provincial eclecticism' in architecture and design, an idea very much in harmony with the case I am advancing for 'devolved' cultural centres.

34 *Ibid.*, p. 49.

35 *Ibid.*, p. 17.

36 It was removed in 1915 after protests from Scottish soliders stationed nearby.

37 *The Earl of Mar's Legacie to Scotland and to his Son, Lord Erskine*, ed. Hon. Stuart Erskine, (Edinburgh: Scottish History Society, 1896), pp. 141–243.

38 Terry Friedman, 'A "Palace Worth the Grandeur of a King" Lord Mar's designs for the Old Pretender, 1718–30', *Architectural History*, 29 (1986), pp. 102–18.

39 This drawing is the National Archives of Scotland, RHP 13256/65.

40 For this and parallel questions, see Macaulay, *The Classical Country House in Scotland.*

41 Margaret Cook Hay Stewart, 'Lord Mar's Plans, 1700–32', (M Litt. dissertation University of Glasgow, 1988).

42 *Ibid.*, p. 5.

43 *Ibid.*, p. 61. The original drawing is National Archives of Scotland, RHP13256/23.

44 *Ibid.*, p. 73. The drawing for the monument is National Archives of Scotland, RHP13258/38. See also Ludovicus Innes, *Relation du feu d'artifice et des illuminations qui ont esté faites au College des Eccosois de Paris le 8 Juillet 1688* (Paris, 1688).

45 A discussion of the phenomenon is found in Judi Loach, 'On Words and Walls', in David Graham (ed.), *An Interregnum of the Sign: The Emblematic Age in France* (Glasgow: Glasgow Emblem Studies, 2001), pp. 149–70; the classic account is Karel Porteman, *Emblematic Exhibitions at the Brussels Jesuit College, 1630-85* (Brussels: Royal Library, 1996).

46 This subject is discussed at length with texts and examples in the two volumes of *Europa Triumphans*, ed. Watanabe-O'Kelly, Mulryne and Shewring.

47 See Jane Stevenson's and my transcription and translation of these emblems (from the Venerable English College, Rome, MS Liber 1422): 'Emblems for the *Vulnerata*, Valladolid, September 1600', in Jan Frans van Dijkhuizen *et al.* (eds) *Living in Posterity: Essays in Honour of Bart Westerweel* (Hilversum: Verloren, 2004), pp. 61–8.

48 The social use of emblems of course includes illustrations and inscriptions in the friendship books or *alba amicorum* carried by educated travellers; most of these show to some degree the use of Latin as a supranational language. A particularly fine early modern example has been printed in facsimile, the album of the well-connected scholar Jan Dousa, *Een netwerk*

aan de basis van de Leidse Universiteit, ed. Christiaan Lambert Heesakkers (Leiden: University of Leiden, 2000).

49 I discuss one such, the Marian sodality directed by the English Jesuit Henry Hawkins, whose meditation-text, illustrated and full of emblems, was printed in Rouen in 1633 as *Parthenia Sacra*, in 'The Jesuit Garden', in *The Jesuits II* ed. O'Malley, Bailey, Harris and Kennedy, especially pp. 89–90.

50 Cf. Loris Fontana, *Valsanzibio* (Padua: Bertoncello Ed., 1990).

51 Judi Loach, 'Revolutionary Pedagogues? How Jesuits Used Education to Change Society', in *The Jesuits II*, ed. O'Malley, Bailey, Harris and Kennedy, pp. 66–85.

52 Alison Saunders and Peter Davidson (eds), *Visual Words and Verbal Pictures: Essays in Honour of Michael Bath* (Glasgow: Glasgow Emblem Studies, 2005).

53 Some sense of the flood of emblem-books and visual devotional manuals on this theme can be gained from the magisterial *Corpus librarum emblematum: The Jesuit Series*, ed. Peter M. Daly and G. Richard Dimler SJ (Toronto, Buffalo and London: University of Toronto Press, 2002), pp. 112–85.

54 Richard Crashaw, *Carmen Deo Nostro* (Paris, 1652), pp. 105–6. In the same volume, p. 85 is illustrated by an engraving of St Mary Magdalene borne up by a winged and flaming heart.

55 St Robert Bellarmine SJ, *De Gemitu Columbae, sive de bono lacrymarum libri tres* (Antwerp, 1617), many subsequent editions.

56 Ripa, *ed.cit.*, p. 128.

57 Kalenberg *et al.*, *El retorno de los angeles*, plate 20.

58 Dieter Bitterli, *Der Bilderhimmel von Hergiswald* (Basel: Weise Verlag, 1997) pp. 160, 172, 270, 324.

59 Jennifer Montagu, *An Index of the Emblems of the Italian Academies* (London: Warburg Institute, 1988).

60 O'Malley and Bailey (eds), *The Jesuits and the Arts*, p. 396.

61 Careri, *Baroques*, pp. 84–7.

62 Porteman, *Emblematic Exhibitions at the Brussels Jesuit College*, p. 69, pp. 114–15.

63 Throughout this section on Orthodox Baroque, Dr Jelena Todorović, on whose published work I have drawn extensively, has advised on every detail and has most generously provided texts, illustrations and translations.

64 Natalia Pylypiuk, 'The First Panegyric of the Kiev Mohyla School', *The Kyiv-Mohyla Academy*, [special number of] *Harvard Ukrainian Studies*, 8: 1 and 2 (1984), pp. 45–70.

65 This whole process could be confirmed and duplicated from the instance of the evolution of a distinctive local Baroque in the Lutheran churches of Scandinavia. Altarpieces and the fine wooden monuments, *epitaphia*, have elements which derive from the international circulation of prints and emblem-books, but the elements derived from local tradition, particularly in ecclesiastical woodcarving are equally strong. The result is the usual 'third term', the emergence of a distinctive Scandinavian Baroque. Cf. Arne Gunnarsjaa, *Norges Arkitekturhistorie* (Oslo: Abstrakt Forlag, 2006); Peter Gillgren, *Gåva*

och själ (Uppsala: Uppsala Academic Press, 1995); Sigrid Christie, *Den Lutherske ikonografi I Norge inntil 1800* (Oslo: Forlaget Land og Kirke, 1973).

66 There is a full discussion of these emblem sources and of transitional Baroque in Dejan Medanković, *Putevi Srpskog baroka* (Belgrade: Nolit, 1971).

67 Teofan Prokopovich, *Sochinenia* (Moscow: Izdatelstvo Akademii Nauk SSSR, 1961).

68 Jelena Todorović, *Entrances and Departures* (Ph.D. dissertation, University College, London, 2004), pp. 140–2; see also Paula Lewin on Ukrainian school drama, *The Kyiv-Mohyla Academy*, pp. 93–123.

69 Todorović, *Entrances and Departures*, pp. 133–4.

70 *Ibid.*, citing Erćić Vlastimir, *Manuil Kozačinskij injegova 'Traedokomedija'* (Novi Sad: Matica Srpska, 1980).

71 This fine manuscript is in the University Library of Wrocław, MS IV fol. 88s. A full modern study of it is Jelena Todorović's *An Orthodox Festival Book in the Habsburg Empire* (Aldershot: Ashgate, 2006), from which I draw all my information on Orfelin's use of the flaming heart, pp. 132–8.

72 The sources for Orfelin's calligraphic heart are discussed in full in Todorović, *An Orthodox Festival*, pp. 133–4.

73 Benedictus van Haeften, *Schola Cordis* (Antwerp, 1635); Francesco Pona, *Cardiomorphoseos* (Verona, 1645).

74 Maurizio Fagiolo dell'Arco, *La festa barocca* (Rome: de Luca, 1997), p. 223.

75 *Ibid.*, p. 224.

76 The oldest example of several such copy-manuscripts appears to be Stonyhurst MS A.v.27. The edition by Davidson and Sweeney, *The Collected Poems of St Robert Southwell*, is based largely on this manuscript.

77 For this reading I am indebted to discussions with Dr Anne Dillon and to Dr Anne Sweeney, whose exemplary reading of this poem is in her *Robert Southwell, Snow in Arcadia, Redrawing the English Lyric Landscape, 1586–1595* (Manchester: Manchester University Press, 2006), pp. 278–9.

78 Alan R. Young, *Emblematic Flag Devices of the English Civil Wars* (Toronto: University of Toronto Press, 1995), p. 2.

79 The image is engraved by Jean-Baptiste Letourmy, cf. Françoise Demange, *Images de la révolution, l'imagerie populaire orléanaise à l'époque révolutionnaire* (exhibition catalogue, Orléans: Beaux Arts, 1989).

80 See Nikolaus Pevsner, *The Buildings of England: North Somerset and Bristol* (Harmondsworth: Penguin, 1958), pp. 128–9.

81 Nicolaus Pevsner and Bridget Cherry, *The Buildings of England: Northamptonshire* (Harmondsworth: Penguin, 1973), pp. 300–1.

82 Cesare Ripa, *Iconologia*, ed. Piero Buscaroli (Milan: Tea Arte, 1992), pp. 97–8.

83 Cf. Praz, *Flaming Heart*, p. 205.

84 This anagram and the Latin monostich developing it were printed in the prefatory pages to Vondel's *Maria Stuart of Gemarteleerde Majesteit* (Keulen, 1646).

85 D'Ors, *Du baroque*, p. 171.

Epilogue

It is sometimes possible, even now, to experience a baroque work of art in a way analagous to that in which one imagines it would originally have been experienced.

Giardini Buonaccorsi

By an extraordinary series of coincidences, a flower garden laid out on one of the symbolic plans published in the treatise on the flower garden *De Florum Cultura* (Rome, 1633) by the Italian Jesuit Giovanni Battista Ferrari (*c.*1580–1655) survives in Italy to this day. The Giardini Buonaccorsi near Macerata are famous for their extraordinary statuary and for their preservation of a layout dating in the main from the early eighteenth century. (Indeed, the gardens are almost crowded with eighteenth-century statues of high quality, an element which makes a solitary visit a most remarkable experience of populated emptiness.) They also preserve on the uppermost terrace, between the villa and its chapel, a mid-seventeenth-century *giardino segreto* laid out from Ferrari's plans and maintained in accordance with his precepts.

The source is unequivocal: the seventeenth-century Conte Buonaccorsi's copy of the 1637 reprint of *De Florum Cultura* survives in the section of the *Biblioteca Nazionale da Napoli* kept at Macerata.[1] This layout, with its statues and little obelisks, its stone-edged geometrical beds, gives the fullest sense possible of the ambitions and pleasures of the baroque flower garden which Ferrari sought to transplant from the Low Countries to Italy.

This upper terrace is laid out from the first of the symbolic garden plans published in Ferrari's treatise: it evokes both the Celestial City

and the Garden of Eden. The central part of Ferrari's plate 25 is repeated
four times in the *giardino segreto* of the Villa Buonaccorsi, symmetrical
about a central fountain which evokes the unfallen garden with its fountain from whence flowed the four rivers of Paradise, while the whole
in its symmetries of fours answers to Ferrari's apprehension of the 'mystical mathematics of the city of heaven'.[2]

> If it might be to anybody a pleasure to design within the bounds of a gar-
> den the blessed seat of the Holy City in its eternal stability, laid out in
> four quarters of celestial beauty, and to acclimatise something heavenly
> on the earth, this is proposed here since the diagram divides the garden
> into patterns of fours.

The rare visitor to the Giardini Buonaccorsi is privileged to experience an aspect of baroque experience and aesthetics which survives
nowhere else. Deserted but not abandoned, kept in wonderful order
by local custodians, the garden spreads in its terraces down the slope.
On the middle terraces, the statue of Flora still sprays water from her
bouquet and crown at the unsuspecting visitor, and a hedge of jets of
water arises to imprison them amongst the statues and obelisks at the
centre of the garden. In the grotto on the lowest terrace (more disquieting, somehow, than any ossuary, than any bones dressed in gold
brocade) the skeletal automata of a Turk and a Pierrot stand (motion-
less now) in their eighteenth-century rags. Under the villa itself is a
grotto of rough stone (in the tradition of all the ruin rooms, the artificial
caves) inhabited by statues of monastic hermits in ecstasy, and furnished
with an automaton of a devil who springs forward like the cuckoo out
of a clock.

But the most remarkable survival of all is the original *giardino segreto*, the three-and-a-half centuries' survival of an ephemeral flower-
garden laid out on the symbolic plan of the Jesuit treatise. And the
precise sense in which a visit to it is an exploration of the sensibility
of the Baroque is that it offers a double experience: the garden of the
senses is full (very unusual for the south) of scented flowers. It is ornamented with wonderful statuary, disposed on the bright hillside with a
prospect of olive groves across the valley. The garden is 'paradisal', and
yet, knowing its purpose, reading the hieroglyphic of the disposition
of its geometry, it is a limited simulacrum of the otherworldly garden
of Paradise and, accordingly, carries within it an admonition to dissatisfaction with its transient beauty. *Post hoc exilium*. Baroque time.
Simultaneous gratification and disquiet is a complex sensation at the
heart of baroque aesthetics.

The opera of *San Francisco Xavier*

Another extraordinary access to the Baroque was an invitation to a performance of a fabulous rarity, never performed in Britain before, the opera *San Francisco Xavier*, composed in the remote 'reductions' of the Chiquitos, in lowland Bolivia (see pp. 144–50 above). By the determination and enterprise of the Hispanists of Nottingham University, scores were obtained, and two able Englishmen were coached in the arduous text, sung entirely in the Amerindian language of the region where the opera was composed. It is only after two centuries and more that the work has begun of deciphering, and disseminating world-wide, the music produced in those Jesuit towns of Spanish America.

The Amerindian opera in performance brought many ideas to focus – about works written, as it was originally, for young performers, and also about the fearless internationalism of the baroque arts. There are only two named performers, representing St Ignatius of Loyola and St Francis Xavier. It is scored for two trebles, but originally the performers would have been more of university age – early modern diet ensured that most seventeenth-century boys' voices remained unbroken into their late teens. The modern performers, baritone and tenor, were singing consistently high in their ranges, part of the sense of strain which, in the end, became a vital part of the performance. The enjoyment of the contemplation of strain is, I suspect, a vital part of Baroque aesthetics. The two students who represented St Ignatius and St Francis Xavier were singing as if singing was like ice-climbing, as if their lives depended on holding the thread of the figured bass. Thus they sang with hallucinatory attention to the difficult text which they had worked to master, and the tension in the singers was the spring which drove the whole. There was a lesson to be learned in baroque aesthetics: the sense that watching the two performers stretched to the limits of their skill and concentration was to watch an action of catechesis.

In opposition to this tension was the content of the piece: a succession of arias and duets filled with rejoicing, with a scarcely imaginable happiness. '*Au nipostij Tupas ape, cheanapî nauxîxîquis, cheanapî maquietis, cheanapî niquîpuras*' – 'in Heaven, in the house of God, there is no cold, nor wind, nor thunder'. The palpable, anxious tension of the two young men came from the difficulty of the music (dance music deepened as far as it can be deepened), but when the two voices came together, there was a sense of the creation of authority, of the witnessing of a truth. Usually voices singing in thirds, wreathing around each other in imitative phrases, express sexual love: here the duets were something unfamiliar – music full of energy and expressive of love, but wholly sexless.

As I listened to the two young men in their soutanes and Roman collars singing in the language of the red-earthed lowlands of Bolivia it came to me more and more that this enterprise was inhabiting a remote, but absolutely contiguous, region of a familiar world. It was a matter of being overwhelmed by a weary love for that world of the tireless Baroque, loving the hugeness and permeability of the Hispanic territories, most themselves when most intensely hybrid. It was a matter of remembering with reluctant, sombre affection the whole cultural landscape lying behind those two youthful figures in soutanes, singing familiar mysteries in an arcane tongue.

It was partly an appreciation of history and partly a recollection of the manifestations of that history remembered from childhood. Then I recovered the precise memory and recalled the weeping images in Spain in Holy Week, passing along the Alameda by torchlight (I was told that their tears were pearls and diamonds), the pauses in the drumbeats, and the songs – *Saetas*, arrows of song, sung to them out of the crowd as they halted. The style of those songs of love, addressed to the statues of the Virgin with the swords in her heart, was the style of the music which still came out of the radios in the cafes in those days: the incorporation of the local popular tradition into an universal commemoration. Another example of feeling and being in two modes (idioms, tones, languages) at the same moment. *Barrocos fuimos siempre.*

Notes

1   It is due to the great kindness of Dr Gabriele Cingolani and Prof. Carlo Vecce that access was obtained to this remarkable place, not currently made available to the public.
2   Giovanni Battista Ferrari SJ, *De Florum Cultura* (Rome, 1633), p. 29.

Bibliography

Manuscripts

Bodleian Library, Oxford, MS Eng Poet b. 5
Cambridge University Library, Bradshaw collection 5311, Hib. 7.664.33
East Sussex Record Office, Glyne MS 314
National Archives, London, SP 12/254/67
National Archives of Scotland, Edinburgh, Clerk papers, GD 18/4538/5
National Archives of Scotland, Edinburgh, RHP 13258/38, RHP 13256/23
National Library of Scotland, Edinburgh, MS 1782
Royal Irish Academy, Dublin, MS 24 K 43
Salamanca University Library, MS 1343
Stonyhurst College, MS A.v.4
Stonyhurst College, MS Anglia.v.IV
Stonyhurst College, MS Anglia.v.27
Venerable English College, Rome, MS Liber 1422
Wrocław University Library, MS IV fol. 88s
Yale University, Beinecke Library, MS Osborn Shelves fb 228

Primary Sources

Anonymous Paraguayan master (*c.*1740), *Cantos Guaraníes y Moxeños*, ed. Piotr Nawrot SVD (Cochabamba, Bolivia: Editorial Verbo Divino, 2000)
—— *San Francisco Xavier*, ed. Piotr Nawrot SVD (Cochabamba, Bolivia: Editorial Verbo Divino, 2000)
Ascham, Roger, *The Scholemaster, or plaine and perfite way of teachyng children, to vnderstand, write, and speake, the Latin tong* (London: John Day, 1570)
Ashrea: or, the Grove of Beatitudes, represented in Emblemes: and, by the Art of Memory, to be read on our Blessed Saviour Crucifi'd: with Considerations and meditations suitable to every Beatitude, and to the holy time of Lent (London: W.P., 1665)
Bellarmine SJ, St Robert, *De Gemitu Columbae, sive de bono lacrymarum libri tres* (Antwerp, 1617)

Benavides, Alonso de, *Memorial of 1630* (Washington, DC: Academy of American Franciscan History, 1954)

Caus, Salomon de, *Hortus Palatinus: die Entwürfe zum Heidelberger Schlossgarten von Salomon de Caus, 1620* (Worms: Werner'sche Verlags Gesellschaft, facsimile edn, 1980)

Chearnley, Samuel, *Miscelanea Structura Curiosa*, ed. William Laffan (Tralee: Churchill House Press, 2005)

A Collection of the Most Celebrated Irish Tunes (Dublin, 1724)

Crashaw, Richard, *Carmen Deo Nostro* (Paris, 1652)

Donne, John, *Selected Prose*, ed. Neil Rhodes (Harmondsworth: Penguin, 1987)

Dousa, Jan, *Een netwerk aan de basis van de Leidse Universiteit*, ed. Christiaan Lambert Heesakkers (Leiden: University of Leiden, 2000)

Drummond of Hawthornden, William, *Forth Feasting: a panegyrike to the King's most excellent maiestie* (Edinburgh: Andro Hart, 1617)

Erskine, John, Earl of Mar, *The Earl of Mar's Legacie to Scotland and to his son, Lord Erskine*, ed. Hon. Stuart Erskine (Edinburgh: Scottish History Society, 1896)

Fanshawe, Sir Richard, *The Poems and Translations of Sir Richard Fanshawe*, ed. Peter Davidson, 2 vols. (Oxford: Clarendon, 1997–99)

Ferrari, Giovanni Battista, *De Florum Cultura* (Rome, 1633)

Gage, Thomas, *The English-American* (London: Routledge, 1828 [1648])

Geddes, William Duguid (ed.), *Musa Latina Aberdonensis*, 3 vols. (Aberdeen: New Spalding Club, 1892–1910)

Gheyn, Jacob de, *Waffen handlung von den roren, musquetten undt spiessen* (The Hague, 1608)

Gibb[s], James Alban, *Carminium Jacobi Albani Ghibbesii* (Rome, 1668)

Haeften, Benedictus van, *Schola Cordis* (Antwerp, 1635)

Herbert, George, *The Works of George Herbert*, ed. F.E. Hutchinson (Oxford: Clarendon, 1945)

Herrera, Antonio de, *Historia General de los Hechos de los Castellanos* (Madrid, 1615)

Huygens, Constantijn, *Heilighe Dagen*, ed. L. Strengholt (Amsterdam: Buijten and Schipperheijn, 1974)

—— *A Selection of the Poems of Sir Constantijn Huygens*, ed. Peter Davidson and Adriaan van der Weel (Amsterdam: Amsterdam University Press, 1996)

St Ignatius of Loyola, *Personal Writings*, ed. and trans. Joseph A. Munitiz SJ and Philip Endean SJ (London: Penguin, 1996)

Ijsewijn, Jozef, *Companion to Neo-Latin Studies*, 2 vols. (Leuven: Leuven University Press and Peeters, 1990, 1998)

Innes, Ludovicus, *Relation du feu d'artifice et des illuminations qui ont esté faites au College des Eccosois de Paris le 8 Juillet 1688* (Paris, 1688)

Ixtlilxóchitl, Fernando de Alva, *Obras historicas*, ed. Alfredo Chavero (Mexico City: Editora Nacional, 1952)

Johnson, Arthur (ed.), *Delitiae Poetarum Scotorum* (Amsterdam: Johann Bleau, 1637)

Jones, Edward, *Musical and Poetical Works of the Welsh Bards* (London, 1784)

Jones, Inigo, *The most notable Antiquity of Great Britain, vulgarly called Stone-Heng on Salisbury Plain* (London, 1655)

Juana, Inés de la Cruz, Sor, *Obras completas*, ed. Francisco Monterde (Mexico: Porrua, 1989)

Keirney, Barnabas, *Heliotropon* (Paris: Cramoisi, 1633)

Kircher SJ, Athanasius, *Ars Magnae Lucis et Umbrae* (Rome, 1646)

—— *Mundus Subterraneus* (Amsterdam, 1665)

—— *Romani colegii Societatis Jesu musaeum celeberrimum* (Amsterdam, 1678)

Knox, John, *An Answer to a Letter of a Jesuit called Tyrie* (St Andrews, 1570)

Lom, Iain, *Orain Iain Luim*, ed. Annie M. Mackenzie (Edinburgh: Scottish Gaelic Texts Society, 1964)

Melvill, James, *The Autobiography and Diary of Mr James Melvill*, ed. R. Pitcairn (Edinburgh: Wodrow Society, 1842)

Melvill, James, *Ad Serenissumum Jacobum Primum . . . ecclesiae scoticae libellus supplex* (London: George Thomason and Octavian Pullen, 1645)

Montaigne, Michel de, *The Essayes of Michael Lord of Montaigne*, trans. John Florio (London: Oxford University Press, 1910)

—— *Oeuvres complètes*, ed. Albert Thibaudet and Maurice Rat (Paris: Gallimard, 1962)

Nieremberg, Johannis Eusebius, *Historia Naturae* (Antwerp: Plantijn-Moretus, 1635)

O'Carolan, Turlough, *The Complete Works of O'Carolan*, ed. Graínne Yeats (Cork: Ossian Publications, 1984)

Oldani SJ, Louis J. and Philip C. Fisher SJ (eds), *Jesuit Theater Englished* (St Louis: Institute of Jesuit Sources, 1989)

Ó Tuama, Seán and Thomas Kinsella (eds), *An Duanaire 1600–1900* (Portlaoise: Dolmen Press, 1981)

Peacham, Henry, *Henry Peacham's Manuscript Emblem Books*, ed. Alan R. Young (Toronto: University of Toronto Press, 1998)

Plancarte, Alfonso Méndez, *Poetas Novohispanos, primer siglo (1521–1621)* (Mexico City: University of Mexico, 1964)

Pona, Francesco, *Cardiomorphoseos* (Verona, 1645)

Pope, Alexander, *The Works of Mr Alexander Pope* (London: Lintot, 1717)

Prokopovich, Teofan, *Sochinenia* (Moscow: Izdatelstvo Akademii Nauk SSSR, 1961)

Ribas SJ, Andrés Pérez de, *History of the Triumphs of our Holy Faith*, trans. Daniel T. Reff, Maureen Ahearn and Richard K. Danford (Tucson: University of Arizona Press, 1999)

Richeome SJ, Louis, *Les Oevres du R. père Louis Richeome . . . revues par l'autheur avant sa mort* (Paris: Sebastien Cramoisy, 1628)

Rinuccini, Giovanni Battista, *Commentarius Rinuccinianus* (Dublin: Irish Manuscripts Commission, 1932–49)

Ripa, Cesare, *Iconologia*, ed. Piero Buscaroli (Milan: Tea Arte, 1992)

St Rosa de Lima, *Celebridad y Fiestas, con que la Insigne y nobilissima Ciudad de los Reyes Solemnizo la Beatificacion de la Bienaventura ROSA DE S.MARIA SU PATRONA Y DE TODOS LOS REYNOS Y PROVINCIAS DEL PERU* (Lima, 1670)

Sarbiewski, Mathias Casimir, *The Odes of Casimire, Translated by G. H[il]* (London: Humphrey Mosley, 1646)

Sigüenza y Góngora, Carlos de, *Glorias de Querétaro en la Nueva Congregación Eclesiástica de María Santissima de Guadelupe* (Mexico City, 1680)

—— *Seis obras*, ed. Irving A. Leonard and William G. Bryant (Caracas: Biblioteca Ayacucho, 1984)

Sousa SJ, António de, *Relación de la real Tragicomedia* (Lisbon: Jorge Rodriguez, 1620)

Southwell, St Robert, *The Collected Poems of St Robert Southwell*, ed. Peter Davidson and Anne Sweeney (Manchester: Carcanet, 2007)

Verduccioli, Felice, *In Funere Iosephi A Giaceto Castelvillani Comitis &c. Oratio Felicis Verduccioli* (Perugia: Typographia Episcopali, 1643)

Verstegan, Richard, *The Restitution of Decayed intelligence in Antiquities* (Antwerp: Robert Bruney, 1605)

Vondel, Joost van den, *Maria Stuart of Gemarteleerde Majesteit* (Keulen, 1646)

Wadding, Luke, *A Smale Garland of Pious and Godly Songs, composed by a devout Man, for the Solace of his Freinds and neighbours in their afflictions* (Ghent, 1684)

Secondary Sources

Auer, Alfred, *Ambras Castle* (Milan: Electa/Vienna Kunsthistorisches Museum, 2000)

Bailey, Gauvin Alexander, *Art of Colonial Latin America* (London: Phaidon, 2005)

—— *Art on the Jesuit Missions in Asia and Latin America, 1542–1773* (Toronto: University of Toronto Press, 1999)

—— *Between Renaissance and Baroque: Jesuit Art in Rome, 1565–1610* (Toronto: University of Toronto Press, 2003)

—— *The Jesuits and the Grand Mogul: Renaissance Art at the Imperial Court of India* (Washington: Smithsonian Institution, 1992)

—— 'Le style jésuite n'existe pas', *The Jesuits: Cultures, Sciences and the Arts*, ed. John W. O'Malley SJ, Gauvin Alexander Bailey, Steven J. Harris and T. Frank Kennedy SJ (Toronto: University of Toronto Press, 1999)

Bann, Stephen, *Under the Sign: John Bargrave as Collector, Traveler and Witness* (Ann Arbor: University of Michigan, 1994)

Bath, Michael, *Renaissance Decorative Painting in Scotland* (Edinburgh: National Museums of Scotland, 2003)

—— John Manning and Alan R. Young (eds), *The Art of the Emblem* (New York: AMS Press, 1993)

Baur-Heinhold, Margurete, *Baroque Theatre* (London: Thames and Hudson, 1967)

Bérchez, Joaquín (ed.), *Los siglos de oro en los virreinatos de América* (exhibition catalogue, Madrid: Museo de América, 1999)

Binns, James Wallace, *Intellectual Culture in Elizabethan and Jacobean England* (Leeds: Francis Cairns, 1990)

Bitterli, Dieter, *Der Bilderhimmel von Hergiswald* (Basel: Weise Verlag, 1997)

Blunt, Anthony, *The Art and Architecture of France, 1500–1700* (London and Baltimore: Johns Hopkins University Press, 1953)

Brading, David, *The First America* (Cambridge: Cambridge University Press, 1991)

Briesemeister, Dietrich, 'Inszenierungen des Fremden in Frankreich und Portugal (1550/1619)', in *Die ganze Welt ist Bühne, Festschrift für Klaus Pörti* (Frankfurt: Peter Lang, 2003)

Burke, Peter, *The Art of Conversation* (Cambridge: Polity Press, 1993)

Burton, John Hill, *The History of Scotland from Agricola's Invasion to the Extinction of the Last Jacobite Rebellion*, 8 vols. (Edinburgh: William Blackwood & Sons, 1897)

A Calendar of the Manuscripts of the Most Hon. the Marquess of Salisbury, KG, &c., Preserved at Hatfield House, Hertfordshire (London: Historical Manuscripts Commission, 1888–1973)

Calligaro, Thomas, *et al.*, 'PIXE Reveals that Two Murillo Masterpieces Were Painted on Mexican Obsidian Slabs', *Nuclear Instruments and Methods in Physics Research*, 240:1–2 (October 2005)

Careri, Giovanni, *Baroques* (Princeton: Princeton University Press, 2003)

Le chant de la Jérusalem des terres froides, audio CD, Studio de Musique Ancienne de Montréal directed by Christopher Jackson (K617 Records, 1995).

Chaves, Jonathan, *Singing of the Source: Nature and God in the Poetry of the Chinese Painter Wu Li* (Honolulu: Hawaii University Press, 1993)

Christie, Sigrid, *Den Lutherske ikonografi I Norge inntil 1800* (Oslo: Forlaget Land og Kirke, 1973)

Coffin, David R., *The English Garden: Meditation and Memorial* (Princeton: Princeton University Press, 1994)

Croce, Benedetto, *La storia di l'età barocca in Italia* (Bari: Laterza, 1957)

Daly, Peter M. and G. Richard Dimler SJ (eds), *Corpus librarum emblematum: The Jesuit Series* (Toronto, Buffalo and London: University of Toronto Press, 2002)

Davidson, Peter, 'The Entry of Mary Stewart into Edinburgh, 1561, and other Ambiguities', *Renaissance Studies*, 9:4 (December 1995)

—— 'The Jesuit Garden', in *The Jesuits II: Cultures, Sciences and the Arts, 1540–1773*, ed. John W. O'Malley SJ, Gauvin Alexander Bailey, Steven J. Harris and T. Frank Kennedy SJ (Toronto: University of Toronto Press, 2006)

—— 'Marvellian Questions', *TLS* (3 December 1999)

—— 'The Theatrum for Claudia de'Medici, Urbino 1621', in *Court Festivals of the European Renaissance*, ed. Elizabeth Goldring and J.R. Mulryne (Aldershot: Ashgate, 2002)

Della Vida, Giorgio Levi, *George Strachan: Memorials of a Wandering Scottish Scholar of the Seventeenth Century* (Aberdeen: Third Spalding Club, 1956)

Demange, Françoise, *Images de la révolution, l'imagerie populaire orléanaise à l'époque révolutionnaire* (exhibition catalogue, Orléans: Beaux Arts, 1989)

De Simone, Roberto, *Il presepe popolare napoletano* (Turin: Einaudi, 1998)

Dorsten, Jan A. van, *The Radical Arts* (Leiden: Leiden University Press, and London: Oxford University Press, 1970)

—— 'Mr Secretary Cecil: Patron of Letters', in *The Anglo-Dutch Renaissance: Seven Essays* (Leiden: Leiden University Press and London: Oxford University Press, 1988)

Dowling, Patrick, *The Hedge Schools of Ireland* (London: Longmans, Green & Co., 1935)

Eliot, Thomas Stearns, *The Varieties of Metaphysical Poetry* (London: Faber, 1993 [1926])

Fagiolo dell'Arco, Maurizio, *La festa barocca* (Rome: de Luca, 1997)

Farrelly, Peter V., *600 Years of Theatre in Kilkenny, 1366–1966* (Kilkenny: P.V. Publications, n.d.)

Fiske, Roger, *Scotland in Music* (Cambridge: Cambridge University Press, 1983)

Fletcher, Alan J., *Drama and the Performing Arts in Pre-Cromwellian Ireland* (Cambridge: D.S. Brewer, 2001)

Fontana, Loris, *Valsanzibio* (Padua: Bertoncello Ed., 1990)

Friedman, Terry, 'A "Palace Worth the Grandeur of a King": Lord Mar's Designs for the Old Pretender, 1718–30', *Architectural History*, 29 (1986)

Gaunt, William, *Bandits in a Landscape* (London and New York: The Studio, 1937)

Gillgren, Peter, *Gåva och själ* (Uppsala: Uppsala Academic Press, 1995)

Gisbert, Teresa, *Iconografiá y mitos indigenas en el arte* (La Paz: Linea Editorial, Fundación BHN, Editorial Gisbert y Cia, 1994)

—— and José de Mesa, 'Ángeles y arcángeles', in Kalenberg, *et al.*, *El retorno de los angeles*

—— and José de Mesa, *La tradición biblica en el arte virreynal* (La Paz: Los Amigos del Libro, 1986)

Gockerell, Nina, *Nacimentos* (Munich: Bavarian National Museum/Taschen, 1998)

Gregson, Ian, 'Camp's Out', *Poetry Review*, 86:3 (Autumn 1996)

Grierson, Sir Herbert, *The First Half of the Seventeenth Century* (Edinburgh: Blackwood, 1906)

—— (ed.), *Metaphysical Lyrics and Poems of the Seventeenth Century* (Oxford: Clarendon, 1921)

Gunnarsjaa, Arne, *Norges arkitekturhistorie* (Oslo: Abstrakt Forlag, 2006)

Harbison, Robert, *Reflections on Baroque* (London: Reaktion, 2000)

Heikamp, Detlef, *Mexico and the Medici* (Florence: Edam, 1972)

Illari, Bernardo, *Fiesta Criolla*, booklet accompanying audio CD (K617 Records, 2003)

—— 'La ópera y el Otro: *San Ignacio de Loyola* en las reducciones jesuíticas' (unpublished essay)

Jackson, Kenneth Hurlstone, *A Celtic Miscellany* (Harmondsworth: Penguin, 1971)

Jensen, Minna Skafte (ed.), *A History of Nordic Neo-Latin Literature* (Odense: Odense University Press, 1995)

Johnson, David, *Music and Society in Lowland Scotland in the Eighteenth Century* (London: Oxford University Press, 1972)

—— *Scottish Fiddle Music in the Eighteenth Century* (Edinburgh: John Donald, 1984)

Jones, Barbara, *Follies and Grottoes* (London: Constable, 1974)

Kalenberg, Ángel *et al.*, *El retorno de los angeles: barroco de las cumbres de Bolivia* (exhibition catalogue, Montevideo: Museo Nacional de Artes Visuales, 2000)

Kendrick, Thomas Downing, *Mary of Ágreda: The Life and Legend of a Spanish Nun* (London: Routledge, 1967)

Kennedy SJ, T. Frank, 'Jesuits and Music', in O'Malley and Bailey (eds), *The Jesuits and the Arts*

King, John N., 'Patronage and Piety: The Influence of Catherine Parr', in *Silent But for the Word*, ed. Margaret P. Hannay (Kent, OH: Kent State University Press, 1985)

Kinsley, James (ed.), *The Oxford Book of Ballads* (Oxford and New York: Oxford University Press, 1989)

Klarwill, Victor von (ed.), *Queen Elizabeth and some Foreigners: Being a Series of Hitherto Unpublished Letters from the Archives of the Hapsburg Family* (London: John Lane, the Bodley Head Ltd, 1928)

Leonard, Irving A., *Baroque Times in Old Mexico* (Ann Arbor: University of Michigan Press, 1966)

Lescarbot, Marc, *Les Muses de la Nouvelle France*, ed. Bernard Emont (Paris: Harmattan, 2004)

Llewellyn, Nigel, *Death, Passion and Politics* (London: Dulwich Picture Gallery, 1995)

Loach, Judi, 'On Words and Walls', in David Graham (ed.), *An Interregnum of the Sign: The Emblematic Age in France* (Glasgow: Glasgow Emblem Studies, 2001)

—— 'Revolutionary Pedagogues? How Jesuits Used Education to Change Society', in *The Jesuits II: Cultures, Sciences and the Arts 1540–1773*, ed. O'Malley, Bailey, Harris and Kennedy

Lo Sardo, Eugenio (ed.), *Athanasius Kircher, il museo del mondo* (Rome: de Luca, 2001)

Lyall, Roderick J., *Alexander Montgomerie: Poetry, Politics and Cultural Change in Jacobean Scotland* (Tempe, Arizona: ACMRS, 2005)

McCabe SJ, William H., *An Introduction to the Jesuit Theater* (St Louis: Institute of Jesuit Sources, 1983)

Macaulay, James, *The Classical Country House in Scotland, 1660–1800* (London: Faber and Faber, 1987)

McFarlane, Ian Dalrymple, *Buchanan* (London: Duckworth, 1981)

Manieri-Elia, Mario, *Barocco leccese* (Milan: Electa, 1989)

The Manuscripts of the Marquis of Ormonde, preserved at The Castle, Kilkenny (London: Historical Manuscripts Commission, 1895)

Mauriès, Patrick, *Cabinets of Curiosities* (London: Thames and Hudson, 2002)

May, Steven W., *The Elizabethan Courtier Poets: The Poems and their Contexts* (Columbia: University of Missouri Press, 1991)

Medanković, Dejan, *Putevi Srpskog baroka* (Belgrade: Nolit, 1971)

Meslay, Olivier, 'Murillo and "Smoking Mirrors"', *The Burlington Magazine*, 143:1175 (February 2001)

Montagu, Jennifer, *An Index of the Emblems of the Italian Academies* (London: Warburg Institute, 1988)

Mosser, Monique and George Teyssot (eds), *The History of Garden Design: The Western Tradition from the Renaissance to the Present Day* (London: Thames and Hudson, 1991)

Mowl, Timothy, *Elizabethan and Jacobean Style* (London: Phaidon, 1993)

Nenner, Howard, *The Right to be King: The Succession to the Crown of England, 1603–1714* (Chapel Hill: University of North Carolina Press, 1995)

O'Malley SJ, John W. and Gauvin Alexander Bailey (eds), *The Jesuits and the Arts, 1540–1773* (Philadelphia: Saint Joseph's University Press, 2006)

Orgel, Stephen and Roy Strong, *Inigo Jones and the Theatre of the Stuart Court*, 2 vols. (London: University of California Press, 1973)

d'Ors, Eugenio, *Lo barocco*, ed. Ángel d'Ors and Alicia García Navaro de d'Ors (Madrid: Tecnos/Alianza, 2002)

—— *Du baroque*, trans. Agathe Rouart-Valéry (Paris: nrf/Gallimard, 1968 [1935])

Parry, Graham, *The Arts of the Anglican Counter-Reformation* (Woodbridge: Boydell, 2006)

Peck, Linda Levy, 'Women as Court Brokers: Queen Anne's Household', in *Court Patronage and Corruption in Early Stuart England* (London: Routledge, 1993)

Pevsner, Nicolaus, *The Buildings of England: North Somerset and Bristol* (Harmondsworth: Penguin, 1958)

—— *The Buildings of England: South and West Somerset* (Harmondsworth: Penguin, 1958)

—— and Bridget Cherry, *The Buildings of England: Northamptonshire* (Harmondsworth: Penguin, 1973)

Pollen, J. Hungerford (ed.), *Unpublished Documents Relating to the English Martyrs*, 2 vols. (London: Catholic Record Society, 1908, 1914)

Porteman, Karel, *Emblematic Exhibitions at the Brussels Jesuit College, 1630–85* (Brussels: Royal Library, 1996)

Praz, Mario, *The Flaming Heart* (New York: Norton, 1973 [1958])

—— *Secentismo e Marinismo in Inghilterra* (Florence: La Voce, 1925)

Prescott, William H., *The Conquest of Mexico* (London: Richard Bentley, 1854)

Prest, John, *The Garden of Eden* (New Haven and London: Yale University Press, 1981)

Pylypiuk, Natalia, 'The First Panegyric of the Kiev Mohyla School', *The Kyiv-Mohyla Academy, Harvard Ukrainian Studies*, 8:1–2 (1984)

Rincón, Carlos, 'La poética de lo real-maravilloso americano', in *Recopilación de textos sobre Alejo Carpentier* (Havana: Casa de las Américas, La Habana, 1977)

Roldán, Waldemar A., 'Catálogo de manuscritos de música colonial de los archivos de San Ignacio y Concepción (Moxos y Chiquitos), de Bolivia', *Revista del Instituto de Investigación Musicológica 'Carlos Vega'*, 11 (1990)

Rosenberg, Eleanor, *Leicester, Patron of Letters* (New York: Columbia University Press, 1955)

Saunders, Alison and Peter Davidson (eds), *Visual Words and Verbal Pictures: Essays in Honour of Michael Bath* (Glasgow: Glasgow Emblem Studies, 2005)

Shell, Alison, *Catholicism, Controversy and the English Literary Imagination* (Cambridge: Cambridge University Press, 1999)

Shire, Helena Mennie, *Song, Dance and Poetry of the Court of Scotland under King James VI* (Cambridge: Cambridge University Press, 1969)

Sitwell, Sacheverell, *Southern Baroque Art* (London: Grant Richards, 1924)

Smuts, R. Malcolm, *Court Culture and the Origins of Royalist Tradition in Early Stuart England* (Philadelphia: University of Pennsylvania Press, 1987)

Standaert SJ, Nicolas, 'Jesuit Corporate Culture as Shaped by the Chinese', in *The Jesuits*, ed. O'Malley, Bailey, Harris, and Kennedy

Steele SJ, Thomas J., *Santos and Saints: The Religious Folk Art of New Mexico* (Santa Fé: Ancient City Press, 1982)

Stevens, Wallace, *The Collected Poems* (New York: Vintage, 1982)

Stevenson, Jane, *Women Latin Poets* (Oxford: Oxford University Press, 2005)

—— and Peter Davidson, 'Emblems for the *Vulnerata*, Valladolid, September 1600', in *Living in Posterity: Essays in Honour of Bart Westerweel*, ed. Jan Frans van Dijkhuizen *et al.* (Hilversum: Verloren, 2004)

Stewart, Margaret Cook Hay, 'Lord Mar's Plans, 1700–32' (MLitt. dissertation, University of Glasgow, 1988)

Stolzenberg, Daniel (ed.), *The Great Art of Knowing: The Baroque Encyclopedia of Athanasius Kircher* (Stanford: Stanford University Libraries, 2001)

Stone, Lawrence, *The Crisis of the Aristocracy, 1558–1641* (London: Oxford University Press, 1967)

Sullivan, Edward, J.T. Gilbert and Sir Henry James (eds), *Facsimiles of National Manuscripts of Ireland*, 5 vols. (Dublin: Public Record Office of Ireland, 1874–84)

Sutton, Dana F., 'The Queen's Latin', *Neulateinische Jahrbuch/Journal of Neo-Latin Language and Literature*, 2 (2000)

Strong, Roy, ' "My Weeping Stag I Crowne": The Persian Lady Reconsidered', in Bath, Manning and Young (eds), *The Art of the Emblem*

Swain, Margaret, *The Needlework of Mary, Queen of Scots* (Carlton: Ruth Bean, 1987)

Sweeney, Anne, *Robert Southwell, Snow in Arcadia: Redrawing the English Lyric Landscape, 1586–95* (Manchester: Manchester University Press, 2006)

Todorović, Jelena, 'Entrances and Departures' (Ph.D. dissertation, University College, London, 2004)

—— *An Orthodox Festival Book in the Habsburg Empire* (Aldershot: Ashgate, 2006)

Vlastimir, Erčić, *Manuil kozačinskij injegova 'Traedokomedija'* (Novi Sad: Matica Srpska, 1980)

Waquet, Françoise, *Latin, or the Empire of a Sign*, trans. John Howe (London and New York: Verso, 2000)

Watanabe-O'Kelly, Helen, Ronnie Mulryne and Margaret Shewring (eds), *Europa Triumphans: Court and Civic Festivals in Early Modern Europe* (Aldershot: Ashgate, 2004)

Wheen, Francis, *Tom Driberg* (London: Chatto and Windus, 1990)

Williams, Franklin B., 'The Literary Patronesses of Renaissance England', *Notes and Queries*, 9:10 (1962)

Wyatt, Michael, *The Italian Encounter with Tudor England: A Cultural Politics of Translation* (Cambridge: Cambridge University Press, 2005)

Young, Alan R., *Emblematic Flag Devices of the English Civil Wars* (Toronto: University of Toronto Press, 1995)

Index

EU authorised representative for GPSR:
Easy Access System Europe, Mustamäe tee 50,
10621 Tallinn, Estonia
gpsr.requests@easproject.com

www.ingramcontent.com/pod-product-compliance
Ingram Content Group UK Ltd.
Pitfield, Milton Keynes, MK11 3LW, UK
UKHW021826150726
7214IPUK00017B/329